Life Behind the Silence

Life Behind the Silence

Gina Azizah

Copyright © 2013 Gina Azizah

The moral right of the author has been asserted.

Apart from any fair dealing for the purposes of research or private study, or criticism or review, as permitted under the Copyright, Designs and Patents Act 1988, this publication may only be reproduced, stored or transmitted, in any form or by any means, with the prior permission in writing of the publishers, or in the case of reprographic reproduction in accordance with the terms of licences issued by the Copyright Licensing Agency. Enquiries concerning reproduction outside those terms should be sent to the publishers.

Matador
9 Priory Business Park
Kibworth Beauchamp
Leicestershire LE8 0RX, UK
Tel: (+44) 116 279 2299
Fax: (+44) 116 279 2277
Email: books@troubador.co.uk
Web: www.troubador.co.uk/matador

ISBN 978 1780881 317

British Library Cataloguing in Publication Data.
A catalogue record for this book is available from the British Library.

Typeset in 11.5pt Adobe Garamond Pro by Troubador Publishing Ltd, Leicester, UK
Printed and bound in the UK by TJ International, Padstow, Cornwall

Matador is an imprint of Troubador Publishing Ltd

SURREY LIBRARIES	
Askews & Holts	12-Jun-2013
362.7609 HEA	£9.99

CHAPTER 1

Malaysia

The days spent at school when I was a child were relatively few, so I didn't learn much about my own country. But, with the passing of the years, I have read books and become more familiar with my culture and the roots to which I am bound by blood and birth. Indeed, I am now very proud of my own country and its people.

Malaysia has a population of over 27 million people. The capital is Kuala Lumpur and our language is Bahasa Malay. We also speak several Indian and Chinese languages. The majority of Malaysia is covered by tropical forest. But with new developments, large shopping malls and a few five star hotels being built, the country is becoming very modern and our greenery is fading.

The main exports are petroleum and liquefied natural gas, chemicals, palm oil and electronic equipment. The economy relies heavily on oil, rubber from plantations and the mining of tin, which is principally found in the states of Perak and Selangor, on the west coast. In the region of Kedah, the main resource generating income is the rubber tree.

In Malaysia, three different cultures coexist: the Malays, the Chinese and the Indians. Historically, the Malays were involved in agriculture, public administration and the army; the Chinese devoted themselves to commerce, industry, and mining and the Indians took care of the rubber plantations. Sunni Islam is the official religion of Malaysia, and 54% of the population follows this religion. Buddhism makes up 18% and Hinduism 7%. There is also a Christian minority of 7%. Although Bahasa Malay is the official language, English is also spoken and several varieties of Chinese and Indian languages.

Malaysia is developing slowly. We were once considered a very poor country, but we are now experiencing a degree of prosperity, largely thanks to the Petronas Twin Towers in Kuala Lumpur, which, until 2004, were the world's tallest buildings. I think they are wonderful. The Twin Towers include a world-class shopping complex and the shops there sell designer clothes and many beautiful things from all over the world. As I love shopping, I would go to the boutiques and let my credit card do the talking. The complex includes several good restaurants as well. There is a wide variety of Asian food in Kuala Lumpur. There is a choice of Indian, Chinese and Malaysian and you will find many of these foods in the food courts in the shopping malls. I am overwhelmed by the choice of foods in my country. I would get a whole meal with fish, meat, vegetables and rice for under £3, and then I would wash it down with a fresh coconut juice, served from the actual coconut. It was delicious and I love food.

I love Kuala Lumpur International Airport (KLIA), a large, modern facility with air conditioning and plenty of natural light inside. The journey from the airport to the city takes about an hour and offers a beautiful view, with colours everywhere.

Primitive, prehistoric cave paintings depicting animals and human figures have been found in Malaysian caverns. Contemporary Malaysian artists create some very interesting jewellery and metalwork. The fabric produced for traditional clothes is bright and cheerful. Pottery is also an important craft, and there are a number of artists at work in every part of the country.

Kuala Lumpur is a must-see stop for anyone who wants to see Malaysia. There are many beautiful islands and beaches, but if I had to choose one, it would be Penang Island in the north because it has beautiful beaches. I love to walk on the beach, watch the beautiful ocean and run along the shore, taking in the fresh air; it is so peaceful. The smell of the sea makes my mind feel clean. The pressures and tensions that I have in my life seem to clear on Penang Island. For me, it is a beautiful place. The island has one of the largest tropical forests in the world.

There are many large shopping malls, but my favourite is a night food market on Gurney Drive, where I can find lots of local foods. What I love about it is that the food is all cooked in front of me. I place the order and watch while the food is prepared. It is just mouth-watering.

Another favourite place of mine to dine is a wooden deck by the beach which offers a spectacular view of the sunset. I love to watch the sun go down behind the sea in a blaze of red while sipping a refreshing cocktail and enjoying a romantic candlelight dinner. It's the perfect way to end a perfect day and a great start to the night.

CHAPTER 2

Rainy Season

Rain in Malaysia; I love that smell. An afternoon of rain on a warm day in the jungle brings a special and particularly cool fresh air, and when I breathe this special air, it revives me and cleans me from the inside. The Malaysian rainy season starts most afternoons about 2 pm, raining sometimes for thirty minutes and sometimes for hours at a time. In most of East Asia, we joke that the year is divided into two seasons: the rainy season and the rest of the year. The rainy season's other half is the summer, when the sun invades everything, lighting up the bright colours of the jungle flowers and bringing to life more shades of green than one could describe.

Allow me to introduce you to the rest of my family. My grandmother, Fatima, died and left my mother an orphan when she was fourteen years old. She was a native Malaysian who had converted to Islam. She died giving birth to my aunt Salma, her seventh child. In all, there were four girls and three boys. The first to be born was my uncle Mustafa, second was my aunt Ramlah and the third was my mother. Next was my uncle Zainol (who is my favourite uncle and with whom I am very close), then another girl, Jamilah. The sixth child was another boy, Abdul Halim, and last was my aunt Salma.

When my grandmother died, the responsibility of taking care of Jamilah, Zainol and Abdul Halim fell upon my mother; and she retained this responsibility until she was married. My grandfather returned with a new wife after my grandmother's death, but she didn't want to take care of his children. When my mother married my father, the other children got separated and went to live with other families. As newlyweds my parents lived in the house that had belonged to Haji Isa. This is the house where I grew up as a young child.

My parents were married in Kampung Bikan, the house of Haji Dolah, during the rainy season in November 1965. My mother was only eighteen years old and my father even younger, only sixteen. These days, marrying at that age might seem like folly, but at that time in the villages of Malaysia, marriages took place at a very early age. It still seems very young to me; making my parent's marriage work, especially when it was arranged by my maternal grandfather and paternal grandmother, seems an impossible task, but it was the norm for the day. My parents did not marry for love, which I believe is the only thing that can keep a family together, so it should be no surprise that my mother ended up having the life that she had. Because I am the daughter of a loveless marriage and have suffered its consequences, I have come to realise that without love we are incomplete.

Yes, my parent's marriage was arranged, the result of an agreement between Haji Isa and Mariam, my father's mother. Haji Isa arranged my mother's marriage purely for financial reasons. My father was orphaned when his father, my grandfather Hussin, died. Then, because he was the only male child, he inherited the family estate. In those days, within the confines of his rural community, he was considered rich, although the fact is that his entire fortune amounted only to his own house, a little money and ownership of some land. I always say to myself, in the country of the blind, the one-eyed man is king. My father inherited everything because he only had one sister, Fatimah, and she had already married. My grandfather wanted to arrange the wedding because of my father's money and gave little consideration to the thoughts or feelings of that ill-fated couple.

In the beginning, my father was fond of my mother. My mother, in contrast, was never fond of Abdul Wahab. She had another man in her life, Omar, who had paid some attention to her, and my mother felt attracted to him. The young suitor was twenty-three and very handsome, with clear skin and a fine body. When Omar presented Harisun with a ring, Haji Isa became very angry, because he wanted her to marry Abdul Wahab – he had more money. When Abdul Wahab discovered what had happened, he threatened my mother, claiming that if she married the other man, he would kill her. Harisun returned the ring to her lover, cowed by the pressure of her father, and was married to Abdul Wahab, but she was never able to love him. One of the reasons, she said, was because he never allowed himself to be loved.

The wedding was celebrated one rainy day in Kampung Bikan, in the village, in the house of my grandfather's brother, Haji Dolah. It was the same house I would be born in within a year. Muslim ceremonies in the countryside are simple and very basic, with no religious authority in attendance. The bride and groom declare something like "I'm married to you" and then they sign a marriage contract. The family had little money for the ceremony. Someone had made my mother's very simple blue wedding dress, and my father did not buy a wedding ring for her. The reception was a very small family affair with fewer than twenty neighbours and friends in attendance. It was not a grand event but rather an intimate gathering. Haji Isa didn't attend the wedding because his new wife wanted nothing to do with my grandfather's family. None of my mother's brothers or sisters were at the ceremony, and that saddened her a great deal. Not even my mother wanted to be there; she did not want to be married to my father, a man she did not know or love.

The wedding lasted a day. My parents stayed at the house of Haji Dolah for three days. After the third day, my mother gathered up her clothes in a plastic bag and left for Haji Isa's house, where no one was living. My father had been living with his mother up to this point.

Harisun became pregnant within one month of taking her marriage vows, and when she broke the news to Abdul Wahab, he immediately became suspicious of her fidelity, believing that the baby couldn't be his. He did nothing until her seventh month of pregnancy, and then, driven nearly mad with anger and jealousy, he started to abuse my mother.

He was a young man of very bad character, and his youth and ignorance aggravated his violent temperament. Before he left Harisun, Abdul Wahab showed a terrible, hateful violence towards me, the unborn life in my mother's womb. He threw things at my mother's stomach, including a mango, which caused her three days and nights of terrible pain. One time, he threw a knife at her, and the knife stuck on the floor only inches from my mother's stomach; she was so lucky. Another time, he tried to strangle Harisun; she was down to her last breath, her tongue sticking between her teeth, when her younger brother Abdul Halim coincidentally turned up just in time to save her. Abdul Halim quietly grasped a piece of wood and threatened to smash my father's head with it if he didn't let her go. He released my mother as soon as he saw Abdul Halim moving towards him.

After that my father left my mother, giving her no choice but to return to her uncle Haji Dolah's house to give birth. Harisun was very tired when she arrived at the house of Haji Dolah. Due to lack of funds, she had come on foot in the rain from Kuala-Nau, even though it was a long and difficult walk, particularly for a woman about to give birth for the first time. Having no

Life Behind the Silence 5

knowledge about childbirth, my mother knew little about what was about to happen to her. All she knew was that she was in pain and frightened and that no one was there to help, not even her husband.

Sum, Haji Dolah's wife, envied my mother and she didn't want Haji Dolah to help the poor, pregnant young girl at the door. Most women would have lent a hand under such circumstances, but not Sum. But my grandfather's younger brother did take her in, and for the birth called in an old lady in that area who would help her during the delivery. My mother felt abandoned and alone in that most crucial moment: the birth of her first child, a girl.

As is the Malaysian custom, my mother's relatives had a great deal of influence over the choice of a name. It was decided to name the baby a most common name, one that was even considered vulgar: Azizah. I would in time grow to hate my name, and that was why I renamed myself Gina, given from someone special.

My full name is Azizah Binti Abdul Wahab. Binti means 'daughter of'. I am the daughter of Abdul Wahab, even though he never accepted me as his daughter and I have never considered him my father. When I was born, my family circumstances were complicated, and it was difficult for my mother. I knew nothing of these difficulties. I cried, slept and wanted to be fed, just like any other baby. It would be many years before I would understand the mystery and complications of my childhood.

I was born in the middle of the rainy season. It was September 23rd 1965, during a hot, damp night. We are a Muslim family, and the title of Haji is given to men who have made the pilgrimage to Mecca. Women who have made this pilgrimage use the title of Hajah. My grandfather, Haji Isa, was present at my birth. The house where I was born is in northern Malaysia. The village where one is born is known as one's kampong. Rural Malaysia has a beauty all of its own, and all of that beauty was there for me. My mother, Harisun, was eighteen years old when she gave birth to me, and she was a very beautiful woman, brown–skinned with black eyes and dark hair. She wore a baju kurung, the tropical dress of the women of that generation. When she was young, she never covered her head with the traditional head cover that is associated with Muslim women today. She did not know it at the time, but she was an independent woman, and that independence would be passed on to her new daughter, born to her that rainy September evening.

It rained without end. Haji Dolah's home had none of the conveniences that we take for granted today. A humble rural dwelling with few comforts, it had neither water nor electricity, exactly like most of the houses in the area. Sum had two children of her own and had experienced the same agony of birth under similar conditions, but somehow, unbelievably, she avoided helping out and even tried to obstruct the normal common courtesies extended to new mothers by relatives and neighbours. Sum neither cooked nor cared for my mother. I later thought that people can turn into savages if they are allowed to become carried away by excessive jealousy and envy. But such people exist in the world and, unfortunately, Sum's graceless and surly behaviour towards Harisun would not end with this episode.

Harisun did not recover well after the birth. She bled for three days, and there was no one in the house that would help her. I, her newborn child, was crying so hard that my mother put her hand out of the window to beg for help from a woman who happened to be passing by. The kind woman, a complete stranger, helped her when no one else would; not even my mother's sister's kin offered to help. She was the one who took care of my mother when she bled. She cooked some food for my mother to eat. When Sum returned home, she found out that someone had been helping my mother; she was not very happy and was angry with my mother.

My mother knew from the beginning that Sum was not very happy that she was staying at her place, but my mother had nowhere else to go. My mother was very upset, because everyday she received bad treatment from her. After three weeks at Haji Dolah's house, Harisun and her new baby decided returned to Kuala–Nau, which is what we called our house. No one was living in the house, so it was a difficult time for my mother, alone with a baby. There was no one to take care of her, no one to help her take care of me, and she hardly knew what to do. She struggled to try to figure out where to get food, how to meet our most basic needs and how to take care of this new baby. And it kept on raining.

The rain kept feeding the earth, and I grew, or at least I survived as best I could, thanks to the tender care of my young mother. In spite of the scarcity of money, help or anyone to care for us, my mother somehow found a way to carry on living. The truth is that my mother had very little food, no money and no work. The rain made things even more difficult for Harisun. At times she could barely leave the house to look for the food we needed to survive because of the never-ending rain. The very rain that fed the earth was preventing us from feeding ourselves.

To feed us, Harisun would gather plants either from the forest or from a plot of land close to the house that had belonged to my grandfather. She couldn't go into the jungle unless the rain was lighter or starting to clear, and then she would collect berries, weeds and a kind of fresh green vegetable from the trees. Today we might call it a salad. My grandfather's plot of land enabled my mother to eat and to feed me during those first months of my life, although at times my mother hardly ate anything herself, giving almost everything to me. She even chewed the food for me so that I could easily swallow it, as I didn't yet have teeth.

My mother did manage to scrape a little money together in the dry season by collecting sap from rubber trees. The rubber tree contributed a lot to my early development, and it is still my favourite tree. The milky sap (actually a raw latex) obtained from the rubber tree provides a raw material that is used to manufacture latex gloves, tyres and many other products.

My mother would take me with her into the jungle so as not to leave me alone in the house. There she would rock me until I fell asleep and then go a short way off to work her rubber trees and find food. Occasionally she popped back to check that I was OK. Apparently I slept deeply, but I tended to be bitten by mosquitoes, and on more than one occasion my mother had to scare off monkeys that were approaching me. On another occasion, when she popped back to check on me, I was already awake and was playing with the sap that she had put in the container, and I had rubbed it over my hair. As soon as my mother saw me, she began screaming and ran to get me. She took me to the river and tried to wash my hair quickly before the sap started sticking to it. But it was too late because the sap had turned to rubber and was stuck all over my hair. My mother tried to remove as much as she could, but I was crying in pain. As soon as my mother got home, she rubbed cooking oil in my hair so she could pull the rubber out more easily. The jungle could be a dangerous place; the area was full of a number of wild animals, including tigers, wild boars, elephants and especially snakes. Even today one hears of rubber tree workers being attacked by wild animals.

Despite this constant danger, my mother frequently went into the jungle in order to collect the sap in the early morning, when it flows in greater quantity than in the afternoon. She would fix a flashlight on her head, similar to the ones miners wear, and with a machete she would cut the bark of the rubber tree so that the latex oozed out into a small pot for collection. Each day she would collect the sap and then sell what she had collected. She only slept a few hours a day, but we survived. The rubber tree can only be worked when the weather permits, never when it rains, because the sap then mixes with the rainwater and becomes unusable. Malaysian raindrops are huge and fall with tremendous power, flooding everything.

When the rain was too heavy and Harisun couldn't go out to search for food, she would ask a neighbour for a handful of rice. And more than once, driven by hunger, my mother snuck out at night to steal potatoes from the neighbour. My mother would dig the potato plant out of the ground, remove the potatoes and then put the potato plant back into the hole, nice and neat. I know everyone was always hungry, and there was a constant search for something to eat. Conditions were not very favourable for us. Indeed, life was harsh and unforgiving. Oblivious to any hardship, I was starting to crawl just like any other baby, except that in my case, I crawled in the jungle.

During those first three years, my mother did everything in her power to ensure that I would have a normal upbringing. This took a tremendous toll on her and would affect her for the rest of her life. At times she would become very depressed. I was malnourished and became very thin, almost to the point of dying. Luckily, an elderly woman happened to pass by one day, and she felt so sorry for me that she took me with her to the house of the old man who sold traditional medicine. They quickly gave me some medicine, which saved my life, and nursed me back to health. My mother felt a great hopelessness during this time, because she had actually failed to notice my condition. In her opinion, she was very happy when I was not crying because she could have a rest. She even used to forbid anyone from waking me up but what she didn't know was that I was going to die. My thanks go to that woman who saved my life. The continuing absence of her husband or any support at all left my mother with the belief that it was futile to carry on. This was the beginning of bouts of depression that would continue all her life.

CHAPTER 3

Early Years

For Harisun and her new baby, life in Kuala–Nau, in the Malaysian region of Kedah, turned out to be one of monotony and utter hopelessness. Our house was more of a miserable shack than a home, with neither running water nor electricity. We had none of the most basic comforts. There was just a single unfurnished room that served as dinning room, living room and bedroom. The house had never been furnished, and as far as I remember we had to sit on the floor to have a meal.

The plot of land where the house sat provided little food. Garden crops grew wild, because no one had tended them in a long time. We were alone in the Malaysian jungle without a man to take care of the kinds of tasks that make life and survival possible. With the help of my mother's love, I was able to grow and develop. My mother told me many times that in spite of the difficult circumstances, she was very happy when I was born. It gave her joy to look at my face and realise that it was she that had given me life.

When I was little, my mother would sing me a song to put me to sleep. I still remember it and enjoy it even today. It had a sweet and gentle melody, and these were the words:

Lagu tiga kupang
Sagu penuh padi
Enam ekor burung
Masuk dalam kuali
Bila sudah masak
Burung nyanyi saja
Tentu sedap makan

Beri pada raja
Raja dalam rumah
Buat kira – kira
Dayang tepi kolam
Mahu jemur tepung
Datang burung hitam
Patuk batang hidung
Hidung, hidung, hidung!

The lyrics speak of abundant rice harvests, the birds in the trees, the king and the princess. I love to sing this little song, and I love more to hear it sung in my mother's voice. When I was three years old, my mother and I were walking along one day, singing this song, when suddenly her voice fell silent. A figure was approaching the house – it was my father! Abdul Wahab had returned home after having abandoned us for more than three years, and he wanted to get back together with my mother. Because she yearned for the security companionship of a man, my mother accepted him back. She had to have someone – she could no longer continue alone with so much on her shoulders. The capacity of the female heart to forgive is amazing.

Harisun accepted him back, and time proved that to be a very bad decision indeed. Soon my parents began to fight. The arguments always revolved around me: my father hated me, and my mother tried to defend and protect me from his cruelty. During one of these serious arguments, Abdul Wahab got hold of a large knife and attempted to kill my mother. Harisun fled into the jungle, hiding in a cave. After a while, she fell into an exhausted sleep on the top of a rock. I was still at home. She awoke in the dark, hearing the sound of an elephant or some other large animal coming towards her, and although she couldn't see it, she felt its presence near her. Despite her fear, she quickly ran back to the house. There she found me playing alone outside – in the dark. Abdul Wahab was inside the house, making no attempt to look after me. Harisun took me inside and, in spite of her fear, she washed and fed me.

During her work on the rubber trees, my mother managed to save some money so she could buy some jewellery for me. She bought me a gold necklace and bracelet. At that time, gold was not that expensive, so she could afford it. I wore them constantly after my mother put them on me, until one day she noticed the necklace and bracelet were no longer there. Obviously I could not even talk yet, so I could not tell my mother who had taken my jewellery. But my mother knew it was my father who had taken and sold it, and used the money for himself. He was such a bastard husband to my mother, and a useless father to me.

Even with all these awful domestic scenes taking place, my mother once again became pregnant, and within a month my father left home again. This time they were to be divorced. No papers were signed; there was just a spoken agreement between the two of them. I was four years old. On February 23rd 1969, my first brother, Redzwan, was born.

I was a very talkative four year old little girl. I loved to pretend and would sit alone and talk to myself. Once I got hold of one of my mother's handbags and went outside, coming back in immediately, saying: "Hello, Harisun! What are you doing?" as if I was a friend coming by to see her. My mother would respond and play with me, and this would keep her company and make her happy. She thought I was very funny and still remembers and talks about what I did back then. I smiled a lot and talked to everybody, and I picked things up very quickly. My mother told me that she always worried when I went to the shops to buy something because I would say too much and accidentally reveal my family secret – one about my mother and father.

When I was still five, something happened which I have never forgotten and which is still a vivid and painful memory. As always, my mother had gone to work and left me and my brother Redzwan in the care of a relative. He had looked after us well until this one particular day. Once my mother had gone, he asked me for a dish of cooking oil. As I didn't know what he was planning, I obediently brought some to him. Without warning, he grasped my body and pushed me on the floor, pulled my skirt down and opened both of my legs wide, and then he smeared oil between my legs and attempted to penetrate me. I was just a little girl; naturally, I didn't know what was happening, except that something was hurting me. A voice in my head told me I was in danger, so I bit him as hard as I could on his hand and kicked many times at his body before he got any further and then I ran away from him. But he gave me a warning not to say anything to my mother otherwise I would be in trouble again when my mother went to work the next day.

I hid myself in a bush, waiting for what seemed like an eternity, until I finally saw my mother approaching. I ran and embraced her tightly, but I told her nothing as I had been warned. Also, I was afraid she wouldn't believe me. The next day, when my mother got ready to leave the house, I tried to follow, imploring her to take me with her. I was in a flood of tears, but she called this relative to come to get me. I clung to her as hard as I could and held tightly on to her dress but to no avail. Harisun managed to leave the house, and I remained in the presence of my attacker.

I saw my mother run and I tried to chase her as fast as I could but she was a faster runner, and within minutes she had disappeared from my view. If I had known where she worked, I would have gone to her. I was crying loudly and was too scared to go back home, scared the same things would happen again. I decided to stay in an alleyway and wait for my mother to come home. I stayed there for many hours playing on my own, ignoring my hunger and at the same time avoiding my relative. As soon as I saw my mother, I ran and clung onto her with so much relief, but I kept my secret.

It would be many days before I could play normally again. Even now, I still give thanks that I escaped in time and that it was only an 'attempted' rape. It could have been much worse. I never understood why he wanted to do that to me, but from that moment I hated him and didn't want to see his face again for the rest of my life.

I was five years old when I entered a period of my existence that would cause me much suffering and leave me to endure heartache for the rest of my life. My father returned home – and once again my mother let him stay. He warmly embraced my little brother, Redzwan, but not me. As soon as he saw my face, he told my mother to keep me away from him otherwise he would kill me, so I was taken by my mother to live with others, and there I remained, away from my family, for some considerable time.

At the age of six, I went to live with my auntie Fatimah, my father's sister. She didn't get along with my mother, because her husband liked to have a joke with her, so she got very jealous, especially because my mother was a very pretty women. Although my auntie was horrified by the behaviour of her own brother, she could do nothing to prevent it. Nobody could. My father would become so aggressive when he saw me, or when my name was mentioned. My mother was very worried about my well-being and begged Fatimah to take me in. Fatimah was married to Mat Piah and had four children. Of my cousins, the two girls, Khatijah and Rosni, were older; the two boys, Rosli and Roslan, were much younger. We got on very well.

I was very well looked after in that house, growing up strong, healthy and protected from my father's aggression. But I was already starting to think for myself, and I couldn't understand why I had to leave my own family. Why didn't my father love me? Why did my father behave so differently with me?

Why did he hate me so much? What did I do? These questions have tormented me all my life.

I spent about three months, or maybe less, at Auntie Fatimah's house. Then I was taken to the house of my mother's sister, Aunt Ramlah, and was there for a few months. I am very fond of my auntie; she is such a lovely lady, softly spoken and she was very kind to me. I had some wonderful moments at her house. She had seven children, and with these cousins I had a great time. I didn't return to my parent's house until I almost seven years old. I could happily play with my cousins and could do a lot of things that I couldn't when I was at my own home. My life felt so free, I wasn't scared of anything. But out of the blue, my mother and her friend turned up to take me home. I was crying and didn't want to go home, but she took me and put me on a motorbike, her friend driving and my mother sitting behind me, so I was in the middle of them and couldn't do anything. I hated my mother at that time; why did she want to destroy my happiness? Why did she want to take me home to my father? Didn't she feel sorry for me when Abdul Wahab abused me? I cried all the way home.

Later, I understood the reason why my mother took me away from my auntie's house; it was because my mother received the news that my uncle wanted to arrange a marriage between me and his son, my cousin, who was six years older than me. My mother did not agree with my uncle's plan, and she told him that I was still a little girl, and that when I was mature enough, I could make my own decisions about my future. If the arranged marriage had happened, by now I could have had a few children, be wearing a sarong, be in the kitchen all the time, peeling onions and potatoes and cooking for everyone in the family. That is what my cousin's wife does now. My cousin lives in the countryside with his wife and they have four children. His wife is a lot younger than me but all her front teeth are missing. She doesn't know how to dress; every day she wears a sarong with a T-shirt, covers her hair, wears no make-up, not even lipstick, and walks everywhere in slippers. Even today, my mother is always making fun of me, saying, "It's lucky I took you away from your uncle's house otherwise your life would be exactly like his wife's, and of course you wouldn't look the way you do now, and you'd obviously never have dreamt of London." I look at her and smile. Now I appreciate what my mother did for me and owe her a million thank yous. She saved my life.

It was a return to utter hell. Once my father was back in my life, the abuse was cruel and continuous. The physical pain from the beatings and the accompanying mental anguish ruined my childhood. These were my parents: a father who, with no apparent motive, showed me only cruelty and violence, and a mother made weak and vulnerable by her depression and her wretched situation. In spite of all this, the family continued growing, and on September 6th 1971, my second brother, Mohd Zambri, was born.

My brothers and I grew up in great material poverty, with little chance of a proper education. In our rural environment, living conditions were very hard – and we carried the added burden of being a totally dysfunctional family. I consider the normal family bond and the love of its members for each other to be vital to the development of a human being. It is family I most value and respect. I have always regretted that we were not a normal family. In my eyes, we were a complete disaster. But it is this family I love most, no matter what happens.

My father hit me constantly, punching or slapping me every time he saw me. He couldn't stand my presence. I remember many instances of maltreatment, and I still bear the marks on my body and in my weeping heart. As I was the only girl in the family, my mother loved to dress me up. She used to brush my hair into a topknot, with the rest falling loose. I felt beautiful. But one day, consumed by jealously, my father dragged me by the hair to the kitchen and cut off my ponytail with a kitchen knife. This left my hair ragged and different lengths. He also ended up digging the knife into my chest. Fortunately, I am still here to tell the tale. It was an awful moment that is still a source of sadness. He pushed me on the floor and threw my hair in front of me then he walked away. I cried sadly, picked up all my hair that he had cut off and looked at myself in the mirror. That evening, I couldn't stop thinking, I am never going to be pretty again. It was then that I started to hate my father.

He manifested his hatred toward me continually and without respite. His sole aim, it seemed, was to inflict pain. Mistreating me was his obsession and almost his only occupation, since he didn't bother to work or try to support his family.

One night, I was at the house of Ustat, who taught us children to read the Al-Quran. It was late evening; we had finished our studies and were waiting for our parents to come and collect us. While I waited, I fell asleep, but someone woke me and said my father was waiting outside. Quietly I got up and ran straight towards him with my eyes half closed, like a zombie. Without any words, he took hold of the flaming torch he was using as a light and burned my eyes with it until the fire went out. I was in pain and cried silently to hold in the pain, scared that he would do more to me. I walked back home with one eye open. As soon as I got home, I went straight to bed, hiding my face from my mother because if she knew about it, that would cause an argument between them. I didn't want this to happen, especially in the middle of the night, so I covered my head with a sarong and cried silently in pain. But the more I cried, the more my eyes burned and badly stung. The whole night I couldn't sleep. The next morning, my mother noticed and asked me, "What happened to your eyes?"

But at that time my father was there, and he looked at me with his vicious eyes. So I couldn't say anything and walked away before anything happened. But my mother knew exactly who had done it, and as always she protected me and started questioning my father about my eyes. Once again, a big argument erupted between them over me, which was why I hadn't wanted my mother to know. I would rather suffer myself than see my mother being hit by my father. For weeks my eyes were blackened, swollen and painful. Thank god they eventually recovered well without any damage.

On another occasion, I did what all children do sooner or later. I was so tired one evening that I fell asleep very early and had a dream that I used the toilet, so I relieved myself, but when I opened my eyes, I found that I had wet my bed. I was so scared, I didn't know what to do, it was only 8pm. I didn't want anybody notice that I had wet my bed so I pretended to sleep. My mother came to wake me to use the toilet before I wet my bed, but what she didn't know was that I already had. I made myself stiff, but she tried to pull me up and happened to touch my bed, and then she knew what I had done. She raised her voice and said, "You already wet your bed?"

Soon my father heard about it and reacted with characteristic cruelty. He stopped in the middle of having his dinner, took a plate of mashed hot chillies, came towards me and pulled my skirt down. I was crying, begging him not to do it, but he didn't care. He grasped a handful of the chillies and rubbed them into my genitals. I was screaming and jumping in pain, but he slapped me across my face and told me not to cry. I closed my mouth with my hand to stop myself making a noise but it stung horribly, and even today I find it difficult to describe the pain. My mother was in shock and tried to stop him. She asked my relative who had tried to rape me to take me away from my father in order to wash me and try to comfort me. He took me to the little mosque which was not very far from our house, where there was water, and he asked me to wash out the chillies from my vagina, but it didn't get any better, in fact it got worse and I felt like I wanted to die, that is how painful it was. I had to wait until my father was soundly asleep before I could return home. I walked slowly into the house, so as not to wake him, then went straight to bed. I remember the pain that I felt; I cried and was unable to sleep for the rest of the night. For weeks I could hardly walk and had great difficulty urinating. Every time I wanted to urinate, the pain was so strong I would almost faint. I cried as I looked at my red, swollen genitals, and not knowing what else to do, I put cooking oil in my vagina in order to make it easier to walk. Even today, when I look at chillies it reminds me of what happened and I still feel the pain. But strangely enough I still love to eat chillies.

The pain caused me to fall sick with a high temperature. I slept on the floor, covering myself with a sarong, and couldn't stop shivering, despite having a fever. I was almost asleep when suddenly I heard my father's voice from outside; he had just got home from somewhere. I try to get up to get away from him but I had no energy left and within a minute he was standing in front of my face. I started shivering with fear; I didn't know what he was going to do next. But he turned and walked away from me. I was so relieved and closed my eyes and tried to sleep. Suddenly I could hear someone's footsteps. Slowly I opened my eyes and saw my father walking towards me with a bucket of freezing water, which he threw over me with so much anger. I tried to get up and was full of tears, begging him to stop, but then he pushed my body until I dropped on to the floor and then he walked away. For years I received this physical abuse on a daily basis, and I lived in a state of distress.

But heaven had given me a remedy: my inner strength. This inner strength would enable me to eventually overcome the difficulties of my early years. Meanwhile though, life was very hard.

CHAPTER 4

School and Food

I first went to school when I was seven years old then five years later my brother Redzwan came to the same school and I enjoyed having him around. As a child, I was very eager to learn, and I was a good student for the short time that my education lasted.

From the age of seven until I was eleven years old, I had only a morsel of chicken every day. My mother went out every evening and collected chicken eggs for my breakfast the next morning. I was often excluded from the evening meal, but she would always save some food for me. Then, the next morning, after I had dressed in my school uniform, she would hide me in a corner so my father couldn't see what was happening. I would quickly open my mouth wider and my mother would crack an egg into it. Then I had to swallow it down quickly before my father saw. Sometimes I couldn't take it anymore, I got really sick, but my mother forced me, because she thought it had good vitamins in it. A few times I pretended to swallow it, but I keep it in my cheek pouch like a hamster and walked fast until I was away from my mother, then I would throw out the morsel. I just couldn't take it anymore.

Sometimes I just couldn't take the thought that I was not allowed to eat in my own house. My mother was pleased with her accomplishment of giving me what might be the only food I would have to eat until I returned home from school. Sometimes she gave me a little money so I could buy something to eat at school. She would steal this money from my father's pocket the night before and give it to me in the morning before I went to school. But many times my mother didn't even have that small amount of stolen money to offer me, and my father had forbidden the rest of the family from giving me any kind of food or support.

To get to school, I had to walk each way. My father had an old motorbike to get around on, as most men in rural Malaysia did and still do to this day. My brother would walk with me to school, but sometimes my father would take my brother to school and leave me to walk by myself. Every day after school I would walk home with my brother, but then my father would come on his motorbike, stop in front of me and just pick up my brother and leave me to walk alone. Sometimes he would pick up my brother's friend instead of me, and I would watch full of sadness. My friends looked at me and said, "Why doesn't your father pick you up?" There was nothing much I could say so I walked away with a broken heart. Each time my father passed me on the trail, he kept as much distance between us as he could.

I wanted my father to accompany me to school, but this never happened. I would walk for almost two hours along a stony earth trail to get to school, and then walk another two hours to get back home. The walking was very uncomfortable, but that discomfort was overridden by the sharp pain I felt inside each time my father would pass me on the trail. All my friend's parents came to pick them up and left me walking all alone by myself. I survived using my own wits and willpower, collecting fruit from the jungle when I came back from school. I would devour it eagerly because I was so hungry. My mother would try to sneak me food, usually out of sight of my father.

My father would not allow me to be in his presence at home. I could not sit with the family for lunch or for dinner, because my father would get angry. He did not even permit my mother to feed me. My father would have a meal with my brothers and I would sit outside the house waiting until they were finished. I would hear my father say, "Eat it all, don't keep any for her." He hated me that much. As soon as he had finished, I would wait for him to go for his afternoon nap, then I would sneakily eat whatever was left over. If I was lucky, there would be some rice and fish left, or rice with just a fish head. I would gather whatever food was left on the plate and then climb a tree to eat my food hidden from my father. When I had finished, I would look from the top of the tree to make sure no one was around and then I would get down. But sometimes there would be no food left for me and I would be left with an empty stomach all day. To feed my hunger, I would climb the trees around my house and eat their fruits. After eating too much fruit one day, I felt tired and fell asleep on the tree between the branches. I was having such a peaceful sleep on the tree until I fell to the ground! Luckily I didn't break any bones, I just hurt my back and shoulder, but I told no one. Even today I am good at climbing trees but I am scared of heights.

I couldn't understand why my father did these things to me. I was terrified of him and jealous of my brothers. I wanted my father's love and longed for him to care for me.

At school, I was a gifted student. The teacher said I was intelligent – as well as rebellious. Well, at least someone was saying good things about me. I didn't find learning difficult. What was difficult was hiding my studies from my father, who wouldn't allow me to read or to study. I had to do this in secret. The sad thing is, I also got bullied at school because of my name and my face. A singer in the late 1950s sang a song called 'Azizah' and that song became very popular with everyone. So the boys would sing that song to me and I thought, that's not funny. Since that time, I have hated my name. After they saw that I was fine with that, they started picking on me about my father: I am daughter the of Wahab Snail, Wahab Spinach; they told everyone and the whole class made fun of me. I wish they had said that to Wahab and not to me. I was so upset that I asked my teacher if I could go to the toilet, where I cried for hours and hours until my teacher asked someone to look for me.

I used to have a big mole on my palm, and one day one of the girls saw it and made a big issue of it. From that day, if anything belonging to them went missing they said I was the one who stole it even though I never was. Because of that I really wanted to stop going to school, but on the other hand I didn't want to stay at home because of my father. So I decided to remove the mole on my hand with a pin. Everyday I dug and dug at it until my mole became blurry and disappeared. It was very painful but there was more pain in my heart when they said I was the one who had stolen their belongings. I had had enough at home with my father and now everyone was upsetting me at school. I was scared to tell the teacher because I had to walk back home on my own. One time when I was on my way back home from school, a few boys hid themselves in a bush and tried to scare me by throwing stones at me, and that was because I had told the teacher about their behaviour. That gave me a warning and after that I told no one. Obviously I couldn't tell my father, so there was nothing much I could do except continue my journey with a lot of pain in my heart.

My father never bought any toys or dolls for me and neither did my mother, but that was because she was scared of my father and also because she didn't have any money. As a young girl I longed to have dolls to play with like any other young girl but I didn't have any. At home I would make dolls on my own with a napkin and play with my brothers or on my own. But one day, my teacher asked all the girls to bring their Barbie dolls to school and I was the only one who didn't have one. But as I knew how to make one with a napkin, I did, but everyone laughed at me. I was just nine years old at that time. When I looked at their dolls, I really wanted to hold and touch them, because I had never seen dolls so pretty, but none of them allowed me to. I just stayed on my own and watched them playing with their Barbie dolls, dressing them up and brushing their hair. With so much anger and jealously, some evil crossed my brain.

When class was over and it was time to go home, the teacher asked them to leave their dolls at school so we could play with them again the next day. I can't go home without a Barbie doll, I thought, one has to come home with me. I had a plan. I waited until everyone had left the classroom then I made a move, but very slowly, pretending that I was doing something else. I made sure no one was looking at me then I quickly grasped one of the Barbie dolls, put it in my bag and rushed out of the classroom, playing it cool. I didn't feel sacred or guilty at all; in fact, I felt really happy because I got so upset when they wouldn't allow me to play with them, so they deserved it and I got what I wished for. Also, they always said that I was the person who had been stealing things, and now I really was. That made me smile all the way home.

The next day I returned to school as usual, but one of the girls was crying because her Barbie was missing. I pretended I didn't know anything. My teacher asked me but I still managed to deny it perfectly until they believed me. As soon as they stopped asking me the question, I knew I was safe and I smiled happily. At home I had to hide the Barbie from my family, especially my father. So, when I wanted to play, I would go into the jungle and there I would play with the Barbie on my own. I had that Barbie quite some time and looked after her very well. But one day, I hid the Barbie at the top of the tree, and later my father discovered it. He took it and burnt it until it became ash. I was so upset and cried a lot; it made me hate him more than you can imagine. Since that time, I never had another Barbie. If I could turn back the clock and be young again, I would, because I missed my childhood.   My father refused to sign anything from school, so I would have to copy his signature and sign it myself. Luckily my teacher never suspected anything. Neither of my parents cared about my studies or what I needed for school. It was hard for me to study because most of the things that I needed to use at school I didn't have. I didn't have a book, so every time I had to get my chair and search for someone who could share with me. I had to borrow and share almost everything with other students. It came to the time one day when no one wanted to share with me, and then I had to stay at my desk without a book to read and just listen to my teacher; I felt so useless. And for homework no one would lend me the books so I missed all my school work. If I was lucky enough, some of my classmates would let me copy their work. As a punishment, the teacher would cane me on my palm or my bottom and sometimes I had to stand on the chair for a few hours. The teacher was always asking me, "When are you going to buy the book?" and my answer was always "SOON" but the answer should have been "NEVER" because I didn't get any money from my father, but I was too embarrassed to explain that to my teacher. Then soon I had an idea. My idea was to collect an empty bottle every day and sell it at end of the week, and with that money I managed to buy the book that I had needed all this time. From that moment I enjoyed going to school.

My brother Mohd Nazer was born on September 15th 1974. He looked like a little girl with curly hair, very tender and sweet. I cared for him and if I got angry he cried inconsolably. If he wanted something, he would get it no matter what. I was always very close to him. I was close to my other brothers, Redzwan and Zambri, as well. They were both very intelligent and were good students. Redzwan was a quiet boy who never fought with the other children, didn't talk much and was rather docile. But sometimes Redzwan and I would fight, but we always made up. He had a big heart. Zambri, on the other hand, was like my father. He had a quick temper and we always had to listen to him and he was always full of jealousy.

My brothers are very dear to me, and I feel sad when I think about the childhood we had, it was so harsh and difficult. They too have had their share of ups and downs on their journey through life but they were luckier than me because my father didn't abuse them.

When I turned twelve years old, I had to go to a different school. My uncle Zainol, who was fond of me, gave me a bicycle, and from that day on I went to school on my bike. I was very happy to have a bike even though it took me more or less two hours to cycle to school and the same time to cycle back home. I looked after my bike more than myself; my bike was like my best friend. I was in the evening class, so when my father went to work it give me time to prepare my packed lunch. I would cook rice with vegetables for my lunch because I didn't have any money. But if my father was around I would go to school without anything in my stomach and I wouldn't eat until I returned home. At school I had to try and ignore my hunger while I watched my friends enjoying their meals. They asked me, "You don't eat? Where is your lunch?"

I smiled and said, "I am very full because I ate a lot before I came to school." But that was a lie.

My father was a real layabout and didn't work – he didn't even want to work. His days were spent sleeping. He would leave the house for a few days, weeks or months to be with his friends or another woman. It was my mother who had to work, find food and perform all the other household tasks. Sometimes my father came home early and when he found out the meal was not ready because my mother had finished work late, or we had been out looking for something to cook, he would hit her. If one of my brothers cried for some reason, he would hit me because he said it was me who had made them cry.

My mother and my father fought because of the way he treated me – giving him another reason to hit her. I always cried, my heart breaking, when I saw my father hit my mother, but what could I do? Every time they had an argument I would hide somewhere and watch, praying that nothing serious would happen to her. When I saw my mother crying, I felt extremely hurt deep down inside, and I really hated my father being around us. I thought, he is not human, he is an animal. When the argument was over, my feelings were so hurt, I could not bear to see my mother in so much pain. So I would go in to the jungle and just sit on my own, crying for hours. I wondered how long my family would be like this. It would have been so nice to see them hugging each other, like my friends' parents. It would have been so nice if we had been a happy family and had loved each other!

When my uncle Zainol had time off, he would come to our house to see us, and this made me very happy. He really loved me. And I was so in need of love that I was filled with joy when I saw him. But such happy times as these were all too infrequent – I can count on one hand the few instances of affection that relieved my anguish. Most of my childhood was marked by pain, suffering and fear. My life was made a misery by my father, and almost all I can remember are the long hours of bitter tears and the unending hours of grief.

When my father was home, I could never sit around him. I would go into the jungle, search for food and gather wood for my mother so she could make a fire for cooking. We did not have running water in our house, so I fetched water for cooking and drinking. I took a big tank to the well not very far from my house, filled the tank and returned with the heavy tank full of water. I did that every day, it was my routine. I would also clean the house and look after my brothers. Sometimes I went to the river and caught a fish for my mother to cook. How I loved fishing! Catching one requires patience, calm, balance and hope. But when that fish bites, what delight!

My fishing rod was a simple bamboo limb with a rubber band fastened to one end. Worms that I dug out of the soil were the bait. I would wait patiently for the fish to bite, saying, "Bite! Bite!" I would keep repeating the same word over and over until fish bit! Those were very happy moments; catching a fish felt like a real accomplishment.

Then I would make a fire, barbecue the fish and eat it. As soon as I finished eating, I would jump into the river, dive down and find some old bamboo on the river bottom. I would bring it up and pick its layers open to find the small river prawn that lived inside. I ate those raw; and they were delicious. My mother had taught me this survival skill.

Many times, as I waited for the fish to bite, I would take advantage of the solitude and read or do schoolwork that I had brought along. I made use of that time by the river because my father didn't let me study at home. Sitting by myself, thinking about my life and enjoying the afternoon with the soft wind blowing on my face, I often read until I fell asleep. I enjoyed my life at these moments. I was alone and happy because no one was around to bother me, especially not my father.

I loved to sit on my own in the jungle; I could hear many kinds of birds singing with many kinds of melody. I would follow the sound of the birds until I found them, and I also saw a lot of monkeys. Something happened to me with monkey, and it still puts a smile on my face when I remember it. Here is the story: I loved swimming in the river to catch fish and prawns. So, as I always did, I removed my clothes and dropped them on the top of a rock, then I jumped in straight away because I completely naked. Well! I was still a little girl. After a fifteen-minute swim, I crawled slowly to fetch my clothes; but I was shocked to find all my clothes were missing. I sat in the water thinking, I put my clothes right here so where are they? Who the hell has taken my bloody clothes? Suddenly I heard a monkey screaming at the top of a tree, and when I looked up I was shocked and really mad because the monkeys had taken all my clothes to the top of the tree. I tried my best to signal to tell them to bring down my clothes but they screamed even more and shook the branches. One of the monkeys had put my panties on top of its head. It looked like it was wearing a hat but I didn't find it funny at the time because I was so scared and worried about how to get home. I was in the water for half an hour but still nothing happened, and I couldn't stay any longer. I was worried somebody had passed by and seen my naked body; I was worried about a crocodile maybe coming to get me, and my body was getting so cold. I decided to go home naked. If I didn't do that, I would end up in the dark because it was soon going to be night. It was about a twenty-minute walk back to my house, but luckily we didn't have any neighbours. I started to run as fast as I could then I stopped behind a tree, looking around to make sure no one was there, then I quietly ran again and stopped behind another tree, looking around, and I did the same thing until I got home; I was like Tarzan! I think Tarzan was much better than me though, because he had underwear at least. I looked like someone who lives in the jungle and has never seen a human or the outside world before, and is now lost somewhere. Anyway, I was so worried about entering the house because my father was there. But luckily the clothes that my mother had washed were still hanging outside to dry in the sun. I ran like a rat to grasp any clothes that I could put on right away before anyone saw me. I was safe at last, thank God! And since that incident happened, I would never again swim naked in the river, especially on my own.

Our home also didn't have electricity. At night, when the moon was bright enough, I would go outside with my books and study while everyone slept. I took a great interest in learning, and I put as much effort as I could into it. Sometimes I would fall asleep until the next morning. Even today, seeing the full moon reminds me of peaceful moments studying in that clear, bright Malaysian moonlight. I can sit for hours looking at the moon. Tears flow down my cheek as I think of the sadness and unhappiness of my life.

I am a very patient and strong woman, and I always believe that things will get better. Where does moping around feeling sorry for yourself get you? I believe there is an answer to everything. Patience, optimism, looking for answers and physical resilience are the main strengths that enabled me to survive.

CHAPTER 5

Someday

I was just eleven years old, at home, sitting on the floor mats made from special leaves. We had no furniture, but that's the way houses were in the countryside.

My father was watching me with eyes full of loathing and hatred. As always, I didn't understand why he was angry. I had never done anything bad, yet his hatred towards me was ferocious. On this day, I could see a horrible mood rising up in him, and I knew something bad was about to happen to me. I could feel it, and I saw it clearly in his eyes. Abdul Wahab wasn't a man to hide his emotions. He hated me openly.

He went to the kitchen and came back with large knife. My eyes widened as I fixed my gaze on the knife. I was seized with panic and began trembling from head to toe, but I couldn't move. I couldn't believe what I was seeing! Abdul Wahab – I could hardly call him my father anymore – was going to fulfil his desire to eliminate me.

He came towards me, clearly intending to stab me or maybe he was pretending just to scare me. At the last moment, my survival instinct, deeply rooted and powerful, took over, and I sprang out of the door and jumped without putting my foot on the step. Luckily I didn't hurt my foot and I ran into the jungle in a state of absolute terror. Abdul Wahab was right behind me, ready to commit the murder that he had contemplated for so long.

I ran as hard as I had ever run but he was close behind me. Luckily, I was a fast runner – like Road Runner, beep, beep! I could hardly think straight, but I knew that I was in great danger and would have to overcome my terror to survive. I knew I had to protect myself from him, and if he could keep me in his sights, he would eventually be able to catch me. So I ducked down in the lush green vegetation and hid, lying prostrate on the ground, praying hard to God in heaven that Abdul Wahab would not find me.

He was just a couple of feet away. He almost stepped on me. Panic-stricken, I remained as motionless as a statue and as quiet as the grave, listening to the pounding of my heart and feeling that it was about to explode. I feared he might hear my heartbeat! I watched him pass back and forth, stopping now and then to gaze around, trying to penetrate the dense foliage with his eyes, and then moving forward again. For a long time Abdul Wahab kept up his search.

I remained still and silent. My feeling of terror continued. Insects and other creatures of the jungle crawled over my body, I was scared of insects but I did not dare to move a muscle until he left.

Finally he was gone. I jumped high like a monkey to remove some insects from my body, then I hid there in the jungle. At that moment I thought, Abdul Wahab you are evil. Thank God! I am still alive. After my head had cleared and I had convinced myself that he was gone, I finally rested my body against one of the big trees that had protected me. I slowly picked up a small, sharp stone and gently wrote on the tree, careful not to hurt my protector, *Someday I going to tell the whole world what Abdul Wahab did to me today.*

I felt so tired after the run so I slowly closed my eyes and fell asleep. When I woke I saw a beautiful sunset burst in front of me and from that moment I could see how beautiful this world is. I thought, if only I could have a beautiful, bright life like a sunset in Malaysia.

Slowly and with great care, I began walking home. I had no idea what was waiting for me there. After arriving at home, I hid from my father, waiting behind the house for my mother to come into the kitchen. As soon as I saw her I quickly called, "Mum! It's me."

And quickly she came towards me. I asked her where my father was. She whispered, "He's waiting for you, so you better stay in the shed and I will bring food, a sarong, and a pillow later."

While I waited for her, I cleaned myself as best I could in a well not far from the house, then I waited for my mother inside the shed. Not long after, I heard her footsteps then she slowly pushed open the door and walked in, carrying the promised food, a sarong for a blanket and a very soft pillow.

As she looked at me, I could see the sadness in her eyes, but she didn't want things to get worse. She handed me the food and said, "Have your dinner and sleep."

The smell of her cooking made me so hungry. As she is a very good cook, I ate everything; my's mother cooking is the best ever.

I was so happy to stay outside the house rather than be inside the house with the man who had just tried to kill me. After I ate, I wondered around, letting the food settle. I lay in the grass and looked up at the clear night sky. The midnight wind blew softly on my face, and I was comfortable and relaxed. I was alive, even though I had to sleep outside. All night I could hear the songs sung by the insects and frogs, and their wonderful noise helped me to sleep peacefully until the next morning.

I woke to the sound of a rooster. It was a bright, lovely sunrise so I could hardly open my eyes. What a beautiful day. Suddenly I realised that I must hide myself from Abdul Wahab until he left the house. That day, all I could think was that someday I would be away from this place. Someday my father would not be around to create this hell for me. Someday life would smile on me. Someday I would find love and would be treated with the respect I deserved. Someday… someday.

But when would that day come? And when would this nightmare end? What could I do to escape from this situation that was tormenting me? Where would I end up? How could I keep alive my hopes of changing this miserable life into something better? Or would I just keep hoping I would escape from this place?

I wanted to run away. I wanted to shout out to the world about all the suffering that was burning inside me. I wanted everyone to know what my father had done to me. I wanted the world to judge him and find him guilty of being the bad father that he was. I had been lucky this time, and my life had been saved, but what would happen tomorrow or the next day?

I was in anguish over the constant threat posed by Abdul Wahab. How was I going to be able to sleep? I was afraid to close my eyes – what if he came to kill me or beat me? I couldn't predict what kind of craziness would enter my father's head or what plan he might have to inflict further pain. It was impossible to live this way. I was a defenceless child! I didn't know how to protect myself, and I needed someone's help and care. My brothers were younger – still small children. They couldn't defend me. Only my mother could attempt that, but the consequences for her were terrible. My parents had bitter arguments and almost every time my father resorted to his habitual violence and ended up hitting my mother.

One of many violent domestic episodes that I was forced to witness remains etched with fire in my mind. I was ready to go school, but my father wanted to prevent me from going – by force if necessary. Just as he was about to strike me, my mother intervened, putting herself between us, then shouting at me to run from him and go to school. I did what my mother said. I ran but halfway my brain asked me to stop and find out what was happening to my mother. I ran back and saw my father savagely throw her to the ground and then she was on her knees. He grasped her hands and dragged her on the ground all the way to the alley way, then he lashed out, punching and kicking her. She was almost half naked. I watched all this from a rise in the trail, powerless to do anything. I could only weep over this new act of barbarity I was seeing. I couldn't even walk, my energy was gone completely. I couldn't even go to school, worried what would happen if I left my mother. I stayed in the bush all day and kept sneakily looking for my mother, to make sure she was not in danger. I went home at the time I usually finish school and pretended to my mother that I was tired from cycling and hungry. But my eyes were busy looking at her face and she didn't look happy at all. That really hurt me and there were tears in my heart.

CHAPTER 6

Kulim

I was twelve years old and it was the school holidays. In the Malaysian culture, I was considered old enough to think for myself. I could even be married, if my father so wished. I had to do something because most of the time Abdul Wahab was at home and that really worried me. He could not see my face every day or he would kill me. No! I couldn't let him do that – I wanted to live longer.

One afternoon, while I was sitting under one of the wonderful green trees near our house, I was wondering what I would do with myself during the school holidays. I wondered what would happen to me if I just stayed at home. I was sure God would protect me because he loves me more than anyone else does.

Suddenly, out of the blue, one of my relatives, Ismail, arrived. I have no idea why he ended up coming to my house at this moment but there he was, talking with my mother. I wondered what their conversation was about because it was taking so long. I had to stay away, I was not allowed to listen when my mother had a conversation with anyone because that was considered rude. From afar my eyes were focused on them when suddenly my mother called me over; I jumped up quickly and ran towards her. Then she explained to me that Ismail wanted to take me to stay with his family during the school holidays so I could help his blind wife and their four children. My job would be to look after the children and help with the household chores, and then I would come back home when school started again. I could see my mother was not really happy about letting me go, it was just to get me away from my father; she knew he was going to hit me all the time. So for that reason she had no choice but to allow me to go.

I was so happy for the opportunity. I thought: God was listening to me. I was going to get away from the house and my cruel father. At the same time I was worried about leaving my mother but I was sure she would be fine. I hoped that if I was not around my father would have no reason to hit my mother. I was both upset and happy to leave and my mind swam. But my survival instincts pushed me to gather up my few clothes and possessions, and in just a few moments I was ready to leave. Ismail started his motorbike and I sat on it properly, holding his waist tightly. Warm tears were running down my cheek as I said goodbye to my mother. She stood outside the house watching me until I was out of sight. I would not suffer at the hand of my father this holiday!

I was at Ismail's house for more than a month and I was so happy. I had never experienced this type of happiness. There was no fear of death. I could play with friends like other children did. Everyone in Ismail's family was very happy with me. They didn't want me to leave and neither did I. They wanted me to stay because I was very efficient and helpful to Ismail's wife.

So the sudden arrival of my favourite uncle, Zainol, was a sad event for Ismail's family and frightening for me. I ran and hid myself in the toilet, because I knew he had come for me. He waited for hours and everyone looked for me. But then I had no choice; I had to come forward to see my uncle. I was in floods of tears and told him that I didn't want to go home; I wanted to stay with Ismail's family. He insisted he had to take me home and explained that my mother was waiting for me.

And so, full of sadness, I left the only happiness I had ever known. I was on my way to certain death, I was sure of it. On the back of my uncle's motorbike, I was silent and would not speak with him, wouldn't even hold on to him, and I tried to make him angry by opening my legs wider and making them hard like sticks, but he didn't say anything and I thought, he really is a bastard! At that moment, for the first and the only time, I hated my uncle. He had come to take me from happiness to certain misery, if not death. I wanted my life to be full of the love and care I had felt in Ismail's home.

Unknown to me, my mother had run away from my father during my absence, escaping with my three brothers and all the household possessions to a nearby small city called Kulim. My uncle took me to the new house in Kulim. I was so happy when I arrived there and found out that my father was not with us, and for a while I lived in heaven a smile on my face every day.

But the calm didn't last long. My father, or as I had begun to refer him,

Abdul Wahab, found out where we were and came running back to my mother. My heart sank because she accepted him back! There are some things I will never understand and that made me very disappointed with my mother. Why did she want Abdul Wahab to hit us? Once again the clouds were gathering and I was sure it wouldn't be long before my life became impossible again.

And so it turned out. One afternoon, I had just walked in from school. I was still in my uniform and had my bag on my shoulder. The weather was very hot and humid and I was so hungry, I could think of nothing else but that I wanted to eat. But as soon as Abdul Wahab saw me, he called me over and said he wanted me to give him a massage. I told him that I was tired but when I refused, his response was to get up immediately, grab my arm and burn it with his cigarette until the flame went out. After he had done that he again asked me to massage him. I did it because I was scared he would burn my arm again. I massaged his back with tears in my eyes, trying to ignore the pain in my arm. I didn't tell my mother anything, instead I hid the pain and kept it in my heart I massaged him until he said, "That is enough."

I still carry the scar – the mark of burned flesh. The next few days again without rhyme or reason, Abdul Wahab threw something sharp at my face and cut my chin, it stung for a few days but still I didn't tell my mother what was happening. I still bear a small scar on my chin but with the will of God, that scar is not very noticeable. On almost every part of my body he left some scar. Every time I see those scars it reminded of the hell I survived.

Each day that passed, my father tried to commit every type of violence against me that he could think of. But I had grown older and knew how to defend myself or run away. This was my life for several years.

During this time of my life, my problems didn't get any better; they just became more complicated. My grandfather, Haji Isa, came to spend a few days with us. I was his only granddaughter and had been close to him since I was very young. He said I was his favourite and of course I was so pleased to see him, as we had not seen him for a long time because of the family situation.

At that time my house was a rented house, and of course it was a small house, and it was not uncommon for several family members to sleep together in the same room. When I was a little girl I slept with my grandfather every time he came to visit us. But now that I was a grown up young lady, I had become a little shy, especially as I hadn't seen him in such a very long time.

And this particular night, my mother decided that me and my brother Redzwan would sleep in the spare room with my grandfather, which I was quite happy with.

To my horror, in the middle of the night my grandfather tried to penetrate me from behind. I was sound asleep but I woke up when I felt something hard pressing at my bottom. I pretended that I had had a nightmare and screamed loudly than. He let me go immediately and acted as if nothing happened. It was repeated many times as soon as I fell asleep and many times I had to pretend that I was having a nightmare. I wanted to get up but I was scared of my father. All night I was awake and my mouth became so dry from screaming.

The next day I was thinking, my god not my grandfather too! I told no one about it. I tried not to stay at home because I didn't want to see my grandfather's face. All day I tried to think what reason I could give to my mother so I didn't have to sleep with him again. My mother asked me, "Why were you screaming last night?"

I said, "I had a dream, a very bad dream."

When I saw the sun go down and I knew the evening had arrived, I started to get scared. That night my mother sent me and my brother to sleep in the same room as my grandfather again.

This time I told my mother, "Mum, I can't sleep in that room, it gives me horrible nightmares so can I sleep on my own?"

But my mother was angry because she knew my grandfather loved me so much and she said, "Don't worry, your grandfather is with you, he will look after you."

I thought, you are right, Mother, he really will look after me very well. I didn't tell her what had happened as I didn't want to cause any problems between my mother and my grandfather – she had enough pressure in her life from my father. I was also worried she would not believe me because he was her own father; surely she would think it impossible her father would do such a thing to me. I could end up in big trouble, especially with my father at home, so I did as my mother asked.

That night, I was horrified when my grandfather again tried to penetrate me from behind. Again I was lucky and nothing serious occurred because this time I had thought to protect myself by going to bed with pants on and again I cried out loud, pretending to have another nightmare. The next morning, and for the rest of my life, I felt disgusted and uncomfortable whenever I looked at him. Thanks God he was leaving us that day. I have kept this a secret my whole life. I only saw my grandfather once more, in the following year when he was very ill. Instead of sorrow I felt pleasure. He called me to sit beside him but I ignored him and walked away; I couldn't look at his face. That was the last time I ever saw him. I hated him after what he tried to do. He suffered for many years before he died. I am very pleased about that; he did not deserve to stay on this planet.

One calm afternoon, I was cleaning the house with my mother when Uncle Zainol arrived on his a motorbike and asked her if she knew why her husband wasn't at home. My mother replied, "He was working this morning and did overtime last night."

Then Zainol broke the news. "You didn't know that your husband is going to get married tonight?"

My mother was shocked. She stopped cleaning and asked my uncle, "How do you know about this ?"

My uncle said, "Someone in my area who is going to the wedding tonight told."

I was so happy as soon as I heard the news that my father was going to get married. I thought, thank God! He doesn't need to come home anymore; he can stay with his new wife forever. But my mother was very angry. That evening she asked her friend who had a car to take her to the place where my father was going to get married. She got my brothers ready and took us to the place where the wedding was to be held. I was in the car waiting to see the action; it was like something out of James Bond. Many people were at the wedding and my mother waited for just the right moment to make her presence known. The tradition is that the bride and groom sit on the chair in front of the crowd. Everyone watches them.

I saw my father, in his sunglasses and suit, smiling at everyone, enjoying the ceremony with his new wife. When the time came for the guests to approach the bride and groom, my mother took hold of my two brothers and started walking towards them. I love this part. As soon as my father saw them, without saying a word, he got up and ran away, leaving the bride alone on her chair. I cracked up in the car until my stomach got cramp; it was so funny, he ran so fast, like a Road Runner. Zzzooommm…! Beep, beep!

My mother explained to the bride and her family that she was his wife and these were his sons. The bride was very upset because my father had lied to her and her family about not being married. He wasn't getting married that night but because he had already paid all the expenses for the wedding, including the bride's wedding ring, so as not to embarrass the bride's family, they found another groom to marry her. That new groom did not have to pay for anything because my father had already paid for the entire wedding. WOW! What a lucky man this new groom was, and what an idiot my father was.

My mother returned home with us and the whole night she was very upset. I would have loved to comfort her but I didn't feel like it because she still wanted my father in her life. I just sat in the corner in the dark looking at her and cried and hoped my father would never return home. My wish didn't come true because, a few hours later, my father returned home. I took myself away from them, and just hoped my father didn't hit my mother. I returned back in the dark, slowly sneaking to see what was going on, in case anything had happened to my mother. I was very frustrated that night when I heard their voices sounding very romantic in bed. Obviously my mother had taken him back. I walked away and left them in their own world.

In the morning I found both of them in the kitchen. My mother looked very happy, she had a big smile on her face and was joking and laughing with my father. I hid behind the door so I could hear what they were talking about. They talked so romantically, I couldn't understand any of it but before my father left for work he said to my mother, "Call me Abang, please!" Abang means darling.

My mother made herself sound shy, like a little girl, and softly called, "Bye, Abang."

As soon as I heard my mother call that fucker Abang I felt sick, it was disgusting and my heart was on fire. Once he was gone, I went straight to my mother and made fun of her, saying in a flirty voice, "Bye, Abang!"

She got really angry with me for doing that but I didn't give a damn, instead I asked her, "Why are you always taking him back?"

She refused to answer my question, instead she said, "You don't need to know all this, it is not your problem."

Then she walked away and left me alone in the kitchen. I thought, it is my problem because he always abuses me and hits her. It was so painful but I had no power to do anything.

Muslim men can marry up to four times but the majority prefer to follow the example of the prophet Mohammed, who had two wives. Prophet Mohammed married two women for a reason and he looked after his wives perfectly. But many Muslim men marry for enjoyment then after they leave their wives and children without any money. I have seen many women in that situation, first example was my mother. In order to marry a second or third wife, the first wife must give her permission. But Abdul Wahab, knowing that my mother would never consent to this, had decided to get married in secret. Unluckily for him, the news had gone around our small village like lightning, finally reaching the ears of Uncle Zainol.

Another year passed. Now I was thirteen, and knew men found me attractive. I noticed their desiring looks as they passed me on the street. I was one of the most beautiful girls in the area. I had traces of Indian like my grandmother and my skin, although brown, was not as dark as others in the area. Being a little more light–skinned than usual, I was therefore seen as more attractive. I was a little bit different, but not enough to attract negative attention. But I didn't think much of it at the time. I was still very young.

All students in Malaysia attend school in uniforms of the school colour. All the girls have to have two uniforms but I managed to have just one. After a certain age the girls have to wear a uniform with a long skirt that reaches down to their feet, but my skirt was above the knee. This drew the attention of the teachers and the school administrator, who asked me to wear a longer skirt the next day. The problem was that I only had one skirt. I listened to them and got mad, and I decided to cut my skirt even shorter. Why couldn't I have a life like the other girls had? Also, I didn't like the custom and I did not like how the long skirts looked.

Within a minute of my teacher seeing the length of my skirt, I had to be in his office. He warned me, "Your skirt is too short." And my solution? Shorter!

The next day I returned with my skirt cut even higher. I entered the school proudly with a huge smile on my face. I got a lot attention from all the boys, which I liked, but could see all the girls were jealous. Well! Who cares? I was being bullied at secondary school so now it was pay back time. Because the school was aware of my family's situation, no one made much of it. They must have thought I was half wild, but I there were so many reasons why I dressed up the way I did. But most of all it was simply a question of teasing, and even at that age, I had a very clear idea that only I would decide what I liked and what I didn't like.

At the age of thirteen, going to school and learning was my great passion, and it seemed that if I focused all my attention on this mental activity, then I could avoid thinking about the other problems that affected me. I felt better when I studied, and I realised that at school I was considered bright. I was, in fact, a brilliant student, and this made me feel like I had my own identity and that I was strong. At school, I was not the nuisance that I was for my father at home. I was not ignored. I was not invisible. I therefore made a genuine effort to be as a good student as possible. It was school that gave me back the dignity that my father had snatched from me.

By the age of fourteen, I had become an attractive young woman. My main concern was finishing school. I was getting on very well with my homework and preparations for my exams. I believed that if I knew subjects well, I might be able to live somewhere else when I was old enough and work for some company. On the day of the most important exam, Abdul Wahab wouldn't let me go to school. He didn't want me to leave the house. In order to stop me going to school and taking the exam, he took all of my uniform, along with all my school books and papers, and threw them into a dirty pond behind my house, and left me with the words, "You don't need to study because you are stupid." As soon as he left I retrieved my clothes, but they were all wet and smelly so I wasn't able go to school, and of course I missed the exam. I ran to the well and sat on my own for hours, I was crying and very upset thinking about the exam that I had missed. But Abdul Wahab was happy he had accomplished what he wanted. I thought, you, Abdul Wahab, you will see one day, I will show you who I am.

I continued to grow and develop in an environment with almost no opportunities, but even so, I managed to get through it. I consider myself a very strong woman and believe that someone up there is looking out for me. Yes! I am sure about that.

My mother got a job working at a restaurant, helping with cooking and cleaning in the kitchen. I think she was happy because she dressed herself nicely and she looked very cheerful. I was more than happy when I saw her happy. But one day she returned home from work and with her was a young man with a sweet face. My mother introduced him to my father, his name was Johari and he worked as a bread maker at the same restaurant where my mother worked. I didn't pay much attention to him. As far as I was concerned, I was just happy to see him bringing my mother back home safely everyday

But one evening my mother called me over to introduce me to Johari and, as a mark of respect to the elder person, my mother suggested I call him Abang, which means brother but between a couple means darling. My stomach felt sick when my mother suggested I call him Abang. I looked at my mother with my eyes open wide and with anger on my face. But my mother opened her eyes even wider and mumbled something so I knew she was angry. So I had to follow her suggestion and call the bread man Abang, but I thought, yuk! At the beginning I found it very difficult because I was not used to it but as time went on I found it easy to call him Abang.

In Malay the word Abang has a few meanings. The first Abang means older brother. It is often used in Malay families when one addresses their older male siblings. Malay families (mostly) find it rather disrespectful to address their older siblings by their first name alone. So as a sign of respect the word Abang is usually placed before the person's name or nickname, e.g. Abang Jo. This is perhaps the first step towards understanding why Malay women call their sweethearts Abang. It's because it is a nickname that has a feeling of respect, adoration, closeness and, most importantly, love. She calls him Abang. So I called the bread man Abang out of respect but he might have thought that I was in love with him. If that is what he thinks, I thought, then he can go to hell.

Soon I found out that my mother wanted me to be Johari's girlfriend. From then on my mother would leave me and Johari alone to chat. Sometimes I ignored her and left him with my mother and went to play with my friend. But my mother got very angry and gave me a warning, she said if I didn't pay attention to Johari, I would not be allowed to leave the house. I thought, this is madness, why does she have to force me to be with someone that I don't like? He was a very nice boy but I was just fourteen years old, I needed to be with friends rather than sit with a man with whom I had no idea what subject I was going to talk about. But when I was at school, I was the girl who knew how to flirt with the boys and who always had letters left in my desk. I had an afternoon class and the person who sat in my place in the morning was a boy so he would receive my letters and we would fall in love through the letters. Well! At that time, when I received a love letter I fell madly in love with that person, but actually I didn't know the difference between love and like because I was too young to understand.

My father had been getting really pissed off since Johari had entered our lives. I was going to school at the same as my mother was going to work. My mother worked from morning until evening, and then she came home with Johari, who would stay at our house until almost midnight, so my father didn't have much of a chance to hit me. I was so happy about this but knew I had to make the most of it as I didn't know how long it would last, it could end tomorrow or any time.

At fourteen year's old, I was quite naughty and very cheeky. I would arrive at school wearing my uniform but I would have spare clothes in my school bag. After school I would go to the toilets to change into a T-shirt and skirt then go to a coffee shop and have a glass of water with a male friend or go to the cinema. But sometimes I would go to Penang Island to meet my other boyfriend; I was so daring at that time. When I got home I would say that I had had an extra class. Sometimes when I got home Johari was there waiting for me. But most of the time my mother kept him company. I started to feel bored with him because he came to see me every day. I was bored when he talked about love because I really didn't know what love was about. He always talked romantically, which I hated. I wanted him to tell me a joke so I could laugh but he couldn't do that because he was such a good boy. We always stayed in the house and my mother never left us alone, she watched over our every single move. I totally understand that she didn't want anything to happen to me, especially as I was still so young. Sometimes Johari could be a very cheeky boy because as soon as my mother left us to have a shower or something, he would quickly hold my hand. His gentle touch made my heart beat faster; my whole body grew warm and I wanted him to be close to me. I thought, this strange feeling could be love. I started to like him and after that time I allowed him to hold my hand and sometimes he touched my hair. I knew he was really in love with me.

One day, I had just returned home from school when my mother asked me to be very polite because Johari's father had come to our house especially to see me. I thought, why do I have to be polite for his father? I found out that my mother and Johari had arranged for his family to come because he wanted to propose to me. I thought, fuck! I'm not going to get married at the age of fourteen. I'm not going to be in the kitchen cooking for him and I am not ready to have children. So I thought of an idea to make his father call off the proposal. I pretended that I was going to have a shower but I had to go to the well to do so. So I removed my top and just wore my underwear, then I started running like a chicken to the well in front of Johari's father while they were having some discussion. I could see my mother's face turn very red, she was obviously embarrassed. Even Johari's father was shocked but he smiled at me. After they had left my mother got really mad with me. She came towards me and pinched me hard on my thigh until it became badly bruised. She can pinch as much as she wants, I thought, as long as doesn't ask me to marry that bread man. Then my mother said, "You really embarrassed me and now I am sure his father will cancel the proposal."

I said, "Good! That is what I want."

Then she said, "Stupid girl!"

I raised my eyebrows, turned my back and left her alone. The next day Johari came to tell my mother that his father had said, "Not at this time because she is too young."

I thought, thank God! I was so glad but Johari continued to come to our house and even began to love me more.

Physically, I was strong and I was generally resistant to illness. But one day my habitual good heath was shaken by a serious chill and I spent several days with a dangerously high fever. I couldn't even get out of bed.

At one point, my mother was still at work and my brothers were outside playing, which left me hopeless, unable to move and alone in the house with Abdul Wahab. I was shivering in bed; suddenly my father came to my bed and began hugging me from behind and my shivering got even worse. My heart seemed to stop beating, my brain went completely blank and I didn't know what to do. Soon I felt something hard touching my bottom. Thank God I was dressed, even though I was in bed. I was horrified and scared and didn't move my body at all. I did not have the energy to defend myself. The high fever had left me completely debilitated.

Abdul Wahab hugged me tightly from behind. He started to talk to me tenderly and that made me so scared because he had never done that before in my entire life. I curled my body tightly to my chest while I felt something hard trying to penetrate my bottom and my mind went completely blank. Then he turned me over towards him. His face had the look of a hungry tiger looking at fresh meat. He started rubbing my body. I was lying like a piece a wood, wondering what was going to happen to me. He almost threw himself on top me, when suddenly my mother returned home. Abdul Wahab heard the door and he immediately let go of me and jumped to his feet. Providence had again smiled upon me and, for the third time, I was lucky and escaped being raped.

I detested Abdul Wahab for this continual abuse of every description, for his cruelty and for making my life so difficult. But, above all, I detested him for the lack of love he showed me as a father. The most painful thing of all was that he was my father, and yet he did not love me. When I looked at my friends and the presence of a man they called 'Father', sometimes I was very jealous of their happiness.

All my life, I have kept this pain inside me. My heart was continually broken during my first fourteen years of life, but I never asked anyone why he did these things to me. I never asked my mother and of course I never asked my father, since he never spoke to me like a father would a daughter. I continued trying to live my life, not understanding anything. I was unable to comprehend why he hated me as he did.

It was during this period of my young life that the answers to this mystery were revealed to me. I was finally told what had happened, but that only served to confuse me further, especially considering who told me and in what way.

When I was finally cured of the fever and the days returned to their normal routine, Abdul Wahab became enraged at me one day and he shouted, "You're not my daughter, you're a bastard! When I die, don't come to visit my graveyard!"

And that reminded me of a time I had called him 'Father' and he had shouted at me and said, "Who is your father? I am not your father so don't called me Father." From that time on I never again called him Father. If I needed to talk to him, I just talked directly to him otherwise there were no conversations between us.

When I heard these words I was speechless. I dimly began to comprehend. Was I in fact not his daughter? Was that why he hated me so much? I walked away with a broken heart and crying without tears. I was completely drained. I wanted to talk to my mother about it but I couldn't do it at first.

Only after a while did I work up the courage to ask my mother to explain her version. She told me that Abdul Wahab didn't believe he was my father but in fact he really was. My mother told me that she had become pregnant one month after their wedding, but that Abdul Wahab thought the child must be another man's. He was too young and ill-informed about pregnancy, and he thought it was not possible for my mother to be pregnant after such a short time.

I now felt like a stranger in the house. I was very confused by this turn of events. In my mind, the two versions became mixed up. How could I know for sure if I was his daughter? I wasn't sure if my mother was telling the truth and I lived with these doubts for a long time. It was not until I was twenty that I decided to believe my mother. I began to think that I was indeed his daughter, I looked a little like him, although I never felt for him what I thought I would feel for a father.

Life Behind the Silence

Meanwhile, the abuse continued. My mother tried to defend me and every time I became the subject of an argument. One afternoon, I arrived home from school and was just about to walk in but I could hear them having a big argument. So I slowly closed the door and went behind the house, waiting for the argument to settle down.

I tried to hear what they were saying. Tears came to my eyes as I heard my father say, "I can't bear to see that bastard's face anymore."

My mother answered, "She is my daughter and if you want to continue hitting her, we had better get divorced."

The previous separations had simply been verbal agreements but this time the separation was more permanent. They signed divorce papers and were legally divorced in 1980. When I was sure the divorce was really happening I became the happiest person in the world. I had never felt so happy and free in my all life. I never thought this miracle would happen and this became one of the most joyful times in my life. I went around with a constant smile on my face at the thought of a fresh beginning and a new life without that crazy man, Abdul Wahab, in our lives.

CHAPTER 7

Broken Heart

My mother, my three brothers and I moved to another house, this time in a different area of Kulim. We all carried the hope that we could live a happier life. It was more than hope in my case. I longed for it with all my heart.

This time, life did indeed start down a different path and things changed. In retrospect, I can't say whether they changed for the better or not but at the time it was certainly a change.

But Johari kept coming as usual and this time more regularly; almost every night he slept at our house. My mother still worked at the same place but Johari got a new job as a teaching assistant at a secondary school. After he finished work, he would go to my mother's work and take her home. I could clearly see the happiness between him and my mother, as they joked, laughed and slapped each other. Seeing my mother happy made me share that happiness in my heart. My mother would eat with him but not allow me or my brothers to be around. Well! Nothing bad crossed my mind, in fact I was happy for Johari because my mother was more experienced and could look after him better than I could. I was happier leaving them alone as I was free to do whatever I wanted. But as time passed, my mother became very strange. She started to get very angry when she saw me and Johari having a conversation. From her anger, I could see her jealously. I thought, this is weird, and day after day wondered why she was behaving so differently.

Her jealously got worse, she started to control Johari, telling him he couldn't be close to me. If Johari was at home, my mother would stay close to him and never leave him, even for a second. She would tell me what I should do to keep myself busy so I would not be around them. My mother would ask me to heat the food, but as I was not allowed to take the food to Johari I would have to call her as soon as it was ready. She would come and get the food and they would both eat together and leave me alone in the kitchen to wait until they had finished having their meal. Then my mother would leave all the dirty dishes for me to wash. I felt like a servant.

One afternoon I was sitting on my own on the veranda and my neighbour walked past and stopped to have a chat with me. The conversation started with a basic things then she told me about my mother's relationship with Johari, something that I was not happy to hear about. I looked at her with a smile, without saying a word, but my head was full of questions. Before she left me, she told me not to tell my mother because she didn't want to cause any problems between her and my mother. I agreed. I felt so sad but I didn't believe all this gossip. My mother was a pretty women and she was divorced and always with Johari, a young, good-looking man. I was sure this jealously was coming from this neighbour because she not happy to see my mother's happiness. So I let my mind rest peacefully rather than think such silly things, especially as she was my mother. She would never do such a thing to her own daughter.

My parents had just divorced and my father had taken my three brothers to live with him, only I stayed with my mother. I would visit my brothers every day and look after them, especially my little brother Nazeri. I spent as much time as possible with them and then I would leave before my father returned home. I prayed and hoped my mother would bring my brothers to live with us soon. It was the first time I had been apart from them and I couldn't live without them much longer. My brothers were my soul mates; I did everything with them and I felt very sad without them around me.

Usually I entered our house through the front door but one day, for no particular reason, I entered through the back door, walked through the kitchen and straight into the living room. I was shocked to see my mother and Johari hugging each other. Not just that but Johari was inside my mother's sarong. Soon Johari noticed me, and he jumped out and smiled at me. I couldn't believe my eyes. I turned my back and walked away with nothing in my mind. I didn't feel hurt, angry or jealous, just so frustrated with my mother's behaviour. I sat in the bedroom, not knowing what to think or what to do. She was my mother and Johari was my boyfriend, so why did they do this? From that day I felt my relationship with my mother became really weird. I was so confused and wanted to ask my mother about it but I was too scared. I waited for her to tell me something but she just acted like nothing had happened and so did Johari.

Every time I looked at them it left me with so many questions. This is something that I have never understood.

A month later my three brothers came to live with us. I was so happy. With them around to keep my brain occupied,I put to one side what had happened between my mother and Johari.

One night something that I had not been expecting happened between my mother and Johari. As always, my mother asked him to sleep at our house. Her reason was that when there was no man in the house during the night she was very scared. As we only had one room so my mother my brother's and I slept together in one room and Johari slept in the living room. But on that particular night, for some reason I couldn't sleep so I wanted to read a book and do my homework. For no reason, my mother did not allow me to that. But I insisted I stay awake and that we keep the light on so I could read. I looked at her face; she really was not happy with me and she said angrily, "Turn off the light and go to sleep."

I said, "I can't sleep, and I want to do my school work."

She looked at me with her big eyes and, with her voice even stronger, she said, "The bill will cost a lot of money, you want to pay?"

I thought, why is she forcing me to sleep? I ignored her warning and continued reading. She got mad and switched off the light while I was still reading. She went to bed and left me in the dark. I thought, why has she become so evil, like my father? I slowly crawled in the dark and put my book in the corner and then crawled to bed. I tried to sleep but my eyes were still open wide. I whispered to myself, "Come on eyes! Help me, please sleep."

I lay like a piece of wood, worried that my mother would notice that I was still awake as she would surely get mad. Suddenly I felt her make a move. She slowly got up and walked on tiptoe out of the room. I wondered what she was doing and why she was awake. Then I heard her wake Johari up but I couldn't hear what they were talking about because it was too quite. It didn't bother me, maybe my mother had something to talk to him about, but why couldn't it wait until morning? Whatever it was, I didn't care. As my eyes were beginning to close, I suddenly heard a funny voice coming from the living room. It was my mother's voice. I was sixteen years old and old enough to know what was happening. My heart broke into pieces; I was really hurt this time, hurt because I did not know why she would do this to her own daughter. My soul was screaming and crying in the dark silently. I was left with one word: WHY?

After one hour she returned to bed and went straight to sleep. I tried to hold my breath quietly so she would not know that I knew what had happened. All night I couldn't sleep, thinking of all the bad things that had happened in my life. I thought when they divorced I would live in peace but again I was having to suffer.

In the morning, the birds start singing and the day light punching through a small, small hole in the window. My body felt so tired and my tiredness really affected my mind I could hardly get up from the bed. I could see my mother get up and walk out from the room than I could hear both of them talking. My mother returned to the room and grabbed a towel for him to have a shower and then she went to the kitchen to prepare breakfast for him before he went to work. I wouldn't come out of the room until he had left the house. Surely he was ready to go because I could hear their voices outside the house. As soon as he left my mother shouted at me to get up and tidy the house .I whisper to myself, mum! I got up long time before you and before sunrise to bright this world to see what was happening in this planet earth. Good ended with bad and happy ended with sad so this is what life about. I woke up and woke all my brothers up too so I could tidy the bed. Everyone rushed to have shower before my mother screamed at them and left me alone to do the work. My mother walked in the room and found me mumbling to myself and she asked, "What are you talking about?"

Then I said, "Nothing."

Without seeing her face I walked out from the room. Then she came to find me in the kitchen, I walked outside to find something else to do. Because of what happened last night I try to avoid face to face confrontation with her as much as possible. I kept myself away from her as much as I could. I just wanted to be on my own without talking to anyone. I felt my mother was like a stranger. I loved her dearly but at the same time I hated her behaviour and I lost my respect toward her. I might have been young but I am still human and I have a heart too, that make me can't forget and can't forgive her. Maybe one day when I mature enough to understand why she doing such of things or she might be come forward tell me. Who knows what going to happen in the future but whatever is she still my mother and I love her deeply in my heart and as I have promise myself I will do everything for her life until the day I die.

One evening Johari came around my house and my mother happened be at work still. I left him by himself but he kept calling me. So hard for me to face him but I tried to hold the pain that had cut inside me and I walked slowly towards him. I sat far away from him and looked down on the floor like a stupid girl. I fight with my soul and look at him straight in his eyes without single blink and my brain whisper, you will never see me again, you are so disgusting and I hate you forever, stupid man!

He just kept smiling at me; he must have thought that I was in love with him still because of the way I looked at him. I didn't even know how to start conversation with him, only him keep talking to me. Then suddenly I could see my mother come home with her bike. Her face changed when she saw me and Johari chatting. I quickly got up and run in to the house but instead, I hid behind the door and tried to listen to what was happening. My mother got so upset with Johari because he left my mother to come home on her own, especially when my mother saw Johari and me talking. Then he went to sit near my mother and touched her shoulder. When I heard my mother's voice getting softer than I left them alone and I did my own things. Life full of foolish and people around makes me really sick.

The relationship between my mother and Johari was getting even closer and I was suffering from depression for the second time in life after I received abuse from my own father. Day by day I was getting so hurt to see their relationship. I tried so hard to be patient and this is the hardest things that I have to deal with in my life. I always thought I wanted to run away but I didn't know where to go. And I didn't have any money. I prayed every day and night that someone would come to get me out from this house full of hell.

A few months after the relationship between my mother and Johari were torn apart. Obviously I didn't know what was happening but I could see they had arguments all the time, then Johari stopped coming to our house. Very strange, my mother's character has changed as I can see in her face, she was very sad and she looked like someone who had heart broken with love. Not long after she decided to move to a different house but still in the same area. I was sure she wanted to run away from Johari or maybe something else. I would love to know about what happening but she always been to tuff toward me and that make me so scared to her. I don't know what the meaning of love and I had never been in love. I loved Johari just because I wanted to be loved because I never received any love from man called a "Father". Even though I had no feelings towards him but still hurt me badly because he plays with my mother's heart who just divorced with my father. And at the same time he was in love with me, wished I could read his dirty brain, what exactly was his plan. I really hoped he was not coming to my house anymore. I would be very happy and I hoped not to see him again for the rest of my life. I was sure my mother was in love with him but why did she have to take mine. I guess love must be blind. It hurts me to see my mother's had heart broken with her lover and hurt me constantly because she is my mother and I love her.

    I was so happy to see my mother back to her life and back to work at the restaurant helping around the kitchen and she always brings back the food left over for dinner. Sometimes I tried to make it last for a couple days by reheating it everyday. I tried to do the best I could at home, cleaning the house and looking after my three brothers especially my little brother Nas so when she returned home, I want to see her smile after being work all day.

    Being the elders child was a big responsibility, especially as my parents were divorced which left my mother, my brothers and me without much money. Even though I was still at a young age it hurt me badly to watch my mother struggle to find money for our basic daily survival. She worked hard for us but there was one thing that I really didn't like about her character; when she got tired she would throw her anger towards us and she would swear and use bad words at us. At that time I couldn't even have a conversation with my brothers because she would get mad and shout at me. When my mother at home my relationship with my brothers never been close because of my mother anger. She never sat and had a conversation with me or played with my brothers. As my brothers were still very young kids, I knew my brothers needed love from my mother. I thought when she divorces with my father my life was going to be different. Yes! The difference was I was saved completely from the abuse of an evil man called Abdul Wahab; but I still received mentally and physically from my mother. Because of her stressful life makes her trough all the nasty words and anger towards me.

    I remember one day I took my friend to my house and my mother really upset me by saying to me, your friend is very pretty and you are not. It really hurts me and at the same time really was embarrassing but I just kept silent because she is my mother. She always says not very nice things about me, just to put me down, I really did not understand for what reason. She wouldn't walk with me; she asked me to walk a long distance from her. The reason was, she was embarrassed if people knew I was her daughter because I was not pretty like her, it hurts me a lot. I really suffered with my mother's behaviour but I was still in her life. At that age of sixteen I had many works to help her with some money but whatever I did still didn't make her happy. When I got home she always found reason's to get angry with me. If I returned home late because of work then she would say, that I was going to meet up with a man. This made me so frustrated I would rather stop work and look after my brother's at home. For one reason I did not understand, why she had done this to me after I have abuse from my father. She safe my life and she give up her life with my father because of me. This is left me huge question mark and massive confusing in my head.

Before I always thought to run away from her because of what happened between her and Johari. But now I have program in my brain that one day I would run away, just because I couldn't take her character anymore. Well! I was not pretty like her and she was embarrassed to tell people that I was her daughter, sooner than later I would go from her life, and maybe without me she would be happy only god knew how hurt I was. I cried when I thought about Johari but thank god I did not marry him. If I had married him, surely the relationship between me and my mother was going to be a disaster and we would have hated each other. I spent another year with my mother, and then, at the tender age of sixteen, I moved to Kuala Lumpur the capital of Malaysia.

It happened one afternoon, as I lay in the veranda taking a nap. All of sudden, I was awakened by my mother, who came home early this particular afternoon. She had not only come home early but she had brought a middle aged woman with her. I didn't know who this woman was and she did not even look at me when they arrived.

While my mother and this lady sat and talked, I played with my brother outside. Suddenly my mother called me to join them. Without any discussion about it, I was informed that I would be going with this lady to stay with her sister in Kuala Lumpur.

When the woman said she wanted to take me to Kuala Lumpur, I almost fainted. My heart began to race as I thought of travelling to the big city, full of glamour and famous people. It was my dream to live in the big city and also I wanted to run away from my mother because of what she had done to me. She also would always swear and get angry at me when she was under immense pressure to look after us and to find money to get our daily basic food and to pay bills and rent, and for all those reasons I just couldn't wait to get away. My mother did not seem very happy about my leaving, but I begged her with tears on my cheek, and at end of the day she sadly agreed to let me go.

In the next few hours I packed a small bag with the few clothes I owned and I left my house, my mother, and my three brothers. I didn't feel sad at all to be leaving them. I was very excited about the trip I was about to take and the thought of seeing the big city was the only thought in my mind, even though I was leaving the only family I had ever known.

I lived with a married couple who had two children. They knew that I still wanted to study and as a promise they took another girl as a maid and her job would be cooking and cleaning. And my job was just look after her two children and study whenever they were a sleep or during the night.

I loved the children, even until these days. In addition to having a nice home to live in, I earned a small wage from the work I did for the family. It was not much but for a girl of seventeen who had previously had nothing, this small amount of money was like a fortune. My room was very small but allowed me a certain independence I had never experienced before. At the same time, I continued with my studies, progressing with my A levels at home. The family was very encouraging and kind. At that time I was overwhelmed with work and with the additional pressure of my studies and I had almost no time for myself.

After a few months I had received the letter to tell me which school I had to go to for the exam. My women who I called her auntie took me to school and when the exam was over, she picked me up and brought me home. This was a wonderful change for my life, when my own father had never done such a thing for me. The students looked at me when I arrived with big car and I am so proud, some of the students asked me; who was that lady. And my answer was, she is my auntie. They must think that I came from a rich family. Well! Who cares? The exams lasted more than a week. One month after I received a letter from school, it was the result of my exam. My heart bumping fast I was so scared to open it, in case I failed the exam and I would feel frustration for myself, embarrassed, guilty to them, because she took time off work to send me to school. If that happened I would get out from they house. I locked myself in the toilet and opened the letter a bit by bit until I could see the words passed, and with a good mark. I was jumping and my heart was screaming with happiness, I looked at myself at the mirror, smiled and splashed my face with water and I felt on top of the world that I did it, all the hard work had paid off. This was the first time in my life I had taken the exam properly and for the first time ever someone who really care about my education even just a very shot time but is mean a lot to me. Thank god! For giving me such happiness that I never had before. And thanks to them for giving me the opportunity to learn and to understand my dream. They were so happy for me when I told them the news.

But then the happiness didn't last long when the other girl broke the news that she wanted to stop working. The woman I called auntie, she asked me to stay and promised to find another girl to help me. But in the mean time I had to do all the domestic chores: looked after the two children, clean the house, ironing the clothes and cook for them. But I had never done much cooking in my life, so I had to learn how to cook from a cookbook. Took me hours and hours to cook just for one dishes and this led to some bouts of tears because I hated cooking and the kitchen. As far as I was concerned, cooking was a hassle. But to show appreciation for what she had done for me I stayed with it and learned and today, thanks to the experience I know how to cook very well.

Some how their character towards me has changed, they became so serious, only talked when they needed too and never smiled at me. She put a small table and one chair in the corner of the kitchen, and there I waited for them to finish the dinner. Soon as they finished, she would find me in the kitchen to ask me to clear up the dining room. After I had done everything then I had dinner in the kitchen, I would eat whatever was left but sometimes they left me nothing. I couldn't go anywhere, because I had so much work at home. She decided not to take anybody else on to help me. Everyday I was getting so tired with work with so much stress. I wanted to go out from that house but I didn't know where to go, I didn't want to go back home. Everyday and night I was hoping something will happen so I can go out from that house for good.

One day, I was at home taking care of the children as usual, when there was a knock on the door. When I saw who it was, I stood there in shock; there stood my mother – in Kuala Lumpur, completely unannounced! And alongside my mother were an old man and two good looking young man that I never meet before. I was unhappy seeing my mother and I was scared of the family and scared to asked them to enter the house without permission from them. But because of my own mother with no fear I asked them to come in. I didn't pay much attention to them because I was busy with two children under my care. My mother just sat with old man and looked at me than she asked, "So you look after the children and where the family are? "

She asked me like a stranger and her face look very arrogant and I thought, you as a mother never care what I go trough in life instead you embarrass me but I answered, "Still at Work."

I didn't talk much with them, but I noticed the three of them discussing something, which I don't know, what? Whatever it was, I didn't care.

Life Behind the Silence

This is how I learned that my mother had married an older man with two grown up children from a previous marriage. I was more than a little surprised. My mind was in a whirl. So many things went through my mind I could not even focus. All I could think was what? Another husband! This an old man going to treat her same like my father done? How did she meet this man? And how did she find my address? And where are my brothers?

I became so confused and mad at the same time, all I could think to do was shout at her. In stead, I said I was busy and did not have time to talk to her right now; and I told her not to come here again. In truth, I very scared the family will return home any moment. I was rude and did not even offer them something to drink, as is the custom in Malaysia.

I could not even look at them as they left, all I could think was, he was a lot older and he could hurt her more than my father. When the family returned home, I didn't tell them anything, I was doing my job as usual pretending nothing happened. But I was so upset the rest of the evening and that night I could not sleep.

The following week, my mother came to see me with her new family again. I told her not to come here anymore because I was afraid about everything at the moment. Even though I was not happy where I was now but I would rather be a slave then follow her back home. I looked at the time, the family would return home any moment and I had not even fed the children, and not even cooked dinner yet! If they realised just how dysfunctional my real family was-they might ask me to leave.

The family did not like people entering the house when they were not at home. After some discussions we came to a solution. I agreed to talk with my mother just outside the house.

The conversation didn't last long but at least we started catch up on the latest and hope she would answer the question that burned in my mind: How did you get my address? And why you married with an old man? I am very protective of her and I just don't want to see her suffer again. It turned out that my mother was now living in Kuala Lumpur, just as I was!

After I left Kuala Lumpur, Harisun had changed to another restaurant helping around kitchen. The owner of the restaurant was a very nice young woman of about thirty named Rosita. Everyday she talked to my mother, tried to find out my mother's background without my mother noticing. She loved my mother because my mother was such a hard worker. Also Rosita came to respect my mother because of the way she maintained a positive outlook in spite of her past life. Funny enough, her father who lived in Kuala Lumpur was looking for a woman to spend his life with and for that reason; Rosita asked my mother if she would ever get married again. But at first, she said, "Never " then after sweet talk from Rosita at last, my mother said she would if a good man came along. Rosita was so happy and decided to telephone her father, Rahmat, an older man who was considered attractive. Without wasting time, over the next few weeks, he came to Kulim in order to meet my mother and the following months they got married. For me that was very quick. More than eighty people attended the wedding. The bride wore a wedding dress of bright colours and of very good quality. After the ceremony, the happy couple decided to live in Kuala Lumpur, not very far from the city where I live.

I also received news about my brothers. My mother told me that only my youngest brother, Nazeri, had come to live with her in Kuala Lumpur, and that my two older brothers were living with my uncle and that is what she told me, I really hoped their were ok. Anyway I was very unhappy to learn that my two brothers were living with someone else, even if it was my uncle. I didn't trust anyone in our family to look after my brothers.

I was completely unaware of all that had happened and I was still not happy to see my mother with her new husband an old man. My mother was a very beautiful woman, still young, so why did she have to choose this old man with grey hair. I didn't think she should have got married so soon; I was afraid this new husband would hurt her as my father had. I was very worried for her. I have only one mother she had already had such a difficult life with my father.

As I feared, my mother asked me to come and live with her and her new husband. I made the decision to follow my mother because I was worried about her with her new husband if I was with her at least I could do something.

Not long after the family came home, as soon as she saw my mother, her face changed. She just said, "Hello "then went straight to the kitchen.

I followed her in the kitchen; I saw her face was very angry; I stood in the corner with so much worry. As she had never met my mother before so she asked me, "Who are these people?"

I said, "She is my mother and I told her about the news, that my mother came to take me to stay with her."

She looked at me with shock, anger, frustration and then she left me in the kitchen and returned to living room to said, hello to my mother and the rest. I went and sat in my little room nervously waiting, what going to happen? Half an hour someone knocked on the door and quickly I run to the door, it was her with unhappy face and she said, "You can go."

I gave her a little smile and said, "Thank you".

I started gathering my clothes with happiness, relieved from all the housework that I had to do. Even though sometimes she could be very nasty to me but I have learned a lot about life and human character. It was a sad time to leave the children that I looked after for quite sometime. I thanked her kindness the time that I was with her then I look for the last time to her two children under my care, hold my tears and walk away without looking back.

CHAPTER 8

My Life Becomes Independent

I started a new life with my stepfather and I hoped this would bring me the happiness that I searched for for a long time. If his character was bad like my father's, it would be really difficult for me to stay with him. Because my life had been hell with Abdul Wahab I didn't want that to happen to me or my mother again. What I hoped I would get from Rahmat was happiness. I hoped he would be a good father to me and a good husband to my mother because she deserved it. All I wanted was a fresh new life to begin.

It didn't take long to see that my mother's new husband, Rahmat, was a good man and made my mother happy. I saw that my mother had found contentment in her life at long last – a happiness she had never had before. I was very happy for her. Her heart began to recover from the past abuse. This old man kept surprising me with his treatment of me and my mother. I started to love him as a father, with feelings I had never felt before, certainly not for Abdul Wahab. But the biggest and most wonderful surprise was yet to come. One day, he asked me to call him Daddy.

Rahmat had a son from his first marriage who was about thirty years old. His name was Rosli and he worked in a hotel. As I couldn't speak English very well at that time and so I could gain some work experience in a hotel he recommended me as a housekeeper and, with his help, I got the job. I was so happy when I got the job but at first I didn't realise that I would have to clean more than ten rooms a day. I was not worried about cleaning the rooms but I was worried about making the beds. I hardly knew how to make my own bed let alone ten. I was relieved when I found out that the supervisor had asked someone who had experience to teach me.

I was now ready to start my new job. As I was a new worker I followed those who had been working there for a long time. I followed whatever they said. One of the girls handed me a sheet and the sheet told me which floor I had to go to and the number of the room that I had to clean. Also she showed me the trolley that I had to take. I thought, fuck! I have to push the trolley, and I started to hate the job. Even though I didn't enjoy my work I was fine because one girl was always with me when I cleaned the rooms and she taught me how to make the beds, clean the bathroom and the rest. It was hard work but I still managed to do it as long the guests were not in the room. If they were, I couldn't clean the room and make the bed in front of them because I am a very shy person. For exactly one week the girl accompanied me then she left me and told me that I had to work on my own from now on. I had no idea that she was only with me to train me. I thought she was going to be with me all the time. Now I was really worried and felt under pressure working on my own. I was not worried about doing my work but felt pressured when I thought about the guests. I just didn't want them in the room because I would be too shy to do my work. Every day before I started work, I would hope and pray the guests were not in their rooms and then thank God for listening to me if he gave me what I asked for. But sometimes if I heard guests footsteps while I pushed the trolley, I would quickly hide my face behind the trolley. It was like that until I stopped working there.

The most exciting part of my work was when I entered the room. I would walk straight to the bed to see if there was any money on the bed, as that would mean that the money was a tip and belonged to me. Whenever I got a tip it was a happy day for me and today every time I stay in a hotel I always leave tips for the housekeeper because I know it will mean a lot to them. And the other happiest time of my work was when I cleaned the checkout room, because sometimes guests would leave something that they didn't need anymore, such as an apple. At that time I hardly got to eat apples, only people who had money could afford to eat apples, so for me it was special. I could eat one apple for two days. But the experience that I can't ever forget was when I found a condom on the bed for the first time. I thought it was a balloon. I wanted to blow it up but it was a little slippery, so I washed it properly and tried to blow, but I found it was an unusual balloon. Then I decided to keep in my pocket and show it to my friend and my friend laughed and explained to me what it was. I felt so stupid and so embarrassed. It was a good experience working as a housekeeper. It taught me how to make a bed and clean properly. Every day I learned new things and I gained even more independence.

My mother got pregnant and in the months that followed we noticed a big change in her. Her character changed drastically. She was very irritable and depressed because of the pregnancy. Almost every day, she asked her husband to divorce her and every day she stirred up problems, but her husband just ignored her behaviour. My mother started screaming and swearing at me again. Every day I had to run to work, otherwise she would stop me. When she asked her husband to divorce her she said she would leave Rahmat if he didn't and go back to Kulim by herself. I prayed and hoped she would not do such a silly thing.

One day, she left Rahmat and me without a word. I was ashamed to stay at Rahmat's house without my mother, so I gathered my clothes and left that house. I went to the train station, thinking, where should I go? I didn't want to go back home to my mother. At that moment I felt like a bird that had lost its mother and was learning how to fly on its own. The question was, why had she done this to me again? Many questions were buzzing around my mind and for almost one hour I sat in the train station on my own, I didn't know where to go. Then I decided to call my friend and I had to wait another hour for him to arrive. When he arrived, he quickly found me and asked me what was happening. I explained to him and, with the little money that I had saved, he said he was willing to help me find a room for rent. But it would have to be the next day because it was now too late to look for a house. That night I didn't know where to sleep and of course he wouldn't leave me alone. As he lived with his parents, he was a bit worried to take me home, especially as we were still young. But he was very brave and took me to his parent's house. We arrived almost at midnight, but before we entered the house I said, "I don't want to go inside, I am scared."

He said, "Don't worry, you wait here for a minute, I will go inside to explain to my parents."

I waited in the dark, thinking a snake might come to bite me or maybe a ghost might come to scare me, many stupid things crossed my mind. I was so scared I didn't dare move, a few mosquitos were sucking my blood but I still stood like a statue. I just hoped he had not forgotten about me waiting outside. After ten minutes I saw him open the door and walk towards me then he said,

"Sorry! But I have talked with my parent and explained everything to them, so come on inside, they want to meet you."

I was very nervous but his mother was such a lovely woman and made me so comfortable. After we had chatted about a few things, she took me to the room where I was going to rest for the night. I was so tired, as soon as she left me I closed the door and went straight to bed, where I stayed until the morning.

As he had promised, the next day my friend took me on his motorbike to go and find a place to rent. After two hours of searching we saw a piece of paper hanging on a gate which said 'Room Vacancy'. Without wasting any time we entered the house and asked about the room. I was very lucky, they accepted me and I moved in the same day. I stayed in a double storey house with three bedrooms and with three new friends sharing. One of my housemates, Zai, became a very good friend of mine. She worked at the checkout counter at a club for VIPs, and she got me a job there as a waitress. I was so happy going to work in a smart uniform, I looked so pretty. I worked in the lounge serving soft drinks and alcohol. There I started to learn to speak English and met a lot of good people. Most of the customers were Malay, Chinese, Indian and European. One day a group of Europeans walked in and sat in the lounge. I was scared to take the order because of my English, so I hid myself behind the bar but unluckily my supervisor found me and he said, "Go and get the order for that table."

Without argument, I came out and walked straight to that table but when I was halfway he said, "Get a pen and paper."

I turned around, looked at him and said, "I have them in my pocket."

When I got to their table I was very nervous and in my mind I was counting; there were eight of them. I hoped I could understand what they said. Then I brought out a pen and paperand asked in my broken English, "You like drink?"

They looked at me with a smile and then one by one placed their order with me. My nerves let me down completely and my eyes concentrated on my supervisor. He was staring at me, making me even more nervous. I thought, fuck off, just leave me alone. My brain went blank and I forgot the order that I had taken, the only drink that I remembered was Campari. But what I heard was 'ikan pari', which means 'stingray' in English. I thought, why do these foreigners want to drink ikan pari? As far as I know, Ikan Pari can only be eaten, and how do they know about that fish? Very weird. I walked to the bar, where my supervisor was waiting for me to give him the order.

He asked, "Give me they order."

I said, "Sorry, I didn't write it down and I only remember one order, which was ikan pari."

He looked at me then he said, "All though there are eight people you remember only one drink?"

Still I didn't say a word, I just stood in front of him and looked down at the floor. But then he asked me go to the coffee house and ask the kitchen for ikan pari. While I went to the coffee house, he went to take the order all over again. In the coffee house I asked one of the staff for ikan pari. As soon as I mentioned that word they all laughed at me and made fun of me. Then the chef said, "We don't cook ikan pari in the club. Who asked you for it?"

I was so embarrassed and was brought to tears but one of the waiters from the coffee house, who was in love with me, took me outside to comfort me. I learned a lot after that incident and every time I saw a foreigner with white skin, blonde hair and blue eyes walk into the lounge, I would quickly go to the bar and have a shot of vodka, which is my favourite drink, then I would feel confident enough to speak English and take their order. It was very cheeky of me; if my supervisor found out I had been drinking, I would surely have been fired.

Usually my friend and I would take the bus to work, but sometimes, if we were working the night shift, we could catch a ride in the club's car, which was reserved for employees. I worked there for more than a year. I felt very happy with my new lifestyle. I had freedom and that was important to me. I knew how to appreciate it after spending so long confined by my father.

I suppose the bad times my mother had experienced during previous pregnancies had left their mark on her. Harisun returned to Kulim and there gave birth to my sister, Nurul Fatima. Nurul Fatima was born a year after my mother's wedding, on February 11th 1985. Soon, Harisun went back to work on the rubber trees again, earning a wage collecting sap from trees that belonged to someone else. Her life never changed. She had once again cycled back around to where she had begun.

I moved into a different house, this time with a couple of different girls. There were two rooms with two girls living in each room. My roommates were very nice and I got along fantastically with them. I moved into this new house because it was convenient for my new job. I was now working in an electrical store as a shop assistant. I was earning a little more money and continuing my part-time studies.

Soon after that, I was offered a job in Melaka, a major city about three hours from Kuala Lumpur, in a foreign exchange office. I moved to Melaka with one of the girls from my house. She had also landed a job in the same office. We travelled there together and, almost immediately, we found more work as waitresses in a club in Melaka, where we usually worked the night shift. It was part of a Portuguese restaurant, next to the beach, where a lot of tourists would come to eat and have a drink. By that time I was confident with my English.

One night I met a gentleman from Australia at a club. He was twenty-five years old, tall and very handsome. This was the first time a white man had paid attention to me, and I was very proud of myself because in my country, whoever was with the white guy was considered to be the lucky one. I enjoyed going out with a good-looking man but didn't fall in love with him. I discovered I liked to play around with men's minds. He was very caring, always waiting for me while I finished work, and one night I took him home. I shared with three other friends, so I called all my friends to join me and sleep in the living room. We all slept on the floor but he slept on the sofa close to me and held my hand all night; it was so sweet. The next morning before he left he wrote a note to me saying, 'Gina, I Love You'. That was romantic. It was this man who suggested I call myself Gina. I thought Gina had a nice ring to it and, since that time, Gina has been the name I use.

The Australian man had fallen in love with me and wanted to get married. Although I liked him as a friend, I didn't see him as a potential partner in the way he saw me. I knew myself very well and I was still very young. I had discovered that I couldn't stay with one man for more than a month – if he was lucky! I loved to play with men's hearts and I was happy and satisfied when they got hurt. I did this as revenge for how my father mistreated me.

I lived with three others girls, they were all fantastic friends, but they all took drugs except me. Every day and night they brought male friends to the house. I didn't know any of them but slowly I became friends with all of them. I never smoked and I never took drugs, but I liked to watch them taking and most of the time I helped them do it. One night, one of the guys really wanted me to try it. I insisted I wouldn't take it but they followed me everywhere that I went and challenged me to do it. I hate people challenging me and for that reason I took drugs for the first time. After a puff, I felt the world turn upside down then I collapsed on the floor. I didn't know what was happening, but I knew I was safe because they were my good friends and they would look after me. The next day I tried to remember the feeling the drugs gave me. It was so different and I could forget all the problems that I had in my life. Since that time I took them every day and became addicted for some time. Life for me at that time was fantastic; I did not need to think about my life or anyone in my family.

But one day I was so upset and had been crying all day, my eyes were very swollen and this was noticed by someone who I knew at work. He was about thirty-five and was so in love with me, but I never gave him any attention because he was much older than me. But that evening he saw how upset I was and he was so caring towards me, giving me the comfort that I needed. I had never met a person with such a good heart in my entire life at that time. My feelings towards him were nothing more than they would be for a father. He gave me so much confidence and I trusted him and, because of that, I told him that I missed my brothers and my mother. But I couldn't go home; I was scared because I had never sent any money to my mother. I wanted to send it but there was hardly enough for myself. He listened without saying anything but the next day he returned to my work with a big smile on his face and handed me an envelope. I looked at him and asked him, "What is this?"

Then he said, "Just look at it."

Impatiently, I opened it straight away. I was shocked and almost fainted because I had never had this amount of money before. I was confused and scared. "Why have you given me a lot of money?" I asked him. "Why have you given me a lot of money? I don't want your money."

Then he said, "For your mother so you can go back to visit them."

It really touched my heart. I didn't know how to pay back his generosity, so I said, "Thank you for your kindness, but I would like you to send it yourself to my mother."

I handed back the RM 1,000 so he could send it to my mother. I was sure my mother would be very happy to receive that amount of money and I was so proud to do that for her even though it was not my own money, but one day it would be.

Not long after, I decided to visit my mother, as she was having a very hard time of it. She got divorced officially; they signed the papers and everything. She never returned to her second husband. My heart fell; I was very upset with my mother. Why did she do this? A good man came into her life and she did not take advantage of the opportunities offered to her by this good man who asked me to call him Daddy. I wanted her to be happy so much, and to be treated with love and care. Well! I guess my father had succeeded in ruining my mother's life as well as mine.

CHAPTER 9

My Sister

When my mother was pregnant with my sister, Nurul, I was in the capital city, and at first I didn't go back to visit my mother and my little sister for some reason. A few years after she was born I decided to go home to visit my mother and the rest of the family. There in front of me stood a little girl. She was so tiny and so sweet, at that time she was only two years old. She just looked at me but never came near me. I guess because she hadn't seen me before she was a bit scared of me, and I was a bit rough with her. Well! I had never had a sister and all of sudden one entered into my life when I was twenty years old, so it was a new experience for me. I felt very strange but I adored her. I looked after three of my brothers, I used to be a servant and looked after two children and of course I love children, but I can be very tough and serious too, and that makes the children scared and nervous.

The next day I took my mother to the hairdresser, as she loves to have her hair cut short. I waited for her in the car and looked after my sister, who slept soundly. Five minutes later she woke up and found out that it was only me in the car. As soon she looked at me, she started to cry. I can't stand it when children cry, it really annoys me. I tried to talk to her as nicely as I could, but she wasn't listening, in fact she cried even louder. I handed her a sweet, and she took it and threw it at my face. That made me lose my patience and I shouted at her, "SHUT UP!" I thought shouting would make her stop, but it was getting worse. She was kicking and screaming – it was non-stop. I had never seen a child cry like this before; none of my brothers behaved like her. She made my head burn, so before I exploded, I took her to my mother in the salon. With anger I handed her to my mother and said, "Take it! I don't want to look after her, she is mad."

Life Behind the Silence 63

My mother said, "What happened?"

I said, "She doesn't want me at all, and she cries like crazy, I hate her."

My mother said, "She is still new to you."

She stopped crying as soon as my mother started breastfeeding her. Ugh… two years old and still drinking her mother's milk. I walked away and waited for my mother in the car, while thinking about my sister. Well! I guessed it would take a bit of time for my sister to get to know me because until now I had never been in her life, so I was a stranger to her. I realised that I was the one who was being silly. After that I went home quite regularly and she started to get to know me, she almost accepted me in her life. But then I left her for a very long time; I disappeared to London for a year without telling anyone in my family except my brother Nazeri, who only knew about it because he stayed with me.

I always stayed in contact with my family because I was worried about them, especially my mother. Obviously I couldn't help much at that time because I was still studying and I couldn't even support myself. When my life was getting harder and times were getting tougher I kept myself in silence and I stopped contact with everyone. The reason for that was that I didn't want to hear about their financial problems. I felt guilty that I couldn't help them. Then a few years later my life got a bit better and I got some work to earn my living. I felt a bit more comfortable about getting in touch with my family. So I sent them a letter with my phone number. Within a few weeks I received a phone call from a man whose voice I had never heard before, so I asked, "Who are you?"

His reply was, "Zambri, Mum wants to speak with you."

I was in shock; the person on the phone to me was my brother. I was lost for words. Then I heard my brother say to my mother to hurry up and speak to me because it was long distance. Soon my mother said, "Hello."

I answered, "Hello, Mum!"

As soon as she heard my voice, she screamed, cried and hardly talked to me. Since then I never left them again, and tried to help them as much as I could until this day. For nearly twenty years I have been in London and that is the first and last time Zambri called me. I can understand as calling long distance costs them a lot of money but I will call them three or four times a week.

One day something happened that I never expected. I received a lovely surprise, a beautiful letter from my sister. I hadn't seen her for many years, she had been a little girl when I left and now she could write letters! I wondered what she looked like now; she must be grown up and a beautiful girl. I still remember her letter, it said, 'Hi sis! How are you? When are you coming home? I miss you and I love you.' The sight of that little letter made me want to fly back home right then. Her letter really touched my heart, it made me so emotional. I burst into tears, thinking, this is the first time someone in my family has said such things, I just couldn't believe it. It was a magical and wonderful feeling that I had at that moment and it made me feel alive again. I really couldn't wait to see her. And I would make sure this time that I would be a fantastic sister to the little sister that I used to hate when she cried. Since that time, she started to send me letters, New Year cards, and she never forgot to send me a card on my birthday. She is just a sweetheart and I adore her. But of course before I lost contact with my brother Nazeri he was the only person who really cared about me and who always worried about my life. My brother Nazeri is my soul, I love him dearly.

After eight years in London I went home to see my family. Kazmin, my boyfriend, took me in his car all the way from the capital city to my mother's city, and the journey took about five hours. He was very kind to do that for me. On my way home I was so looking forward to seeing my mother, my brothers and especially my dear sister; she had been so fantastic to me. When I arrived at my mother's house, I saw my mother standing in front of the door, looking at our car. But she didn't know that I was inside it, and she didn't recognise Kazmin. She had lost a lot of weight but in fact she looked younger. I hurried out of the car and shouted, "Mum!"

She was kind of shocked to hear my voice after seven years and it took her a few seconds before she started screaming and ran towards me. I hugged her and gave her a big kiss, then I quietly said, "I love you, Mum, and miss you loads and loads, sorry for leaving you for such a long time." As soon as I entered the house, I expected my sister to be around and was a little disappointed because she was not in the house so I asked my mother, "Mum, where is Nurul?"

Then my mother said, "She is at school, but she will be back soon."

My mother had met Kazmin before so they just talked naturally without any help from me. I know my mother, she loves to decorate her house, but this time it was really too much. In every corner of the house she had put flowers, and she had even hung flowers on the wall. For me it's okay if the flowers are real, but all the flowers were plastic. As soon as my mother went to

Life Behind the Silence

the kitchen, Kazmin started to look around. I was a bit embarrassed, so I said, "Look at my mum's house, flowers are everywhere and are very colourful and bright like an Indian house."

Then Kazmin said, "Well, that's fine, you have to understand, she lives in the countryside and is it nice anyway."

I looked at him but didn't say anything and I thought, I am not sure he really means it or if he is just trying to be nice to me. My thoughts were interrupted as soon as I saw a school bus stop in front of the house. Then a young girl in her school uniform and with her head covered walked through the gate and entered the house. I thought, she must be my little sister. As soon she entered the house, she looked at me with her beautiful smile on her face and said, "Hi sis!"

As is the custom, out of respect for her elder, she kissed my hand and then she disappeared into her room. Her face looked exactly like my mother's, and she was so sweet and very polite. WOW! She wasn't a little girl anymore, and from that moment I fell in love with her character. How proud I was to have a sister like her. I just couldn't wait to spend time with her, and I knew we would get on well together.

Kazmin left me with my family and he drove back to the capital city on his own. I stayed with my mother for two weeks and had lovely time with my sister. Every day we got to know each other more and we became very close; we weren't only sisters but also best friends. Then after a few weeks I left my mother, my sister and brothers and went back to the capital city, but I promised her that on my next trip I would bring her to stay with me in the capital city. This would be a treat for her, also I was alone as Kazmin was with his wife most of the time. So it would be nice if my sister could stay with me for a few months before I decided to return to London.

A few months after I bought my own car and decided to drive back to my mother's city on my own. As I had promised my sister, I had to discuss with my mother my plan to take my sister to stay with me for a month or two. I was a bit worried in case my mother didn't agree, but thank God she allowed me to take her daughter, who had never left my mother alone. I understood that, with my sister not around, my mother would be lonely, so I promised my mother that I would send my sister back soon. Within a few days I drove us back to my home in Kuala Lumpur. I looked at my sister, who had her head covered like a good Muslim girl, and at myself in my western outfit. I was a bit embarrassed, so I said, "Could you remove the cover from your head please? I don't want you to cover your head when you are with me."

I thought, she is not going to do it because she has been doing that for a long time. But surprisingly she couldn't wait to take it off and as soon as I told her to, she quickly pulled her head scarf off and said, "Thanks sis! I feel so much better."

We both smiled and I thought, poor girl, my family must have forced her to wear it. I said, "That is better, you look even more beautiful."

My comment made her smile and she looked so excited to be in the city. I concentrated on my driving while talking and answering the many questions that my sister handed to me. Soon we arrived in the city that is so full of life, and I made sure she had good time while she stayed with me.

I started giving aerobics classes in many places and I took my sister along with me, in fact I took her everywhere with me. It was so wonderful to have my sister around me. My friends didn't believe that she was my sister because we didn't look alike. We talked about everything in life, she was very mature for her age and I was so proud to have a sister like her. It was so very helpful when she was around me because she could answer the calls from the boys who I didn't want to talk to. I was very bad but, well, that is part of life.

I started teaching her everything so she would know what life is about. At the beginning I introduced her to having lunch at a good restaurant then slowly I introduced her to having dinner at the hotel, which she had never done had before. It was fun and I wanted her to know the kind of life I enjoyed. I took her to the Hard Rock Café to see a live band and she really enjoyed it. She was still underage but luckily no one stopped her. I couldn't believe myself but of course I looked after her. But then I went too far by introducing her to alcohol. It is still fresh in my mind. One weekend, as always, I was out with my friends at a club, but this time I took my sister with me. As soon as we entered the club I explained to my sister about alcohol. I got her a glass of red wine and got a glass for myself. But then I went too far by drinking too much and mixing a few different drinks. I started to feel sick. I told my sister to stay where she was until I came back, and I quickly ran to find a toilet. I was in the toilet for a few seconds then passed out right there in the toilet. I had no idea what was happening to me, and I had no idea that my sister came to look for me, then she passed out as well. Luckily I was well known in the club, and soon the waitress entered the toilet and they carried me and my sister back into the club and put us in a safe place. One of the guys from the live band who was really interested in me asked the staff to send me and my sister back to my place safely. I was completely knocked out that night. The staff knew that I lived at one of condominiums just behind the club so that made things much easier for them. The staff took me and my sister there then they asked the security guard to give them directions to my apartment.

The next morning, I felt heavy and full of alcohol and I could hardly wake up. As soon as I opened my eyes, I found myself at my own place then quickly looked for my sister. Thank God, she was right beside me asleep. I couldn't stop feeling bad about what I had done to my sister. This was the stupidest thing I had ever done in my life. I felt so guilty for what I had done to my sister, and I hoped she wouldn't tell my mother. If she did, hell, my mother would kill me. From that time I learnt from my mistake and it would never happen again. I lay on the sofa and suddenly my doorbell rang. I thought, who the hell is here at this time? I looked through the keyhole, Oh shit! The guy from the live band who was interested in me was outside my door. But why didn't he give me a call before he came? My brain didn't know what to do, should I open the door or should I just ignore it? But he had looked after me and my sister the night before. I quickly told my sister. She was not very happy about it and neither was I. But I had no choice but to welcome him and tell him I appreciated what he did the previous night. I asked him to have a sit while I quickly jumped in the shower.

Soon I was ready and joined him in the living room. We had a chat, then I thanked him for what he had done. He was an Indian guy, very generous, but he was not my cup of tea. I didn't think that he would stay at my place for so long but every hour that passed, I looked at him and thought, come on, get your ass out of here. He was probably waiting for me to serve him lunch. Well, if he was, sorry! I don't cook and my head was still heavy, I couldn't even think straight. At the same time I was worried in case Kazmin popped up at my place. That would be a big disaster. My brain was working fast, trying to think of a good excuse to make him leave. Finally he dragged his ass from my place, thank God. I was so relieved. After that meeting I often went to the club where he played, and we ended up going out as a couple for a while. In fact, I did have a few boyfriends at the same time and I managed very well. I really don't know how I did it but at that stage of my life I needed someone to keep me company because I had too much pressure with Kazmin. But I shouldn't have influenced my sister by introducing her to all my boyfriends. I might be stupid but I am honest too and I know that I am not perfect. I learnt from the mistakes that I made.

The time came for my sister to go home because my mother was all alone and needed my sister more than me. As much as I would have loved my sister to stay with me she needed to help my mother, who always depended on her. I felt sad and lonely without her at my place. Nobody teased me as she always did, and no one chatted to me while I drove to work. I love to swim in the middle of the night but couldn't anymore because no one would wait for me except my sister. I went shopping on my own and it felt very strange. But the most important things that I missed was she was my operator. I could avoid calls from anyone who I didn't want to talk to. She would answer all my calls and she knew what to say without asking me, she was fantastic. I was thankful to my sister for understanding about my life. Even though she only stayed with me for a short time she did a lot of things to save my life. Without her, worse things might have happened to me. We used to talk in the middle of the night outside the house, and look at the full moon. One night I held her hand and said, "Close your eyes and we'll make a wish." We both made a wish.

As soon as she opened her eyes I asked her, "What did you wish for?"

She laughed and said, "I can't tell you."

I insisted, I wanted to know but she wouldn't tell me. Well! She was right anyway. We both promised a lot of things in our life. She is not only my sister, but also my buddy and like my daughter as well. We had a lot of fun times together, laughs every moment. I really missed my time with her and really hoped one day we would be together again. I want to let you know, my dear sister, Nurul, you are phenomenal and I am so proud of you and I love you deeply in my heart.

Almost one year after my sister returned home, I was missing her so much I decided to fly back to visit her and my mother. This time it was not just for a visit. I needed some help from my mother or my brother. Sadly no one in my family helped me except my sister. She told me that she borrowed money from her friend. As I was so desperate for money, I totally trusted her.

On 13th November 2010, about four-thirty on a lovely, cold evening, I was chatting with my sister on the phone; she was in Malaysia and I was in London. For some reason in the middle of our conversation I remembered what she had done for me, and that I would never forget it in my entire life. So I told her that without her help I don't know what would have happened. Before we ended our conversation she mentioned to me that she had a secret to tell me, but she wouldn't tell me until I went back to Malaysia! Ummm...! I thought that was very exciting, she had kept the secret from me for a very long time, and she was scared I would get angry. I didn't like the sound of that, it really made me unhappy, so I said, "Could you tell me what the secret is and don't worry, I won't be angry. Just be honest and tell me the truth."

It took her a few minutes to tell me the secret that she had carried all this time, and then she said, "Sis! I will tell the truth and the truth will come out today."

I listened and waited impatiently and then she said, "Sis, you remember I gave you some money for your flight before? Well, that money was not actually from my friends."

I was a bit confused then I said, "So who was it from? Explain everything to me."

She said, "Okay. I will. It was actually from a Chinese a guy that I knew, and I knew he was the only person who had money. I called him to meet up at some place. He came in his car, and as soon as he arrived I jumped in and explained to him about the problem. He agreed to give me the money but before he handed the money over, he held me and tried to kiss me. I was so scared at that time but to protect myself from any danger, I made myself strong and without thinking straight I bit his hand and slapped his face, then I jumped out of his car. I told him that I was not a prostitute; I just wanted to borrow the money then I would pay it back in a week's time. But at the same time I prayed he would give me the money because I was more worried about you at home. Then he said sorry to me and handed me the money. Without wasting any more time, I grabbed the money and said thank you, and promised to pay him back in a week's time. I walked back home happily with the money in my hand. I just couldn't wait to give to you. I knew you would be very happy to leave the house and I wanted you to go from here too. You are such a happy person and to see you sad every day really hurt me."

To hear what had happened to her really hurt me inside, I felt so guilty. I couldn't imagine how I would have felt if something had happened to her. I would never forgive myself and I would regret it for the rest of my life. Then I asked my sister, "Are you telling me the truth, the whole truth? He only tried to kiss you? Nothing else happened?"

She said, "Yes! It's all true."

I said to her, "Why didn't you tell me? Never ever do such a stupid thing again. I'd rather you didn't get the money for me, it wouldn't be the end of the world. You are more important to me than anything. I am very upset and very disappointed with you but thank you very much for telling me this, you should have told me when it happened, you are a silly girl. You really find trouble for yourself and me but thank God nothing happened to you otherwise I would kill myself."

Even today she is still very naughty and teases me and when I go back to Malaysia we still have a fun time together.

I lay my body on the sofa, slowly closed my eyes and rested my brain peacefully, trying to go to a different world, but suddenly my mobile beeped with an incoming message. I thought, who the hell is that? I never get any peace. That's my fourth; I should turn off my mobile. I was too tired to get up, so I tried stretching my hand to the table and dragged it closer to me so I could get my mobile. I just hoped that I wasn't going to get any hassle from people in Malaysia. Thank God! It was my sister, she wanted to talk to me about something. Ummm…! It didn't sound good to me. I decided to find out what she wanted. I dialled her number and to my surprise she answered straight away, which was unusual for her.

"Hi, sis," she said in her cheerful voice.

"Yep man, wassup?" I answered with an African American accent and before she said anything I continued and asked her, "You want to tell me that you are pregnant?"

"Oh my God, I think you are psychic, yes! I am pregnant, but how did you know that?" she asked me with surprise.

"Well! It's the magic of Gina. Anyway I was just guessing but my guess was right. Congratulations," I told her I was so happy about the news.

"But, sis, as my situation is right now, I am not ready yet for another child and I want to ask you, do you know any medicine or tablets that can make my period normal again?" she asked me with disappointment in her voice.

"Darling, I can give you a few tips but I really can't promise that they are going to work. At the moment what have you been taking?" I asked her.

"I have taken a few things to make my period come, but it still hasn't," she told me in a sad voice.

"Why did you do that? Please stop, it is very dangerous, anything could happen to you." I was very angry as soon as I heard she had taken medication to make her period come. Then I gave her some advice about what she should do.

"Right, sis, I will do what you have suggested," she replied.

Thank God! I was so pleased as soon as she had agreed.

We spent another fifteen minutes on the phone then we said goodbye to each other. As soon as I hung up the phone, I continued to lay on the sofa like a piece of wood. But this time my brain was working like clockwork after having spoken with my sister. I was so happy for her but at the same time I felt so sad for myself because, at the age of forty-five, I still didn't have any children; it just made me so frustrated. And at twenty-five, my sister was going to have three children. She is so lucky, I thought. I felt warm tears starting to leak out and I whispered into my pillow, "Please! Please! Why must this happen to me?" But I wish her all the best for her future and congratulation on her third baby.

CHAPTER 10

It's You

At the age of twenty, I returned to Kuala Lumpur and was initially living alone but soon my younger brother Nazeri, then twelve years old, came to live with me. I had taken charge of his upbringing. My mother was worried but she trusted me. To earn a living my mother made sweets and Nazeri had to wake up at about five in the morning and cycle for about thirty minutes to sell all the sweets from house to house until they were gone. His two older brothers stayed in bed, didn't help at all, and they were always bullying him. I felt so sorry for him and my heart really hurt but he didn't complain. And for that reason I took him away with me. As soon as he found out the news that he was coming with me, a big smile was on his face. I could see that he couldn't wait to get away from the house. At that time I had a car and it took about seven hours to drive from Kulim to Kuala Lumpur. My brother talked a lot about family matters, both good and bad, during that drive. Once in Kuala Lumpur, we settled down quickly. I felt like a mother as I looked after my brother and I took the responsibility seriously. I paid for the school bus, so the bus would come to pick him up and send him back after school. I cooked for him but most of the time we had takeaways because it was only the two of us. I did everything a mother should do for a child, I liked that feeling and we lived happily.

One evening, Nazeri and I were out at a night market buying some vegetables and a few others things. Two men were standing on the pavement close to where I had parked my car. As I crossed in front of them, one of the men whistled, gazing at me intently. I felt embarrassed and nervously continued walking. When I came out of the market, I put our things in the car and drove home. As we unloaded the car, I noticed a car pass my house but as it passed me, it immediately slowed then reversed down the alley way.

I didn't pay that much attention; I thought they were just lost. I looked over and saw two men in the car. One of them called me over.

I called back, "Is it me or my brother you're calling?"

"It's you," one of the gentlemen answered. I thought, what the hell does he want?

I walked over to him, saying, "What do you want?" I thought maybe he needed directions.

One of the men said, "Do you remember me?"

I tried to think, where had I met him? But he reminded me and said, "Remember, earlier at the market? I whistled at you."

Then I said, "Oh yes! I remember you, so what do you want?"

With a cheeky smile he asked me my name and for my phone number.

It was at this moment that I noticed how handsome this stranger was. I felt attracted to him from that first moment. He was tall and slim with slightly slanted eyes – Oriental-looking. His manner was very polite, gentle and tender. So I ended up giving him my telephone number. He thanked me and I went into the house. As far as I was concerned, when I turned my back on him, I was done with him. This was nothing but a flirtation with a stranger.

Ten minutes later the phone rang. I picked up the receiver, there was a pause and I asked who it was. A very sweet voice asked, "Don't you remember me? You just gave me your phone number."

My heart was all aflutter and I couldn't think of anything to say, so I said the first thing that came into my head: "Oh that was quick! Where are you?"

This was a new feeling for me – I was almost out of control with this man! From that moment on, we spoke daily. We talked on the phone for hours, sometimes the whole night through.

We spent the next month just talking on the phone, never seeing each other. I remember that those conversations were wonderful. He would tell me that I had a beautiful voice, that I was good-looking and that I had a wonderful smile. He told me many other romantic things. He wanted to know everything about me including thing about my brother. I answered all his questions and asked him the same too. My new friend's name was Kazmin Kuzi. I wanted to get to know him better even though we had liked each other from that first moment we met. I told him that I had many friends but had never had a boyfriend; this was true. Kazmin insisted on knowing more about me. He seemed a romantic person and I liked talking to him. Kazmin knew how to touch my heart. His manner was always polite and correct and this made me feel safe with him.

One day, I told him that I liked to dance and I was very amused when he informed me that he didn't know how to dance. He then asked me if I liked to kiss and I thought, Ummm how interesting! I told him in a flirtatious tone that I had never kissed a man. His daring response was that he would teach me everything. I answered him full of excitement!

Three months of talking for hours on the phone went by and then we decided to meet up. This would be the first time we would actually see each other since we had met for the first time that evening after my shopping trip.

Like a gentleman, he came to pick me up for the first date. I was polite and a little shy and, from that day on, we went out almost every day and my shyness eventually went away. He always played the song 'Because I Love you' by Shakin Stevens. He kept repeating that song over and over for me. At that time we were really falling in love and that song made our love so romantic. Because of that song I allowed him to kiss me for the first time. It was the happiest day for me and I thought, this is something I will truly celebrate for the rest of my life. He had stolen my heart. But then I started to get really tired because as soon as the song finished he would play it all over again so we could kiss until the song finished. At the beginning I enjoyed this new experience but then it got too much and I grew bored and at the same time my lips were painful.

Kazmin came from a Muslim family. All his sisters covered their heads, as is the tradition in some families. I chose to keep my head uncovered and he didn't mind at all. Actually he was very open-minded and liked me to wear modern, sexy clothes. I wasn't very trendy-looking because I had grown up in the country, but Kazmin taught me how to dress sexily. I know he did this because he wanted me to look good for him and of course I did as he asked because I was falling in love with him. We did not have a lot in common but we were becoming a happy, loving young couple.

In the meantime, my life started getting harder. I lost my job and ran out of money to pay the rent, for my car and the bills. What worried me most, though, was my brother and his school.

I loved sports cars and I even had one, and at that time I drove a Mazda RX7. Sometimes I drove back to see my mother and took her for a drive or shopping. She was not happy at all with my car and said that it was too small and she didn't like the fact that it didn't have a boot to fit all the stuff in. She always asked me to change it and get a bigger car. I just smiled and said nothing. She would never understand why I liked this car. I always laughed when I looked at her sitting in my RX7, I couldn't even see her head, it was hilarious! But then my car was taken away because I wasn't paying my monthly instalments.

The owner of the house came but I didn't come out, I hid myself inside. He was shouting outside and I became so embarrassed because the entire neighbourhood heard about it. It got to the point where I became so depressed because I had almost no money to buy food for my brother. But he was such a wonderful boy, he didn't complain about anything even though he was hungry. I told Kazmin nothing but I was secretly going to see someone to borrow money just for my brother.

I was unlucky, I met the wrong people and that person who lent me the money wanted me to promise him I'd be his lover. As I was so desperate for the money, I had agreed with his solution. For a few weeks I had to pretend that I was falling in love with him. I tried as hard as I could to keep this from Kazmin. But one day Kazmin came to my house without phoning first and at that time the person from whom I had borrowed money was with me in the house. Luckily his friends and my brother were with us, so we were not alone together.

Kazmin walked into my house and went straight upstairs to my room. He was not very happy at all and asked, "Who is that guy?"

I wanted to tell the truth but something stopped me. Instead I told him, "That guy is just a friend."

But he was still not happy; he wanted me to tell that guy to get out of the house that moment. I didn't really want to cause any problems between them, so I begged Kazmin and told him, "I can't do that, they are my friends."

To make him happy so that he would leave my house, I promised Kazmin that I would do whatever he wanted, but in a good way. Thank God he agreed with that. At last he left, but before he did he told me, "I will come back in an hour and I don't want to see him here."

I felt so guilty for playing with his feelings and it was really hard for me to tell him that I was not in love with the other man. But before Kazmin started trouble I had to tell him the truth; everything, the total truth. After I had explained everything to him, he was very upset. Because of his anger he used witchcraft to make me suffer. With the power of witchcraft I suffered for one month. I didn't remember anything and I didn't know what happened to my life and my brother. I had friends who treated me like family and one day one of them came around for a visit. As soon as she saw my situation she took me and my brother to stay with her. She took care of me and took me for a traditional treatment. With her help I slowly recovered and started to ask her what was happening to me. My brother told me what was happening. He told me that I chased him and Kazmin with a knife trying to kill them both. I even tried to get naked and tried to escape from the house, crying, screaming and calling his name. So many things happened, but I didn't remember them at all. Luckily I had my brother and Kazmin, who looked after me before my friends took me for help. Without my brother, I don't know what would have happened to me. After hearing the entire story, I was confused, and I didn't believe it but it happened to me.

Soon I recovered well; I made contact with Kazmin and we saw each other every day. Our relationship was going very well. The following year, we decided to live together. I was twenty-one and Kazmin was twenty-four. I moved into his three-storey house and at first my brother lived with some friends, but the month after I brought him to live with us. Kazmin shared the house with a friend of his named Johari.

I got a new job as an estate agent, earning a small commission for each property I sold. Kazmin had two jobs. He worked for an engineering company and was on commission from another business. Even though we didn't have much money, we were very happy and deeply in love. We travelled together on the bus and did everything else together. He helped me with my work, accompanying me and teaching me how to speak to clients. We spent a lot of time in each other's company. Sometimes he had to attend meetings and I used to wait for him at the bus station for hours. He would come and get me and we would go home together. We always stopped at the roadside food stalls to have something to eat before going home; I would leave money for my brother to have lunch and dinner. It was always late evening by the time we got home, and I would have just enoughtime to have a shower and go to bed because the next day would be another long day. It was like this for quite some time.

It was a difficult period financially and sometimes we had to ask friends for money. My brother was studying at elementary level and wasn't working, so he was unable to help out with the upkeep of the house. I still remember, Kazmin only had two shirts for work. When he got home, he would wash the shirt he was wearing and hang it up on the fan to dry and the next morning he would put on the other one. When we got paid we had to pay back the friends who had lent us money.

At the beginning our relationship was fine but then his character started to change. He always asked me for money. My work at that time didn't pay much but because I loved him I did everything to be with him. Sometimes after work I went out for dinner with someone who was a lord, then after dinner he would give me a small amount of money and the driver would take me home. Kazmin knew about that but he didn't get angry with me, instead he suggested that I go out with someone rich so I could get money and give it to him. I was not happy doing that, but I worried that Kazmin would leave me if I didn't have the money when he needed it. I still remember one day when he wanted money from me and I didn't have it because at that time the lord had been admitted to hospital and Kazmin knew about that. But one night Kazmin said, "Could you call him and tell him that you need money?"

I said, "I can't do that because he is still in hospital."

But Kazmin insisted I call him and put me under a lot of pressure. My heart was so heavy and I felt so embarrassed to call but if that would make Kazmin happy I would do it. I called him and told him that I was having some problems so needed to see him now. I knew that the lord liked me very much and without question he asked me to come to the hospital. I hung up the phone and was very upset with Kazmin. Without saying anything I started the car to go to hospital. I drove the car in floods of tears until I was at the hospital. I sat beside his bed still crying non-stop. He knew about Kazmin, as I had told him about him from day one. He knew that I always got money from him just for the sake of Kazmin, so he said, "What has he done now? He wants money again?"

I just looked down at the floor, it was so embarrassing, but I said, "Yes."

As soon as he handed me the money I went home happily, I just couldn't wait to give it to Kazmin and he was more than happy as soon as I handed him the amount of money that he wanted. I felt so relieved and peaceful without having to worry about him. But my peaceful life didn't last long; he needed money again but a bigger amount this time. Where the hell am I going to get it, I thought. Doesn't he wonder that? I told him that I couldn't do it anymore. But he nagged me every night until I couldn't sleep. He changed and became so moody and didn't talk to me all day. It really hurt me so I said, "I can't get such a big amount of money."

Then he said, "Can you call the lord and get it from him?"

I said, "It is night time and I am not going to disturb him."

Again he put me under so much pressure and insisted that I had to get the money that night because he needed it for something very important the next day. At that time I wished I could get out of his fucking life and go somewhere, but I was not alone, my brother was with me and I didn't want him knowing anything about my problem. Kazmin really put me in a difficult situation. With a heavy heart I called the lord and without question he agreed to see me, but I had to wait for him to finish a meeting.

It was almost midnight. It would take me one hour to drive and meet the lord, so I didn't want to go on my own. Also, it was quite dangerous during this hour. The lord was staying at a hotel that night because of the meeting. Kazmin drove me there. I was silent in the car and started to hate him. When I arrived at the hotel, I had to go to his room, where he would be waiting for me. Kazmin waited for me in the car. He just let me go so easily without worrying that something might happen to me. Luckily the lord was so generous, understood my situation and helped me. He was the one person I could talk to and he gave me a lot of support. As soon as I got the money I walked from the room and to Kazmin who was still in the car waiting for me. I said, "Here is the money you want."

He just took the money without even saying thank you. He was such an idiot and from that moment on I stopped being stupid and stopped finding money for him. I started to use my brain and played my own game; soon he would love me more than the money.

One morning, around two o'clock, I was sound asleep, when suddenly I heard someone enter my room. I wondered who it could be who would dare to enter the room while we were asleep.

Suddenly the light was turned on and I quickly got up and tried to open my eyes. There I saw a woman standing right in front of me. I thought I was dreaming. I rubbed my eyes and this time tried to open them wider. Yes! It was a woman, but why had she entered our room?

We looked at each other and she asked me, "Who are you?"

And the same question I handed to her, "Who are you?"

She replied, "I am Kazmin's girlfriend."

I was really shocked then I said, "I am Kazmin's girlfriend."

I looked at Kazmin, who was sitting next to me looking down looked like a cat, then I asked him, "Do you know her?"

He looked at me and said, "No! I don't know her."

Kazmin just sat between us two girls and he didn't answer any of my questions. He made me so mad and I said, "This is unbelievable, Kazmin."

I left them both in the room and went downstairs with a broken heart and ran into Johari. I asked him to please tell me who that woman was, and begged him to tell me the truth.

Johari's answer shocked me even more. "Gina, I don't want to upset you, but if you want to know, she is Kazmin's girlfriend. She used to stay with Kazmin in this house before you and that is why she has a key to the house."

But Johari didn't know what had happened between them and why she had moved out. And he didn't know what Kazmin had told both of us. That was all that he told me. I was so devastated. I went downstairs and waited for Kazmin for almost six hours. I didn't know what they were doing for so long. At eight in the morning, I left and walked to a friend's house which was a few steps away from our place. I was there waiting for what was going to happen next, when at about midday I saw Kazmin coming. He came and sat beside me and tried to give me a bullshit explanation, but I trusted nothing that he said and just kept on weeping.

He was sorry and begged me not to leave him. Well, I thought, anybody can make a mistake, even two or three times. He had just made one mistake, so I accepted his apology. Even after this incident happened I still loved him. I asked myself, "What is wrong with you, Gina?"

But just because I had forgiven him didn't mean I trusted him and our relationship was not the same after that incident happened. We continued to live together in the same house but I did my things and he did his. We rarely had dinner together; we became two people living two different lives.

I still cared for Kazmin.

One evening while I was watching TV, Kazmin returned home and as he walked in front of me, I could see he had lipstick on the back of his shirt. I almost lost my temper but managed to hold myself together. I knew then he was not the man I used to love and I wondered how much longer I had to be in this situation. I thought, please! Please! Please! I need to get out of here! Day after day the pain in my chest got worse. I was really hurting.

I was waiting until my finances improved, then I planned to move out right away. Every day I searched for a new job. I knew I was, and I felt, independent. I thought, I have been through much worse – much worse and I survived. Life is like a roller coaster, up and down. I was just on the down side then. But I would go up again soon.

But in the meantime, the pain eased and Kazmin and I continued on.

CHAPTER 11

In The Limelight

When my mother realised that I was living with Kazmin, she became very angry. It made no difference that we were not sleeping together. We were not married.

So Harisun came to visit me and my brother in Kuala Lumpur. Soon she realised that life in Kuala Lumpur was difficult and that as I was only a young girl, we needed someone to look after us.

I assured my mother that Kazmin was a good man but she insisted on talking with him in private. This made me a bit worried. My mother told Kazmin all about the incredibly hard life that I had had and how I'd suffered at the hands of my father. She also said she wanted Kazmin to take good care of her daughter at all times, as she did not need any more pain.

I had never mentioned to Kazmin the terrible treatment I had received from my father during my childhood. On hearing the story, Kazmin was anxious to learn more, so I told him the truth of what had happened. He was tender and consoling. He behaved like a husband, friend and father, and he was truly a wonderful person during that emotional time.

Kazmin was my first love, the man who was going to be my future. It was Kazmin who taught me the meaning of passion. I didn't know much about sex. In Malaysia we were never taught about sex, neither at home or in school. I was from the country, so I had only one man in my life. Kazmin and only Kazmin could have taken my virginity.

I still remember the first time he kissed my lips. I trembled thinking I had just lost my virginity, that it was gone because he had kissed my lips. I was so naïve. I am not a romantic person. At the beginning I thought he was a romantic man but I was wrong. From the time I met him, he never gave me any cards, presents or roses and I was very disappointed when I saw my friends receive beautiful, romantic things from their boyfriends. I really wanted to receive such things so one day I said to him, "Today is my birthday, so have you got a present for me?"

He looked at me and said, "I can give you the money and you can buy it yourself."

Well, I thought, just kept your bloody money. I was so frustrated because on my birthday he didn't treat me like I was special, instead he told me to buy my present myself. I was so sad, he was such an idiot. After that time I never asked him again. But he was very kind with a big heart and genuinely cared. If I cried, he would work to find out what was wrong. I am very choosy about food and if I didn't like it, he would run out and buy something I did like.

I have a bad temper when I get angry; I will blow up over anything. This behaviour began the day my father started to abuse me, and it just got worse and worse. I knew I had a bad temper but I couldn't do anything about it. I needed help but I didn't know where to go. When I remembered my father doing whatever it was that I did not like, all of sudden my head started spinning and I turned evil. I would start throwing things everywhere and at Kazmin. Luckily Kazmin was very patient, he would pick up all the things I had thrown and put them back in the right place. Then later I would feel so sorry for what I had done. I should have come forward and said sorry but I am a very stubborn person, I would rather sit on my own feeling guilty and sorry for myself. Each time, rather than being upset with me, Kazmin would simply ask me not to do that again. He seemed to understand. I tried to explain but there was nothing much he could do.

The years passed quietly by. Soon I was twenty-five years old. I loved exercise and I loved to look after myself. One day I joined an aerobics class. In the class I would stay right in front of the instructor. The whole hour I just looked at her body, her movements, her outfit; straight away I fell in love with the job and I knew that it was something that I wanted to do. I went to the class almost every single day just to look at her movements and the way she conducted the class. I imagined that one day I would be exactly like her, maybe even better. A month later, I searched in the newspaper every day looking for an instructor's vacancy. I found a company named Joan Drew, which needed an aerobics instructor. Without wasting any time, the next day I went for the interview. I was so excited but at the same time very nervous and worried that they wouldn't take me, because I had no experience at all.

The interview went very well and I was over the moon, so happy. It was a dream come true because I got the job and they put me in training for three months and soon I started teaching aerobics classes. At that job I discovered my passion. This was the kind of profession I had been looking for. It was a job I could handle with ease and one I enjoyed.

I worked hard to make sure all my students liked me and liked my class. After six months of teaching aerobics, one morning a television journalist joined my class. She was very interested in doing a programme on me and she wanted to interview me for it. I was radiant with joy; it seemed like a fantastic opportunity. The journalist gave me some of the questions that she would ask during the interview, so I could prepare thoroughly.

Every day I put a smile on face and counted the days until I would stand in front of the camera; I just couldn't wait for that moment. I was to practise in front of the mirror, to talk and smile on my own. I already started feeling famous; I would have loved a life full of glamour. The time came to film me and the segment appeared on a programme called Nona, which was broadcast nationally. I was shown entering the sports centre and they filmed me teaching an aerobics class. I answered the interview questions while sitting on a bike. I talked about dieting, but I never dieted myself. I gave information about massages; I listed some of my recommendations for people with back problems and those who were recovering from surgery. Some of the videotape showed me consulting books and sports videos.

I was also shown briefing my manager on the exercise I had prepared for the classes. We recorded a scene next to the swimming pool in the Hilton Kuala Lumpur. It was really good and I had so much fun throughout the whole interview.

I was very proud of myself. It made me realise I knew how to do my job well and as a result of my appearance on TV, I became more self-confident. The onscreen text had shown my name as Gina, which let everyone know that Gina was not my real name, as Gina is not a traditional Muslim name.

I caught the television bug completely. I was famous for a while and I enjoyed it very much. Everywhere I went people almost knew me, and from then on my lucky life started to shine brightly.

Kazmin had asked his sister, who lived in London, for some money to open an investment company. He was very interested in computers and wanted to study them in London. He decided to go to London for three months and take some computer courses.

While he was there, he met another Muslim man called Nasir. They became good friends. Kazmin had received a lot of help from his sister, Nor, who was married with four children and owned a chain of Malaysian restaurants in London.

After returning from London, Kazmin's business took off very well. He was busy most of the time. He had meetings almost every night and usually did not return home until early next morning. I was OK with that and understood about the business; it took a lot of time to get started.

I was not suspicious or jealous. I always asked how the business was going, and I gave him as much moral support as I could.

One day, he had promised to come home early and have dinner with me. I was excited because it had been a long time since we had spent time together. The meal was ready, but where was Kazmin? I kept looking at the time. He was two hours late and had not called; now it was past midnight.

At two in the morning, I was still waiting when he drove up. I heard the engine of his car but he had turned the lights off. Maybe he thought I was sleeping.

I continued waiting patiently on the sofa. He seemed surprised when he opened the door, because I was still awake waiting for him. With a guilty face he said, "Are you still awake? "

I said, "Yes, and dinner is still waiting, that's why I am awake!"

He said, "Don't you think it's too late to have dinner at this hour?"

I replied, "Nope, because I haven't eaten anything yet!"

He tried to give me a lot of explanations, none of which I believed at all. In fact, I wanted to say, "Fuck off." But suddenly his phone rang. I quickly answered it and it didn't surprise me at all to hear a woman's voice; she was looking for Kazmin.

I said, "Who are you?"

"I'm Kazmin's girlfriend," she replied.

I glared at Mr Playboy, Kazmin Kuzi, with so much anger and his eyes kept blinking, wondering to whom I was chatting on his phone. He looked uncomfortable and I could see on his face that he had done something wrong.

I told the woman that I was his girlfriend and we were living together then she replied, "Oh, he didn't tell me that, he told me that he didn't have a girlfriend."

I said, "Ummm...! How interesting. Now you know, so can I help you with anything."

She replied, "Nothing! I just want to talk to him actually; he just left my house."

I said, "WOW! That's even more brilliant! Thank you for your kindness, now I will pass the phone to him."

I handed the phone to Kazmin and waited for him to talk to her, but instead he hung up the phone. Before he started to open his mouth I said, "So you lied to me earlier? While I was waiting at home all night to have dinner, you were having fun with another girl; how great is that? So is she your new girlfriend?"

He was such an idiot, looking at me with those blinking eyes like a pervert, and he didn't say a single word. Of course he couldn't say anything because the truth was out.

I thought, I am just wasting my time and I'm very tired of this type of character. I was so tired of arguing about it, a cheater is always a cheater. I should have known a long time ago but stupid love made me so naïve. I knew for sure I couldn't change him. I knew he loved me and he'd do anything for me but he couldn't stay with just one woman, and I couldn't stay with someone who was always lying. So I went to bed, telling Kazmin to do whatever he thought was best for him.

The next day I decided not to go to work. As soon as Kazmin went out to work, I started packing all my clothes and left that house, and went to stay with my girlfriend until I found my own place. I just left a note to Kazmin that said, 'Sorry I can't stay with you any longer. Now you can go with any girl you like without anyone questioning you. Have a good life!'

Soon after I rented my own place and continued working as an aerobics instructor, and I got my own car. I kept myself busy by working during the day and at night went out with friends. I had so much enjoyment and less pressure without a man in my life. My brother was staying with his friends, but he always came to visit me once a week and I would go to his place to make sure that he was okay. Life was getting better and better.

After a few months, Mr Kazmin came to look for me at work. As usual he came with his charming, gentlemanly character, and showed-off in front of my friends. As my friends didn't know anything about our life, they thought we looked good together, but I naturally overshadowed Kazmin. Because of his lovely sweet words, I took him to my place. Since then, he came every day and sometimes he would wait for me in the car if I was not at home. Soon after we got back together and I moved out of my place and into his.

Kazmin tried to make things better. From that day on, he tried not to leave me at home alone. Sometimes I accompanied him to business gatherings, staying up with him while he attended meetings with his friends at coffee houses in hotels. I did not really enjoy this, but it was the only way he could build my trust while continuing his business activities.

Within a few months, he became a successful businessman. He put trust in me by keeping all his business money with me; it became my job to be his accountant. We moved to a better house in the Chinese quarter, which was safer for Muslims living together without being married. In Malaysia if you are a Muslim man and woman living together without being married, it can create a lot of problems. You can be brought to religious court and your relationship made public.

I was twenty-six years old. My boyfriend had become a successful businessman, which enabled him to give me a boost in my career. In addition to aerobics, a journalist from a magazine called me and asked for an interview as he was interested in my appearance and that I was a Muslim woman working in this type of job. That was rare in Malaysia at that time.

The magazine was called *Wanita*, which means 'Women', and it had a national circulation. I appeared in the December issue of the *Keluaran Khas* in 1991. The article was written by Meran Abu Bakar, the photographer was Raja Jaafar Raja Ali, and the model was me, Gina. The article was called 'Senaman Dari Hujung Rambut Ke Hujung Kaki', which means 'Exercise from Head to Toe'.

I liked doing the interview, and I felt I deserved the fame that came with it. I received a call from a second magazine, and they also interviewed me. When I appeared in this second magazine, I was filled with joy at all the attention. In the back of my mind, I often wondered if my father might have seen the magazine and thought about the daughter he had abused and had tried to kill more than once. Those articles meant a great deal to me, and I still have the magazines in which I appeared.

Kazmin had become a very successful businessman, my life as an aerobics instructor was going better than I had ever expected, and our life together was going well. We were very happy at that time.

CHAPTER 12

London

I loved my job very much and I had the idea of opening my own business someday. In order to do this, I would have to study and be a professional. I wanted to study in London, the place that I had always dreamed of going. I mentioned my plan to Kazmin, and he was very supportive of my idea. He knew that I was very passionate about my job, and so anxious to go to London. He told me he would take care of organising everything and soon he came home with money for the trip to London. All I could do was smile. Yes! My dream was coming true!

Over the next few days, we went shopping for my trip. He bought me a maroon suitcase and filled it with my clothes and he took care of my passport and all the paperwork required for travelling to the United Kingdom. In addition to a ticket for me, he purchased a ticket for a friend of mine who would accompany me to London.

The day before I departed for London in November 1993, Kazmin sat me down so we could go over my trip, my expenses and how to budget my money. Then the time arrived. My friend Nik Ros and I met at the airport and soon we were on our way to London. It was my first long trip on an aeroplane. At the airport I said goodbye to Kazmin and my brother. I was very sad to leave my brother behind, but I was not worried because my mother didn't live very far away, so if anything happened he could go home. And I also told Kazmin to look after my brother. Kazmin and I would be separated for the first time in nine years. I was sad and excited all at the same time. I kissed both of them on the cheek and left my brother and my boyfriend behind. The flight was to take thirteen hours, and Kazmin's brother-in-law, Badrul, would be waiting for us in London. I was twenty-eight years old.

Kazmin had always told his family that I was merely a friend, not his girlfriend. His family didn't know that we had an intimate relationship. He didn't want to reveal the truth to them because I was from such a simple background. I also had Indian looks and was darker-skinned than his family. In Malaysia this is considered uncultured and he thought they would not accept me. So I pretended to be just an acquaintance and friend of his.

Upon arriving in London, I remembered that Kazmin had told me to put on my coat when I arrived at the airport because I would be cold. I had laughed because I had never been in cold weather. I saw that everyone was wearing coats, but I didn't want to wear mine. As we waited for Badrul to arrive, because we had never met him before, we looked at every single Malaysian person who passed by. Suddenly a big man with Indian looks approached us and said, "Are you Gina and Ros?"

We both said "Yes" and he introduced himself to us. We got ready to leave the airport.

He turned to me and said, "Put your coat on, it is very cold outside."

I replied, "I will, later."

However, as soon as we stepped outside, I yelled out, "WOW!" I had never felt cold like that before.

In the car, I didn't talk much; I was amazed to see the city of London. I looked at the trees without leaves, and I still couldn't believe that I was in London. Badrul took us to student accommodation at Bryanston Square, where I rented a room for myself and Nik Ros. Kazmin's sister and her husband owned and worked in the restaurant right next to our hotel. We were there just two weeks; then we moved to Baker Street, into a house with Kazmin's other sister, Izan, and her husband.

After one week in London, Nik Ros and I decided go to Amsterdam for a few days and do the tourist thing. So much for the budget, we went out dancing at night and had a great time. We walked through the streets and ate in the many different cafés. I ordered a sandwich, and when I was offered some drugs along with my sandwich, my eyes opened wide. I was in shock and I explained to the shop owner that I was student, I didn't take drugs. He looked at me and smiled. I thought, what planet is this?

That night we went to a famous street in Amsterdam called the red light district. Women stand half naked in the windows and dance sexily for the men passing by. As I had never seen this before, I left ashamed and could not look at these women. All I could do was stand back and pretend not to see, but all the men had a fun time looking. I did this totally for my friend Nik Ros, because she was the one who had wanted to come to Holland so much. To show that I appreciated that she had come with me to London, I agreed to do what she wanted. All I could think was that Kazmin was going to kill me.

Three days later I decided to call Kazmin and the first thing he asked was, "Where are you?"

I went stupid and said, "Do you know Holland?"

I knew he was going to get mad, but all he could do was ask in his calmest voice, "How much money are you spending? You have to remember, they are not ringgits, they are pounds."

I knew I was in the wrong, so I had better shut my mouth. To make him less worried, I assured him that I had not spent much money. He did not believe me and suggested in a calm, stern voice that I return to London quickly to look for a school rather than wasting time going around doing nothing. Of course he was right but what he didn't know about was Nik Ros!

I told Nik Ros about this, and the next day we returned to London and continued touring the city and sightseeing. Nik Ros had only come to London on holiday, so she returned to Malaysia a few weeks after we returned from our Holland trip. Then I settled into my college life.

I lived in Izan's house, sharing a room with another girl who was there for a while as a paying lodger. I tried not to make it obvious that I was Kazmin's girlfriend; I guarded the secret, exactly as Kazmin had asked. Izan distrusted me because I didn't cover my hair and because I wore jeans and dressed provocatively when I went out at night. Her dislike turned to jealousy as she was worried that her husband would pay attention to me.

For some reason, she seemed to want to hurt me in some way and she began telling Kazmin things that were untrue. Kazmin then called me to ask if what Izan was saying was true. I was shocked by his questions and enraged by his sister's lies, and I told him as much by explaining that I dressed sexily because he had taught me to.

The relationship with Izan grew worse and we weren't getting along well at all. Izan was a gossip. She would tell Kazmin every time I went out at night, always telling him that I was with male friends. Perhaps it's true that I went out at night and that I had many male friends, but they were just friends – nothing more than friends. I found male friends much easier to understand than female friends. Besides, I had only one boyfriend in my heart. Well! At

Life Behind the Silence 89

that time, just one. Kazmin was the one I loved, and he the one who held the key to my heart.

I loved animals, and to give myself a little companionship, I bought a cat that I named Dazzle. He was gorgeous and I adored him. Izan and her husband went on holiday and I was left alone with my cat. I felt so relieved and free. I hoped they would not come back to the house. Their big house had three floors and was in a wonderful part of London: Baker Street, which is in the middle of the city. I signed up for an English course at Radcliff College on Oxford Street. I had studied English in Malaysia from the age of eight, but I wanted to learn more of language.

I liked studying, and life was going well for me. When school holiday time came, Kazmin asked me to go back to Malaysia. I was there for two weeks. He booked a room for me in a marvellous five-star hotel. Kazmin was doing very well during this time and he gave me a lot of money for shopping and generally enabled me to live like a princess. None of my family knew that I was in London, except my brother, Nazeri.

Back in London, I attended the classes like usual, from nine till noon every day, then went to the gym for my aerobics classes in the evening. Kazmin called me every day, sometimes two or three times a day. We were so much in love, and we never got bored talking to each other. So many interesting things were going on in our lives. For the moment, life was perfect.

CHAPTER 13

Kazmin Travels

Izan and her husband returned home from their holiday and once again I started to feel she was spying on me. During this time, Kazmin had asked Nasir, the friend who he had met when he came to London for a short time study, to look after me so I would not feel alone. Nasir had been in London for quite a while and he knew a lot about the city. He agreed to the arrangement; he was kind-hearted, honest and obliging. We became good friends and did a lot of things together. He didn't know that I was Kazmin's girlfriend. Kazmin had told him that I was his friend's sister. That didn't surprise me; nor was I surprised by the problem this secret would create later. Kazmin continued to keep our relationship a secret; only my family knew the truth about us. Five months later, Kazmin needed to come to London on a business trip. I was so happy when I heard the news. He stayed at the house of his other sister, Nor. The morning after he arrived, he came to see me. Izan and I were still asleep when he turned up. The doorbell rang and then I could hear Kazmin talking with his sister downstairs, but I couldn't run down to see him. I waited in my room, and every time he needed to use the toilet, he would come upstairs and would steal a moment to hug and kiss me before he went back downstairs. This put a great deal of strain on me. Kazmin called his friend, Nasir, to tell him that he was in London and arranged to go out for some drinks. Kazmin suggested that Nasir bring me along. Nasir was delighted with the idea of the three of us going out together. The problem was I could not walk as a couple with Kazmin, because Nasir didn't know that we were lovers. We spent a great evening at a club, having dinner and dancing until morning. Then we went to Nasir's place. The three of us sat together on the sofa and when Nasir wasn't looking, Kazmin would touch my hand, withdrawing it quickly every time Nasir turned around. It was so funny but I felt so weird and sorry for Nasir.

We stayed at Nasir's house for several nights. I slept in a bedroom and both of them slept in the living room. During the night, Kazmin would pretend to go to bathroom, but instead he would sneak into my room and quietly jump in and cuddle me in bed. But then as soon as Nasir realised that Kazmin was not there, he would get up and pretend to go to the toilet. Kazmin would then quietly jump from my bed and return to the living room. I felt so uncomfortable and sorry for both of them, but that is what Kazmin wanted. When I returned home I went alone, as Kazmin had suggested. Kazmin killed some time walking the neighbouring streets and then, after a suitable amount of time had elapsed, he returned home to his sister's house, where Izan immediately revealed to him that I hadn't slept at home for the past few nights and that I had definitely been with some man. Kazmin just listened, smiled inwardly and said nothing. Kazmin was in London for two weeks and then returned to Malaysia. I couldn't wait for him to go, because he put me in such a difficult situation as we had to hide our relationship from his family. I did that because I loved him. He was my boyfriend, husband, my best friend, and my brother all in one. He was the only person I could talk about anything. I could cry on his shoulder without any judgment. I could not imagine life without him and he was always near to my heart.

I continued my life as a student, and going out with Nasir. One day I was quite taken back when Nasir revealed that he loved me. I felt confused. When Kazmin called, I told him that his friend had fallen in love with me. Kazmin could sometimes be very naughty but he said he did not feel sorry about what he had done to his friend, in fact he found it funny. Kazmin asked me to continue pretending and not to hurt him because he was a very good friend – but he didn't want me to get too close either. What a situation he was putting me in!

After a year, Izan moved out, leaving me alone in Baker Street with my companion, Dazzle the cat. Nasir came to see me a lot . We got on very well, but I was becoming very worried about his feelings towards me. He wanted to spend more and more time with me. He would come to pick me up from college, waiting for me by the exit. He was becoming jealous and this caused me to worry about the relationship. He would call in the afternoon and if I hadn't arrived home yet, he would become angry. He was checking on me and I was starting to feel uncomfortable with him. In spite of everything, I tried to remain friendly and talkative, because he was a friend of Kazmin. I tried to concentrate on my studies, hardly going out at all in the evening.

Kazmin returned to London about five months later to sort out some business matters, and of course to see me. This time, he stayed at my place because I was the only person living in the house and Izan would not be there to watch over us. As usual, Nasir was invited to go out with us, but this time he was becoming very suspicious. The three of us went out together to a club for dinner and to dance, but this time his eyes kept watch on every move I made. He became very jealous because Kazmin and I kept very close to each other and he could see that something was going on between us.

The situation was becoming rather tense. It was obvious that there was something in the air, but no one wanted to be the first to approach the subject of our relationship. One night, Nasir was watching us the whole time, and he wouldn't leave our sides. He saw Kazmin hold my hand and he pinched me from behind, and I thought, this is silly. But truthfully, I was not sure who was being silly. Kazmin just acted as if he was drunk and it was no big deal that he was cuddling me. Of course, Nasir was not happy. He did not like Kazmin cuddling me and I am sure he was confused and upset. After all the stupid things Kazmin had done to Nasir, Kazmin left me and Nasir and returned to Malaysia. After that I just avoided Nasir as much as I could, I just didn't want to hurt his feelings. Kazmin came to London a third time and on this occasion he was very busy with business and was accompanied by two friends from his company. The three of them stayed at my place – Kazmin paid for the house rent. We all had a great time together, especially Kazmin and I. Kazmin's friends knew about our relationship, so there was nothing to hide, as there had been when Nasir was around. Time passed by very quickly, two weeks were gone and it was time for Kazmin and his friends to go back to Malaysia. After that Kazmin did not come back to London for quite some time; but there was a fourth trip and during that next trip there would be terrible repercussions for both of us.

I had already moved out and was renting a room that was slightly cheaper. This time I could see a lot of difference in Kazmin's character. He was not the man that I used to know, he was not as funny as he was, he didn't talk much anymore and he hardly put a smile on his face. He was very strange and I felt like he was a stranger to me. He was always on the phone, but I didn't know who he was having conversations with, because he always talked in private. I was suspicious about what was going on in his life and just hoped he would come forward and tell me what exactly was happening.

CHAPTER 14

Integration and Rejection

I was starting to fit into London life. I had already made many friends at college and the gym, and I got on particularly well with a man named Andrew, who helped me with my exams. Over the course of several months I studied fitness and successfully passed all my exams. I often went out with Andrew. He was the first Englishman I got to know in London. It was Andrew who showed me a side of London that I had never seen before. Andrew had dark hair, very pale skin and dark brown eyes. He had an honest look about him and a deep, penetrating expression. He was tall, slim and healthy-looking, but despite our good friendship, he was not the type of man that appealed to me.

Andrew was a wonderful friend and we spent many special times together. One of those days was when we went to Kent to pick apples. It was summer time and the weather was perfect all day. The orchard in Kent was just an hour's drive from London, there you could pick your own apples – as many as you wanted.

It was the first time I had seen apples actually growing on trees. In Malaysia, there are many different kinds of trees, but no apple trees. The funny thing is I took my cat with me to the farm and luckily, they allowed us to bring him inside. He behaved very well and didn't run away, but all the other people passing by looked at us with amusement. They must have thought, this couple and their cat are strange. Poor Andrew! He had to put up with all the stares and gossip.

On another trip, Andrew took me to pick strawberries. He knew I loved strawberries.

On the way over there, I was so excited, thinking, I'm going to climb the strawberry trees! I like climbing trees; I always climbed trees when I was a

Life Behind the Silence 95

young girl. Andrew just smiled. He enjoyed my happiness and liked seeing me behave like a little girl. We arrived at the strawberry farm and he handed me a basket and walked in. I saw everyone sitting like birds in a field – and no trees.

"What the hell are they doing?" I asked Andrew, "Where are the strawberry trees?"

He looked at me and said, "Oh dear! All those people over there are picking strawberries."

My eyes and my mouth gaped open. I was shocked and I said, "You're joking."

He handed me a basket and urged me to follow him. We squatted in the field and picked the strawberries that I loved so much, but it was a shame I couldn't climb the trees!

I was very disappointed and grumbled the whole time. Andrew was patient with me – he just laughed at my childish character. There was nothing else he could do! From that day on, I hated strawberries, they seemed different.

Andrew was very good at exercise, every day he would go to a gym called Seymour Place, where they held aerobics classes and where I worked as a crew member at that time. He came almost every day to the aerobics classes, but he was rubbish with his moves. He tried it, but he looked like he was jumping everywhere like a monkey, and his moves disturbed everybody. But he didn't care at all – he just did his own thing. We always stayed together in the class and everyone knew that we had some kind of relationship. All my friends teased me, especially about the way he moves in the aerobics class. I was so embarrassed, but it was hilarious!

He was a very caring person, always asking about my family in Malaysia. I told him everything was fine. He thought my brother was sending money from Malaysia so that I could study in London. He was very helpful a few times when I didn't receive the bank transfer from Kazmin. He would lend me money so I could buy a few essentials. Almost every week, he did my shopping for many weeks. We went to the supermarket together and filled the trolley, and then I had food for the rest of the week. But I paid him back as soon as I received the money from Kazmin. I could never thank him enough. He always behaved like a perfect gentlemen, and I knew he was in love with me.

Almost every weekend, Andrew would pick me up, and we would drive to his flat. There, he cooked a lovely English dinner and dessert. I love dessert, it's my favourite part of the meal. After dinner we would watch a movie and just before midnight he would take me home. He was such a nice man; he just hugged me and would go no further.

Of course he did try to kiss and romance me once, but I told him I could do nothing before I got married because I was a Muslim. And I told him I did not like kissing men because I was a lesbian. This was a complete fabrication – I had never been with a woman. To this day, I don't know why I said such a stupid thing to Andrew. The truth is, I loved him as a friend and for safety reasons and so as not to upset his feelings that was the first thing that popped into my head at that moment.

We went around together for several years and one night I slept at his place. But I warned him beforehand not to do anything to me, and he agreed.

We slept in the same bed and he was very loving, hugging me the whole night, but nothing sexual happened. I trusted him from the beginning and I felt so bad deceiving my dear friend Andrew, he was my best friend in the whole world.

A few times he took me out of London to visit his family and sometimes they would come down to London to visit us. His family were very nice people, I loved them all, especially his father. I have always been close to my friends' fathers, I think because I never really had one. I was very close with Andrew's father but sadly he died before I could see him for one last time. My heart was deeply saddened.

I moved out again. I rented a flat in Maida Vale, which I shared with a couple from Russia. Every evening, I would go to a café on the canal just opposite my house and have a few drinks and watch the people go by. There were also a few shops around, so it was very convenient for me.

One day I was shopping at the local grocery store and met a guy named Ali. He and his brother, two Muslim men from Iran, became friends of mine. They introduced me to their mother, a very nice woman. For me to go to their house and meet their family meant nothing to me, but for Ali it meant we were all but married.

One month later he announced that he was in love with me. He was a good-looking boy, I fell for his looks but he was such a boring person. My feelings towards him became cloudy and I got so bored when I was with him. He was such a jealous person, he started to control my life by following me everywhere, hiding himself in every corner so he could see what I was doing and who I was going out with, and he even waited in the car for hours in front of my house until I got home. Sometimes he came to ring my doorbell at six in the morning to make sure that I had slept at home. If I didn't open the door, he would keep ringing until he disturbed my housemates, and that caused a lot of problems. I felt I was living in danger and finally I had to call the police on him. At last he left me alone and I lived peacefully.

I learned a lesson from this experience: I had to be careful when I met new people.

I sometimes went out with my friend from the gym, Mark, and he became a great friend of mine. He loved cooking and invited me for amazing dinners at his house.

These were happy times. I was getting to know a lot of people and I felt secure in London, the city that had frightened me so much at the beginning. I had become completely integrated and one cannot say that until one has made real friends in a place. And real friends I had.

Kazmin's sister, Nor, discovered that her brother and I were lovers. A Malaysian friend had let the cat out of the bag, telling her that Kazmin and I were a couple and had been living together in Malaysia. Kazmin called me and told me the news and I became troubled and nervous, wondering what the outcome would be. It seemed that Kazmin, too, was very worried about the fact that we had been found out. Because of Nor, the entire family now knew the truth, and it turned out that Kazmin's fear was well-founded. His family rejected me completely and wouldn't accept me because I was from the country and had had very humble beginnings.

In fact, Kazmin's family didn't want the relationship to continue. I had always known in the back of my mind that this day would come. I was now going to be thirty years old and it seemed nothing good had ever lasted long in my life. What would happen next, I wondered.

CHAPTER 15

The Truth, Please

One of Kazmin's business partners from Malaysia came to London on business. Kazmin gave him some money to give to me when he arrived in London. He gave me a call as soon as he arrived and we arranged to meet for lunch at the hotel where was staying.

Along with the money, he gave me something else, namely the terrible news that Kazmin was seeing a woman named Rosnah. She was a famous actress in Malaysia. Kazmin and Rosnah were considered a couple and they travelled together and had even taken trips to the islands together.

I didn't say a word to his friend. I tried to hide my sadness behind the silence. I excused myself and apologised for not being able to talk to him. I could not concentrate on anything and I needed to be alone.

Kazmin's friend looked at me and said, "He is not the only man in this world, look after your self and everything will be fine."

I gave him a smile and left him, tears running down my cheek. I thought, yes! What he said is right. But it is not easy to think rationally at moments like that. All the way home, my eyes flooded with tears. My mind was filled with a million questions and I didn't sleep at all that night. All night, I watched the phone, hoping it would ring, and the clock, counting the hours.

In the morning, when Kazmin telephoned me as he did every day, I told him what his friend had told me and of course he denied it. He said that his friend was jealous of his success and many sweet things came out of his mouth that made me trust his charming words. He said, "I would never do such a thing to someone who I love and want to spend my life with. Do you believe him or me?"

I fell for his words and I told him that I believed him, but the truth is I was confused, then I said, "Why would someone make up a story like that?"

In the Muslim religion, when an unmarried man and woman are discovered alone together in a hotel or house, it is known as Khalwat, and it is considered a very serious matter. So someone had seen Kazmin and Rosnah together in a hotel in Malaysia. Because Rosnah was well known, someone reported them to an Iman (an Islamic religious leader). They were subsequently accused of Khalwat, and it appeared in the local papers. I didn't know anything about it, but this is what I was told.

Kazmin's sister Nor heard the story and called me to break the news. I couldn't wait any longer, I called Kazmin. I was about to go crazy, with a mixture of fear and sadness; I felt as if I were going mad. I told him about the news and he told me that it wasn't him – it was someone else but because their names were the same people mixed them up and put it in the newspapers, so everyone thought it was him.

This was not sounding logical at all. I told Kazmin that I was not stupid. After a long argument and hours of discussion, I almost ended the relationship, but in the end I chose to believe him and to believe that he loved me and me alone. After all, we had been together all those years.

I continued to hear rumours about Kazmin and Rosnah from friends and family in Malaysia. I was uneasy, but I wanted to believe that Kazmin loved me. He called three times a day after this incident, and we talked for hours at a time. The Khalwat matter had been resolved in court; Rosnah had to pay a sum of money. Again, that is what I had been told.

This time Kazmin's trip to London proved decisive for the future of our relationship. He came just to see me this time, so there was no business to get in our way.

He revealed that his company was not doing very well and that his business was less lucrative than before. But I wasn't very interested in money issues. I was glad to see him again and felt more relaxed after so many absurd rumours.

And then something wonderful occurred, although it wasn't the right moment. He asked me to marry him! I was delighted that he asked me; it meant so much to me. Funnily enough, thought he proposed to me, he didn't have a ring. Anyway, my answer, of course, was "Yes, but not at this present time" because I would need to finish my studies first.

His response to this was, "Well! We can marry and you still can study."

I said, "Yes, you are right, but what happens if I become pregnant? I'm on my own? Anyway, if you want to marry me, you have to propose to me in the proper way because I still have to ask my mother's permission."

As soon as I said that he dropped the bomb. He told me that he wanted to marry me in secret, without telling either of our families. In that moment Kazmin broke my heart. No matter how much I loved him, I couldn't do that. My mother was more important to me than anything and a secret marriage would have embarrassed her more than anything else I could do to her.

I felt happy that he loved me in spite of the distance and the opposition from his family, and I didn't want to hurt his feelings after he had come all the way from Malaysia just for this matter. I told him that I loved him – and only him – and wanted to marry him, but I needed one more year in order to complete my studies and to tell my mother.

Kazmin was not very happy with my decision. His solution was for us to get married and for him to get me pregnant. I could still stay and finish my studies. He was adamant that I should get pregnant and stay in London alone with his baby, all the while finishing my studies.

I was very disappointed with his stupid idea. I said, "I don't think that I could do that. If I were pregnant, I would want you to be round me all the time, I wouldn't want you to leave me on my own to carry your baby, what the hell you are thinking?"

I could see that he was very disappointed with my explanation but I told him the truth; that was what I wanted.

Eventually, Kazmin said, "OK! If that is what you want, I will wait for you."

The next day Kazmin returned to Malaysia with an empty hand and an empty heart, but I felt good and that what I had done was for the best.

Three months later, I received the news that Kazmin and Rosnah were married. His sister Nor told me and once again I didn't believe it. I was used to this kind of story so I didn't take it seriously; and I was fed up with being told such silly things. After all, I believed Kazmin loved me and I was sure that he would never marry someone else. He had just promised that I was the only woman in his life and that I would be his wife. Kazmin continued phoning every day, insisting that I come back to Malaysia. I kept telling him I would come back soon, but I didn't know how soon!

After hearing constant rumours about Kazmin and Rosnah, I finally begged him to be sincere with me. I told him that his sister Nor and my family in Malaysia had told me that he was married to an actress.

His answers poured cold water over my dreams. He said, "Yes I'm married."

My heart stopped beating, I was so shocked. No words would come out of my mouth. At the moment I just wanted to be alone so I said, "OK! I will

Life Behind the Silence 101

speak to you later."

Slowly I hung up the phone and started to sob bitterly, my body seemed paralysed; I couldn't move. I sat myself on the corner of the bed, thinking, why must this happen to me? What did I do wrong?

He had no idea how bitter it tasted when he told me that he had settled down and married. I gasped for breath between sobs, choking on occasion so that my face turned scarlet. I am sure his dream had come true and I guessed she gave him things that I couldn't give to him. 'Love Hurts' by Nazareth, that was the song I listened to when he broke my heart by marrying someone else. At that moment I felt his love was just a lie and that he had fooled me badly. Love hurts, but I learned a lot and now I wish nothing but the best for his future with the new woman in his life.

The phone started ringing and it rang and rang. I knew it was Kazmin trying to call me back, but I could not talk to him – not now. I had just lost the only man I had ever loved. My life would never be the same without him. My future was dark because my true love now belonged to someone else.

I didn't want to believe it and the only thoughts in my mind at that moment were, why is he doing this to me? My happiness is Kazmin and now he is gone forever.

The following day he called me to explain. I listened, but I didn't answer much. I was still feeling sick from the day before.

He explained how badly things were going for the two businesses he owned. Everything had gone downhill financially. I couldn't have imagined that his economic situation was so desperate. One of the companies, called Tamara, produced road signs. Kazmin explained that in order to send me money, he had sold his car and the office computers.

He had met Rosnah a long time ago at a business meeting in his office and she had wanted to invest in Kazmin's investment company. Meanwhile, the Malaysian economy had suffered an economic crash and many companies went out of business. Among those businesses were both of his companies – until the intimate relationship with Rosnah saved them. At least that was his story.

I had been busy preparing for my aerobics exams and had also been thinking about Kazmin; hopefully it did not affect my studies. I hadn't realised that Kazmin's finances had gone to pieces in such a manner. I knew that things were not going as well as before, but I couldn't have foreseen the seriousness of the situation. He kept sending money; just as he had done every month.

Later, I found out that he had asked for money from friends, acquaintances – just about anybody – so he could send it to me. Rosnah had helped him a lot. She loaned Kazmin money and allowed him to stay at her house without paying anything in rent. Kazmin told her that he wanted to start another business and she gave him enough money for a fresh start. But instead Kazmin sent some of that money to me. He was lying to her. To think, I was so totally removed from everything that I had no idea what was really occurring. How could something like this have happened?

I felt so sorry for him, and guilty for not appreciating all that he had done for me. So I decided to continue our relationship and have conversations on the telephone as usual. From day one, Kazmin and I had never hidden our problems from one another. He was a good listener and I was a good talker. After he was married, he always told me his problems and I would give him my opinion about what I thought he should do.

Not long after they were married, all I started to hear from him was that the marriage was a disaster. I still wanted him to tell me the real reason he had married Rosnah. He finally told me that Rosnah had found the receipt for the money transfers he was sending me and she had become very angry. Because he had lied to her about using the money to invest in his business, she had made a threat which he was obliged to take seriously; she had said, "Either you get married to me, or return all my money."

Kazmin was already bankrupt, so he decided it was easier to get married than to pay up. That is what he told me, but I still wondered if it was true or not. Either way, it just didn't bother me anymore. But it was then, just before he got married, that he came to London to propose to me. In his mind, if I agreed to marry him, I would be the first wife – a Muslim man can have three wives or maybe more. I try not to be selfish, but I wouldn't like sharing a husband.

My sister sent me a magazine from Malaysia with an article about the wedding of Kazmin and the actress Rosnah. When I saw the photos of their wedding, all I could think was, that should have been me standing beside Kazmin. It should have been me wearing that wedding dress – should have been me Kazmin was kissing. Without me noticing, tears ran down my cheeks and my heart whispered that now I did not belong to him anymore.

In spite of my sadness I made an effort to keep going. I was determined to gain the title of aerobics instructor. With friends I pretended that everything was going fine; after all, nobody knew I had a boyfriend. No one noticed that

Life Behind the Silence 103

I was suffering inside. On the other hand, I had no one in whom I could confide my bitter secret. Luckily, through tremendous effort, I passed my exams with positive results.

Kazmin and I continued speaking on the phone every day, just as before. I could hardly tell any difference between then and before because we continued to carry on as lovers. It was not easy to forget someone that I loved so much. Sometimes I can understand how a Muslim man can have multiple wives.

But our conversations started becoming depressing. He complained constantly about his wife and told me about his financial problems. He said that she was extremely jealous and controlled his every movement. He had no money of his own – she controlled the purse strings. Kazmin stopped being the kind and cheerful person that he used to be; now he talked only about his problems. Knowing that he was so unhappy was soul-destroying for me.

CHAPTER 16

Nor

Muslim men can marry more than one wife but they need the permission of the first wife for subsequent marriages. If she doesn't give her consent, he cannot marry anyone else. Most Malaysian men who cannot get permission from the first wife resort to secret marriages. They go to a registry office or to Thailand and get married without telling anyone. Once they are married, if someone tells the first wife, she is powerless to do anything about it.

In my grandfather's generation, the first wives were scared of their husbands and would permit them to have two or three wives. And some wives allowed their husbands to bring their second and third wives to live under the same roof. What happened was, the first wife cooked, the second wife cleaned and the third wife looked after their children; they worked together as a happy family. And everyone had their own turn; Monday, the husband slept with the first wife, Tuesday with the second wife and Wednesday with the third, so the rest of the week the husband was probably resting after all the hard work. WOW! How lucky that man was. If it were me, he would not even have time to mention the second wife, I would kick his ass.

The difference now is, wives do not live under the same roof. Each wife lives in a separate house and functions with the husband and children as a separate family. The husband comes and goes as he pleases and usually tends to spend most of his time with the first wife. This is one of the reasons I do not want to marry a Muslim man. Kazmin was the first and the last ever Muslim man in my life.

Kazmin had what he thought was a brilliant idea; I was in London at the time and he said to me, "Come back to Malaysia and be with me, I really miss you and I am so lonely so please! And we can get married in secret."

Obviously, whatever happened I was not going to be a second wife. But I didn't want to argue and create more problems, or upset him as he was already under a lot of pressure. So I told him that I would think about it. In the back of my mind I thought there was no way I would leave him because he had done a lot for me and I felt I owed him something.

Nor, Kazmin's sister, started to show me friendship and was very kind to me. I wasn't sure why she was doing that. And sometimes she brought food to my house. I had become rather depressed by recent events and I didn't feel like eating anything. The only thing it seemed I could do was weep; I wept without being able to stop, just as I had done in my childhood.

Nor came to see me often to keep me company. We talked and the more we did, the more I got to know her. She was a rather nice person and I found out the reason for her friendship: she didn't like Rosnah. She told me that Rosnah was older than Kazmin and that Kazmin was her second husband. She had already been married and had three children from the previous marriage. Well! As far as I was concerened there was nothing wrong with that, as long they were in love and had a happy life.

It turns out that Nor would have preferred me as Kazmin's wife over Rosnah. She told me that Rosnah had come from a normal family and when she was young, she was beautiful and had become an actress. She had started to make money and had rich lovers. I was now the person Kazmin's sister liked best and she was tying to impress me and telling me that I should go back to Malaysia and marry Kazmin. This was the same family that had basically caused this mess in the first place. All this misery and now she wanted me to be her friend.

Nor had four children, I loved her children and all of her daughters were good to me. Her oldest daughter, Afida, and I were great friends. She was in her twenties, very funny and with a lovely personality. All of the children called me Auntie. I love children: children and a family is what I wanted from Kazmin but it didn't look like that was going to happen.

Kazmin called me daily; behind his wife's back. Each time, he pleaded with me to go back to Malaysia and to him. He told me that he was having difficulty finding money to send to me. He would support me completely if he had the money. So it became evident that the only choice I had was to go back to Malaysia or to continue my part-time job, but that didn't pay enough.

I had come to love London very much, but it was too expensive, especially as I didn't have a proper job and as a student I couldn't work full time. Also, I still cared about Kazmin. His new business was just starting up and he was living out of his wife's pocket. He was worried about who would look after me if something happened to him. He imagined all the worst case scenarios. What if he went to jail or died? What would I do in London? It wasn't my country. He was very generous and caring and, in my mind, he wouldn't have showed that he cared if he didn't love me. It sounds crazy now, but the fact that he cared during this time made me want to be with him.

I decided to stay in London, even though I knew it was going to be tough without Kazmin's support, but I am a very independent woman, so I would carry on my life in London. I started looking for more aerobics classes, but it was really hard. I had sent my CV to almost all the fitness centres in London. I only had a few responses that asked me to come for an interview. I was so happy and I thought I was doing very well to get interviews, but it was still not enough for them. Some of them said that as I had just qualified, I would have to gain some experience first. I thought, that is such a stupid suggestion. How was I supposed to get any experience if they didn't take me on? I was turned down for most jobs. I was still teaching a cover class, but that was not enough for me to survive. The wages that I received were not even enough to pay the rent. I was getting so worried, because my rent ended four months in arrears.

I would send the wages that I received to my mother every month; she needed the money and I didn't want to tell her that I was finding life difficult. I would always tell her that I was doing well.

Every day I left the house very early in the morning and came home late in the evening, so I could avoid seeing my landlord. I had a few pounds, not even enough for me to buy proper food, so I would buy a loaf of bread and a few carrots; that's what I ate almost everyday. Life became even tougher when, one evening, my landlord unexpectedly came to my place at eleven at night and told me to get out the next morning, if I still couldn't pay the rent. Of course I couldn't, so early in the morning I packed all my belongings and left the house before my landlord came. I walked on the road without thinking about anything, I had no idea where I should go. I had many male and female friends, but I didn't tell anyone about what had happened. I stopped at the bus stop and saw people getting on and off the buses, but not me. I just sat there for hours, thinking, where am I going to sleep tonight? All of sudden it popped into my head, yes! I should go to the park and the only park that I was very familiar was Hyde Park. Even though my brain was feeling so weak, my body still had the energy to get up and pull my luggage in the direction that I wanted to go. I was homeless for weeks. Every evening I sneaked into the park to sleep and woke early in the morning before anybody found out that I had slept in the park. Luckily it was summer time so I didn't have to contend with the cold weather. But I didn't sleep in peace, I was so scared that someone would see me and chase me or rape me; all this was buzzing around my mind non-stop. But I left it in God's hands to save my life because he knew everything I had been through.

But one evening there was heavy rain, like cats and dogs. I had no choice but to sneak and sit outside the church until the rain stopped. By the time the rain stopped it was too late for me to go back into the park, so I ended up sleeping in front of the church. That was the first time I had ever come close to a church, thank God nothing happened. Thank you for saving my life, God, and the next time I come, I will enter inside and say a big thank you. I am sure if any Muslim people heard this they would not agree with what I did. Well! This is my life; no one will tell me what I should or shouldn't do. I have my own opinions and I know what is right and what is wrong in life.

Sometimes I went to the gym in the morning for a shower but most of the time I went in the evening because I worked there as a crew member. I carried on my life as normally as possible without anyone noticing what was happening to me. I smiled, I talked, I laughed, I hid all my problems behind the silence but my soul was screaming for help.

Every day I called Kazmin from a phone box to explain to him what was happening to me and I begged him to send me some money for me to pay the rent. At last, after a few weeks, he sent me the money and with that money I paid for a small room. I was so happy to get my own place and I comfortably slept in a bed for the first time since I became homeless. But my happy time only lasted for a few months then the problem came back again when I could not manage to pay the rent for two months. My landlord kept knocking on my door almost every day. I was getting so worried thinking that I was going to have to sleep outside again. I couldn't go through all that again, so I decided to move out and stay with a close friend of mine for a while.

Even though I stayed with a friend, life never got any better because I don't like to share my life with anyone as my life is very personal and I like to keep to myself. It was a difficult time, I was getting so depressed, it had invaded my soul and left me unable to do anything. My passport was about to expire, and I didn't have enough money to pay for my visa, so I could not extend my stay in London. I even had an offer of marriage from a British citizen, but I didn't want to marry just for a visa. I wanted to marry for love.

With no other option, I decided during the summer of 1999 that I had to return to Malaysia. I had been living in London for seven years and had many things to do in order to prepare for my return to Malaysia. Kazmin was able to help me with some of the expenses. I don't know who he borrowed the money from, but I knew he had many friends who would help him. I started sending some of my boxes of personal items ahead of me by ship. I said goodbye to all my friends – some of them by telephone because I thought it would be too hard to say goodbye in person.

The day of my departure came. Nor and her husband, Badrul, took me to the airport and they both seemed happy and talked about many things. I just agreed with whatever they said. Nor was still advising me to marry Kazmin and take him away from that woman. I was sad and couldn't focus on their conversation. All I could think about was the fact that in a few hours I would be leaving London. At the airport I checked in my luggage and my cat, Dazzle, and said goodbye once more. I walked, with a broken heart, to the gate. I boarded the plane in silence. I am leaving London, I thought. But not for good, I will be back.

Soon the plane took off and I looked out through the window and burst into tears. I couldn't stop thinking about how much I loved London. I cried and cried; I cried because I didn't want to go back to Malaysia, because I didn't know what was going to become of me, because I didn't want to marry Kazmin if that meant I would be his second wife – because crying was the one constant thing in my life.

I was travelling a million miles across the globe and during the thirteen-hour flight, I could barely sleep because of all the worrying that I had in my mind. Who knew how sadly it would all end? I was really not looking forward to seeing Kazmin at all. I was thinking that I would have to find a way to return to London. It was August 2nd 1999.

CHAPTER 17

Love is a Thorny Rose

I was going through immigration at Kuala Lumpur airport when the officer notified me that my passport was being confiscated. In Malaysia, when someone has unpaid debts and court action has been taken, it can affect your passport status. At the time I had no idea what they were talking about, but it soon became obvious. They returned and asked me a few questions all of which I answered correctly, because the debts were nothing to do with me, someone had done it to me. Anyway, the officer let me go through to customs.

I had to wait for a long time for my suitcase to appear on the conveyor belt. I was feeling sad because of leaving London and now, on returning to Malaysia after many years, I had had my passport taken away. I thought, what a good start! I didn't know what was going to happen next. My mind was thinking about my reunion with Kazmin. Just after arriving, I had seen him waiting for me with a little smile on his face. It was the same way he always looked when we saw each other after a long absence. This reunion was different. We did not hug or kiss each other like we used to; I just kissed his hand as is the Muslim custom, to show respect. He picked up my luggage and put it in the car. I was friendly to him, however, my feelings towards him were so different now. I don't know if he noticed or not, but surely he could sense the change in my feelings.

We hadn't seen each other for many years and now the man I used to know as my boyfriend and future husband was sitting next to me in the car as a married man. It was very hard for me, but I tried to pretend to have as normal a conversation as possible. Deep down inside I still felt badly hurt.

He never mentioned his marriage and neither did I, but it was the only subject that I needed to talk about. I wondered what his feelings were towards me now. He broke the silence by trying to make a joke, but it was not funny at all. I looked at him and he smiled, his face looking like a little hamster, and he told me a joke. I looked at him and said, "Yeee! Very funny! So where did you get this joke?" The truth is, I didn't find it funny at all.

He said, "I made it up."

I replied, "Ummm...! Well done."

The journey from the airport to central Kuala Lumpur took more or less one hour. At last I arrived in the city, which was full of light and colour. On every corner I saw many pubs, bars and cafés, and many people walking along the streets. I had not been back for six years and many things had changed. Kazmin drove me around and showed me a few places that had changed since I had been gone. He was trying to show me that Kuala Lumpur was now a beautiful city, and more modern than London. But it didn't impress me at all and all I could do was think about my wonderful London, the city that I had fallen in love with, and that I shouldn't be here.

After the tour of Kuala Lumpur, Kazmin took me to a beautiful five-star condominium he had rented. It was a lovely two-bedroom apartment with a swimming pool and gym. Kazmin always gave me the best and he did it without complaining. But it didn't make me happy because that is not what I wanted; I just wanted a happy life. He rushed out to buy dinner and food for my cat. When he got back, I was surprised to see there was dinner only for me. Even though he hadn't seen me for a long time, unfortunately he had to go off to be with his wife and was unable to stay any longer. As he left, he told me to sleep well and he would see me tomorrow. With that, the love of my life walked out of the door and I looked at him full of sadness. I was so tired after the long journey so I slept soundly.

Kazmin came every day to see me at lunchtime; at that time of day, no one would notice that he was missing. He brought food and we would eat together. Sometimes he would have to leave abruptly. He continued being scared that someone would recognise him. Rosnah was still a well-known person and someone might catch us together. Sometimes he would bring something for dinner as well, but most evenings I would go out by myself. I spent all day and night alone. I needed him but at the same time I knew that I couldn't have him.

Just a month after I returned to Malaysia, I started looking for a job teaching aerobics and soon I was teaching every day at a few fitness centres and hotels.

One day, right before Kazmin came up to my apartment, he made a call to his wife from the public phone in the lobby of the apartment building to tell her that he would be home a little later. He committed a grave error in phoning Rosnah, from the apartment lobby, because as soon as he hung up the phone, she checked to see what number he had called from and was able to find out the location.

Kazmin was lucky – five minutes after he left, Rosnah arrived at my door and rang the bell. I was less lucky; I had to face this tricky situation.

I looked through the spy hole and saw a woman standing outside. I didn't recognise her, so I opened the door, thinking it was one of the building's personnel staff. I had taken off my contact lenses and didn't have my glasses on, so I couldn't see very well.

The lady at the door said, "Is Kazmin here?"

"Kazmin? Kazmin who?" I replied. I thought, my God! Someone has reported that Kazmin was here with me alone. An unmarried Muslim couple alone in a hotel would be committing Khalwat. The person who called the Iman will come to get a statement and take us to the court. And here is someone at my door!

I felt relieved that Kazmin was not in the house with me – otherwise I would have another problem. Then I got surprise when the lady at the door said, "I know Kazmin is here, and you are Gina."

I was shocked and I was becoming suspicious that something was wrong somewhere, but I kept pretending, saying, "No! I'm not Gina!"

She said, "Don't lie to me, I've seen your photo and I know Kazmin is inside your house. Don't hide him from me."

I started getting angry then I said, "I haven't hidden him, I do not even know him, and if you don't believe me, you can come in and have a look." I was becoming very curious. I wanted to know who the hell this woman was.

She stepped inside and we faced each other. She said, "Do you know who I am?"

I thought, what a stupid question and I said, "How should I know who you are if you do not introduce yourself?"

Then the shock came when she said, "I am Kazmin's wife."

I was shocked, but I managed to maintain my courage enough to ask, "Oh! Sorry I do not recognise you, so what do you want? Why don't you start checking around here, maybe your husband is somewhere in this house."

With an angry face, she went straight for the bedroom. The pillow was propped up against the headboard as a back rest, which is how Kazmin tended to arrange it when he sat on the bed. She said to me in a menacing tone, "I know he has been here, because that's the way Kazmin always puts the pillow."

I replied, "Kazmin's not the only person who puts it that way. Anybody could have done that."

Rosnah then went to the bathroom, still looking for her husband, but there was no one there. Then she went into the living room and said, "These cigarettes are the ones my husband smokes."

My response was, "Anyone can smoke those cigarettes."

Upon seeing the biscuits on the table, she said, "Those biscuits are those which Kazmin likes."

Again I replied, "I like those biscuits, Kazmin is not the only one who likes them."

Kazmin had made a trip to Indonesia recently, where he bought a decorative item for his house and another for mine. His wife saw the item sitting there and she said, "Was that from Kazmin?"

I realised this was very silly and I couldn't keep denying her accusations any longer, so at this point I said, "Yes, Kazmin bought me many things, including that. So what?"

Then Rosnah sat down. She showed me a pearl bracelet she was wearing and said that Kazmin had bought it for her. She asked me what else Kazmin had bought for me. I made her even more jealous when I told her he bought me a lot of sexy clothes and had been doing so since we were young. Then she asked the real question: "Is Kazmin still in love with you?"

I told her Kazmin was still thoughtful where I was concerned, but he was not a romantic person. The conversation felt like one between two teenagers having a fight over a boy except this was a lot more serious. Rosnah told me that she knew Kazmin had been sending money to me every month. She told me a lot of other things – among them, that she was constantly in tears because of me. She knew Kazmin had been with me for a long time and that he had supported me from the beginning.

I thought, if she knew Kazmin was with me, then why did she want to marry him without making sure he was not seeing me any longer? I also thought, I did not take her husband; she was the one who took my boyfriend.

I tried to calm her down and told her that she did not need to worry about Kazmin and me. I said I was not in love with her husband anymore because I had a new boyfriend. In fact, that was a lie. I said that just to protect

Kazmin's relationship with her and I knew Kazmin would want me to say something like that to her.

Rosnah calmed down and started to sniffle. I explained that, in the past, Kazmin and I had shared a lot of love and passion. She should understand that and she should also understand that Kazmin and I had known each other for a very long time, we were still very close.

Then I said, "You should have known this before you married him, he was in love with me for many years, but you took him away from me. You thought you had power with your money but maybe now you know that he's not going to change, he is going to be who he is no matter what you do."

Rosnah's sobbing was starting to get even worse now. She couldn't stop crying and tears rolled down her cheeks.

She ended up staying at my house from ten at night until nine o'clock the next morning. Even though I was tired, I listened to her as she spent the entire night snivelling and coming out with ridiculous comments. She appeared to be very jealous.

I did remember to switch off my telephone so Kazmin wouldn't call while she was at my house – that would certainly have made things worse. She still didn't move her ass and leave me in peace. What she wanted now was for Kazmin to show up, so she could surprise him by being here, at my house. So I made up a story about an appointment with the doctor for which I had to leave shortly. Thank God! Finally she left.

To put her mind at ease, I told her not to worry because I knew how she must feel. She gave me her phone number and asked me to call her if Kazmin came over again.

Rosnah had only been gone a moment when I switched on my phone and Kazmin called straight away. I told him everything. He wanted to know everything that we had talked about. So we arranged to meet in my building, but on a different floor, just in case she returned. I told him everything about my conversation with Rosnah. He was pleased with what I had said to his wife to make her trust me.

Meanwhile, I planned to open my own business in the next few months. Kazmin helped me to find the place and negotiate the price. But at the time I was busy giving freelance aerobics classes in many different places. I taught aerobics to women only. One day, after giving a class, I was told that a woman was looking for me and had asked for my telephone number, but they hadn't given it to her because she was a stranger. The woman had come to the centre and asked who they recommended as a good instructor and they had given her my name. It was Kazmin's wife, of course she knew that I was teaching there.

Rosnah called me every day for a while. She had found my number in Kazmin's phone. Stupid Kazmin, why had he kept my number on his phone? Surely he could have remembered to delete it. Every time she called, she tried to hurt me by telling me she knew where I was, calling me a whore, saying I was ugly, a darkie that my boyfriend had married her because he didn't want me anymore. I viewed her behaviour as very immature.

Kazmin decided to move me to another condominium. It was also a beautiful place and I began to feel free and peaceful once more. Kazmin frequently came over for lunch and he seemed to feel relaxed as well, although sometimes he felt he had to hurry off.

I could not stop wondering how long this could go on, but I carried on giving aerobics classes and found a level of peace and fulfilment.

Seven months later, Kazmin's wife discovered my whereabouts yet again. Kazmin had been paying my bills; one of the receipts for my house was in his trousers and she found it.

Rosnah once again started harassing me. I was coming back from shopping with my sister, Nurul, one day and as we approached my home, I recognised Kazmin's car. Naturally I thought it was Kazmin but instead it was Rosnah. My sister was staying with me for a few months at that time. We had a very special relationship.

As soon as Kazmin's wife saw me, she got out of the car and walked towards me. She came right up to me and started poking me with her car key, wailing, "Where is my husband? I know you have him."

I thought, here we go again, but I said, "How do I know where your husband is? Why don't you call him and find out?"

Then she said, "He didn't pick up my call."

I replied, "So what do you want me to do?"

With that, I called him on the spot. Kazmin answered and of course he had no idea what was happening.

I said, "Hello, darling! Your wife is here disturbing me and shouting at me."

Kazmin was shocked and he said, "Just go up to your apartment and call security, ask them to call the police."

Just then, Rosnah grabbed the phone from my hand. She tried to talk to Kazmin, saying, "Hello! Hello! Hello!"

Life Behind the Silence

But Kazmin must have just hung the phone up. Smiling as proudly as I could, I raised my eyebrows at her and said, "So, what's happening now? You know what? I am very tired of this game of hide-and-seek. Now it's serious!"

I did what Kazmin asked me to do. I turned my back on her and walked away. Just as I was at the entrance to my apartment, I heard Rosnah yelled, "You are a prostitute!"

WOW! My ears burnt when I heard that word and my head completely lost it. I stopped, turned to her and shouted back, "Fuck you, you bloody bitch, you're the one who took my boyfriend, shame on you. Now, get out of here, I don't want to see your face anymore, it's disgusting!"

She stood there like a stupid women, blinking her eyes but not responding because I had shouted at her in English and she couldn't understand a word of it. But surely she would ask the person who was with her what I was talking about. I felt so relieved. Don't mess with me, I thought, she was the one who started it.

Before my chest blew up, I found the security guard and told him that I had paid for my apartment and if anybody wanted to see me, he had to let me know in advance. And I told him not to let Rosnah enter my apartment just because she was a famous actress. While I was with the security guard, Rosnah tried to find out about Kazmin and me from my sister. Nurul, the clever girl, told her that she did not know anything. I called her over and we both left with the security guard and went to the apartment. After that incident, she tried to come many times but wasn't sure what she was planning.

After a few months, I took my sister home to my mother. Even though I loved my sister staying with me, my mother was alone at home and she needed my sister more than I did. Also, my life at that moment was not stable, so I was better being on my own. Kazmin moved me to another new place where I could live in peace. Life started to seem normal and I was fairly happy. But then once again Kazmin announced he was having problems with his business and he had to take me to stay with two of his sisters who were on his staff. I was not looking forward to sharing with anyone, especially my belongings, but there was nothing that I could do. The two sisters were quite young, twenty-five and twenty-seven years old. They seemed nice and were kind to me. Sometimes I had no food but the sisters were very generous and always shared their food with me. I was so grateful for their kindness. But one of the sisters kept complaining to me that Kazmin hadn't paid her wages for a few months and asked me to talk to Kazmin. I totally understood that she needed the money and that was not right what Kazmin had done to them. Kazmin keep promising and lying but gave them nothing. Every day she pestered me until I got depressed; another problem that I had to handle. His business was failing because the government was taking too many months to pay their invoices. Things were getting bad, but we carried on together. I was in a stage of depression and spent all day and night thinking, "Damn you, Kazmin, you have given me a lot of hassle since I got back to Malaysia. I thought, what next? What should I do? Stay or get out of here.

The sisters lived in a very basic two-bedroom flat far from town. The area was very dodgy. I did not even know where I was. Kazmin had sold my car because he needed the money and he asked me to stop work for the meantime because of his wife.

Kazmin managed to come and see me only once a week at best. He left me alone with his two sisters. Every time I had to pretend we weren't together as Kazmin had asked me to do so and I was very tired. Kazmin didn't come to see us; he didn't give money to me or to his staff. One of the sisters worked somewhere else so she had some money to buy food. They both were very generous. Every time they cooked, they would invite me to eat with them. But I was starting to become uncomfortable depending on them daily. All this because of bloody Kazmin.

The situation didn't get any better and I began to live under constant tension and pressure from the sisters. Almost every day they would ask me to ask for money from Kazmin for them. When Kazmin didn't have any money to give them, I felt uncomfortable staying at their place, especially eating their food. Sometimes I had to hold my hunger all day and all night. I wasn't free to move around the house and I wasn't free to go to the kitchen to cook because nothing belonged to me. I even worried about switching on the TV because I didn't pay any bills. I ended up staying in my room most of the time. The sisters were very religious; they prayed five times a day and had kind hearts. But at one stage, for some reason, one of them picked on me, which made me lose my temper. We had a big argument and the pressure that I was under at that time made my temper blow up. I screamed and shouted at her, "Fuck you!" I really don't know what got into my head. I could see that she was shocked, scared and in tears. I felt so bad and she had to run to her room.

But the next day their mother came over to stay with us. I thought, WOW! What are they thinking? I'm not that dangerous. Their mother watched over every single move that I made and looked at me like I was a bad person. I am sure she was trying to protect her daughters. I felt like a stranger in this house, no one talked to me. I was all alone. If they were at home, I never came out of my little room. My room had just a small mattress in it and all my clothes hung on the wall, because I had no cupboard. I had no TV; I just lay sadly on my mattress like a piece of wood and looked up at the ceiling thinking, what is going to happen to my life? I ended up in a depressed silence. I was so hungry but I couldn't even go and eat because they had control of the kitchen. Kazmin didn't come and visit me for two weeks. I needed some money to go out and look for work and to do a few things. But he was with his wife having a fun time and I was left with this fucking shit and I looked so miserable. I couldn't take it anymore so I just waited for Kazmin to come so I could tell him my decision.

Three weeks went by and he still didn't come. As my mobile phone didn't have any credit, I had no choice but to borrow a few pence from one of the sisters so I could call Kazmin from a public phone. I felt so stupid for having to do that. I told Kazmin that I had had an argument with one of his sisters and that their mother was staying with them now. I needed to get out of that house that night. I begged Kazmin to come. I went back to my room and packed all my belongings and waited for Kazmin to arrive. In the meantime I told the sisters that I was moving out and apologised to the sister who I had the argument with. Both of them, as well as their mother, seemed very pleased about me leaving. I was more than pleased to get out of that hellish place but somehow I did appreciate very much them letting me stay.

My mobile rang and I thought Kazmin had arrived but surprisingly it was not him, instead it was his friend. Because Kazmin could not leave the house, as he was controlled by his wife, he had asked two of his friends to come and pick me up and take me to the hotel that he had booked for me. His friends were very nice and friendly. They took me for dinner then to the Flamingo Hotel, a four-star hotel in a suburb of Kuala Lumpur that had a restaurant, swimming pool and a lake in the middle of it.

Kazmin was not able to see me because his wife was watching him closely. I was more than happy not to see Kazmin during this time. I had lost my job and income because of Kazmin's wife's constant harassment. Now all I wanted was for Kazmin to pay the hotel bill and leave. At this stage I didn't want to know where he had got the money from, I didn't care less. I just wanted to have my life back. The Flamingo Hotel was to be a temporary fix at first, but after six months I started feeling comfortable there. I jogged around the hotel's lake every evening and the hotel staff were kind to me. I started to look after myself and began to slowly shake off my depression. It was time again to make an appearance.

Kazmin would come round every once in a while and take me out for dinner, just as had done so many years before. Now when we went out together, he would keep a distance between us. Before, we would always hold hands when we walked, but not now. It was a very sad state of affairs.

We couldn't be together. Everything had changed. Never again could we go to a restaurant as a couple. We never dined together like we used to do when we were in love. Now he tried to give me money, clothes and other things – but it was not the money that I wanted. The only thing I wanted was for him to be with me and for us to be happy and now I knew this would never happen.

CHAPTER 18

Goodbye Love of My Life

I met an American, Paul Roberts, who was fifty – four years old, divorced with two children. He was staying at the Flamingo hotel and noticed that I usually ate alone in the coffeehouse. We were on the same floor; our rooms next to each other and we had never seen each other. This was strange, because we had both been living in the hotel for months.

One day as I passed in the hall way he said, "Hello!"

I replied with the same, "Hello!"

I think nothing about this simple greeting. I thought all foreigners were friendly. Then one evening I on my way out jogging than all of sudden he came up behind me and he said, "Excuse me, I don't know if you are married or with somebody, but if you don't, I would like to invite you for dinner sometime. And if you do have someone then I am sorry to bother you."

I looked at him and thought, that was rather than charming. He looked OK and appeared to be a sweet guy. His face was very red, that was funny.

I said, "Don't worry! I'm not married, neither not with anyone."

Honestly, I was so happy to have the chance to get to know someone. We exchanged room numbers and said goodbye for the moment. He left me feeling really pleased and happy. I went jogging for hours. After my run, I returned to my room and as soon as I opened the door I found a little note that had been slipped under the door. It was an invitation from the American guy for dinner the next evening. Ummm...! I thought, he didn't waist his time. Well! Time to go out and meet new people, I wasn't going to wait for Kazmin anymore.

We went for dinner at a restaurant called Steak House. He was an American; so what I expect of course they love they meat. During our conversation, he asked what I did and he told me a little about his business. At first I didn't tell him the true about myself. I said I was on holiday and lived in London.

We had a wonderful time. The conversation and the dinner were fantastic. My heart felt so happy because I hadn't been out like this for a very long time. We have arrived at the hotel lobby; instead back to our room we decided to kill some time to go for a walk around the lake.

We just couldn't stop talking, especially me because I have been keeping my entire problem to myself for a long time. It was so nice getting to know someone who had full sense of humour and we talked for hours. I like people who are such a genuine person like him. So I started be honest and to tell him parts of my life, partly so I could see his reaction and I was interested by the fact that he seemed concerned but not judgmental. We soon realized it was nearly morning. He sent me to my room with a good – night kiss on my cheek which I had returned in kind. He was a perfect gentleman.

We met quite often in the coffeehouse for breakfast and sometimes we would go for lunch. At the beginning of the relationship he was falling in love with me, but then he became a good friend to me and nothing beyond that after I told him that I didn't have feeling towards him. He was so understanding and excepting with an open heart, how wonderful he is. After a few weeks, I started to gain my confidence and told Paul that I didn't work and I was not on holiday. I told him that I did work before, but it was gone because of situation with Kazmin's wife disturbing me at my workplace, and at any places that I use to stay. I revealed the truth about what happened to me and because of that I was stuck in Malaysia also without a passport. All I wanted was to get back to London.

He felt sorry for me and offered to help me. Almost everyday Paul and I would sit and talk about everything that had happened to me. He was a very good listener and he promised me he would do everything in his power to help me.

He introduced me to his business partner and the partner's wife. The four of us would go out for dinner together, which was very pleasant. His partner was kind and I became good friends with his wife.

Later, I introduced Paul to Kazmin. Kazmin felt uncomfortable with the idea of this stranger offering to help me to get my passport fixed so I could return to London. It became obvious that Kazmin didn't care about me anymore. We had an argument over my wish to return to London. He asked me if I had anyone "special" in London. I thought how ridiculous he was and that really annoyed me. He should have known by now that I had waited for him since the start of our relationship, then even when he married, I still came back and waited for him, but all he did was waste almost my entire life. Surely love is blind but he blind in everything.

Paul knew all about my life and still did not judge me. He kept offering to help me with my passport so I could get back to London to start my life.

The story of why my passport had been confiscated went like this. In Malaysia, if a person is found bankrupt, the government confiscates your passport until you have paid the outstanding debt. This happened when I was young, a friend of mine wanted to purchase same home appliances. But the finance company wanted someone to co-sign the loan financing papers. I did not understand what co-signing was; I understood only that my friend needed me to help him by signing some paper. What a good friend I was.

Years later, while I was in London, my friend stopped making payments on the instalments. So the finance company filed documents naming me as a bankrupt person. I had no knowledge of this until I returned to Malaysia and my passport was confiscated at the airport.

Kazmin was not in any hurry because he knew that as long as I had no passport, and no money, I could not go back to London. His plan was working until he moved me to the Flamingo hotel and I happened to meet Paul. Thank goodness Paul knew how to solve the problem. He told is partner, who new a lot of important people and they were able to resolve the issue of my passport. But it was not easy, I have to go trough a lot progression.

Once everything was arranged, I told Kazmin I was going to London. He was so shocked that people were willing to solve my debt problem and my passport was now in order. He had paid the hotel bills, but he hadn't done anything about the passport because he wanted me to stay in Malaysia, but then he had done nothing about our relationship.

I had many reasons for wanting to go back to London. My relationship with Kazmin was beyond repair and I could not go on like this any longer. Kazmin wanted to marry me but he didn't want to divorce his wife, because she is famous and had the money. I brought warmth and the ability to love him but I received nothing as he preferred the frumpy Rosnah, so I nobody. So I decided that I owed it to myself to make my own life and live in peace.

I concluded that money was more important to Kazmin than happiness. He asked me to wait until everything got back to normal and then he would be with me. He wanted me but he also wanted to keep his wife. It was very selfish of him not to consider what I wanted. I thought it would be better to give him some space. I would go away, and there would be less pressure for both of us. Leave him with his own world and I would build my own life back.

Just before I was to leave for London, he asked me if I was happy now that I had my passport so that I could leave him.

I looked at him and said, "Yes! My heart does not belong here and wish you all the best for your life."

After all of that, Kazmin had another bright idea! He suddenly thought it would be a good idea if I went to London as planned, but then he would tell his wife that I was gone and once things settled down, I could come back to Malaysia and marry him.

I just gave him big smile thinking, you are such a looser, you will never see me again and I am never going to be your wife. Who do you think I am?

Incredibly, the day before I left for London, he came to see me and gave me one thousand pounds. He said the money was for me and that he would try to send me money if I really needed it. He told me that I would be fine over there. Then he asked me to look out for myself and call him when I arrived at the London airport.

He gave me a kiss on my forehead and said, "I love you. I'm going to miss you."

I didn't give any respond but I thought whatever. I closed the door as soon as he disappeared from my sight. I dropped myself in bed feeling so relieved that I was away from Kazmin at last. I just couldn't wait to get out from this country and away from the people who gave me so much damage in my life. But at the same time I wept, and was so painful with a thousand memories in my head thinking, money is everything and he chose money over me, but what could I do? I had to follow my own path.

I invited my sister, Nurul to come down from the country and stay with me for a few days before I left for London, she was so excited about that.

The following day my dear friend Paul and my sister Nurul accompanied me to the airport. Nurul helped me with my luggage and I told her not to be sad. She said everything would be all right. It was time to say good bye to both my sister and Paul. A million thanks to you, my dear friend. Without you, I would not be back in London.

As I walked slowly towards the gate, my heart full of happiness at the thought of leaving Kazmin, so looking forward at the thought of being in London again. Before I boarded I did try to call Kazmin one last time. He did not answer; it was early and his phone was off, because he did not want his wife to see his calls.

On the plane I was overwhelmed with sadness and I shed many tears. I wept remembering the story of our love, which had finally run aground. I wept at the thought that he let me go without any regret. I wept because he choose not to married me. But with my tenderness heart I believe that I own everything in life. With my souls full of joy I am very proud of my self as a golden girl who was left with a broken heart in my own country of Malaysia the place where I was born and now on the plane take her back to the city of London where my life belong. Good bye, my love, and good bye to Malaysia.

On February 13, 2003, I arrived back in London. The flight landed at five – thirty in the morning. I watched from the window and when the plane touched the ground all I could think was, here I am, at last back in London again.

Three years had passed. How could all of this have happened? In some ways, it was like a bad dream.

But it was wonderful that I was in London. I passed immigration without any problem, thank god! Then I collected my luggage and I couldn't wait to go outside and feel the cold weather that I missed so much. I had discovered I loved cold weather. Soon as I was outside; I just stood in the cold, letting it seep into my body. This is what I wanted to feel, it was wonderful feeling.

I took a gulp of cold air and blew out my smoky, frosty breath and I whisper, "London, I'm back, back for good!" Everything was new: I was a new person with a new life.

CHAPTER 19

The Book

When I was growing up in Malaysia, we had no electricity, so I sometimes took advantage of the light from the moon to study. I had to hide from my father in order to do my school work and no one could find me when I was studying. But I simply wasn't able to devote the time necessary to learn properly.

Now I study because I have a desire to catch up on what I missed as a child. I enjoy learning and I want to make the most of it. Besides having gained the title of aerobics instructor, I am keen on computers, languages and business. As time goes by, I have the feeling that I am achieving a satisfactory level of education. I take education seriously.

One afternoon during July of 2005, while I was relaxing under a tree in Regent Park after finishing jogging session, I sat and watched the other people in the park. Along with families and children, there were couples holding hands, enjoying each other romantically.

I became sad inside, realising how much happiness I had missed in my life. I whispered to myself that I wanted to do something in life, something that would have meaning. I wanted to do something that would enable me to have a feeling of accomplishment and happiness within.

Then it hit me. My life's story, that is my dream as I had always wanted to tell the whole world. I would write my story in a book. I would write the whole truth for the first time and I would put it out there for everyone to read. I would write a book and publish it.

My mind began to race with the memory of the abuse that I had received. I wanted to get all my suffering out into the open because it was very difficult to keep it all locked up inside. I realised this was something I needed to do. It would be therapeutic and maybe I could even reconcile with my father. Anything is possible and sometimes miracles do happen.

I wanted to see my father's face again. One day maybe he would tell me that I am his daughter. I truly needed to hear those words from him, but the hurt and damage he had caused still showed on every corner of my body. But at this time his love was not as important as my need to tell everyone how evil my father had been to me. I wanted a father, but we had never spoken to each other like a father and daughter should do.

I was beside myself with excitement and at the same time, I was eager to get on with the task at hand. I didn't know how to write a book and I never write a book before. Would it be good or bad for me to tell the truth about myself? What would my family and friends think?

I had lived with the silence and the lies my whole life. I had done that in order to cover the real me. I lived with life behind the silence for my entire life. The book would be good for me. Just the thought of telling the whole truth of my life was refreshing and I already felt my steps getting lighter.

I had grown tired of pretending to be happy and of hiding my sorrow. No one can live with so much pain buried inside for so long. I called a few people that were very close to me and told them what I wanted to do – what I was going to do. The book became my commitment I could not back out of. I had told three people; my mother, Paul and Kazmin, about the things that had happened to me, but now everyone would know.

I was ready with pen in hand. I started writing – and crying. This was going to be more difficult than I thought.

I have a fantastic friend from Chilean named, Mariely, but we called each other Twin as a nickname, because we look alike. She was my housemate and she was a nightmare but in a good way and we had a lot of fun. She was such a generous person and she would do anything to help friend. Because of her beautiful heart which I adore about her she became like my sister. As I am very useless with directions so she helps me a lot with that. Both of us can tolerate any single mistake that we have done and our relationship going on very well even both of us don't have in comment. She would offer me a lot of help and she really cared about me and our relationship became so special. I told her about my project and a little bit about my life. I also asked her if she knew someone who was an author so they could write the book about my life story. But one day she came with good news and told me that she had met someone and that person was an author. I was over the moon I couldn't believe it just can't wait to meet with this person. I thought, Mariely You a my dear friend forever.

Within a few days Mariely introduced me to her, a young lady from Spain. My first impression was, she looks very funny and she can't even speak English very well, so how is she going to write my book? well! I could be wrong. We said hello to each other and that was it, neither one of us mentioned about my project to write the book. Part of me didn't trust this woman but because she was friends with Mariely, I assumed she had to be a nice person. My friend Mariely ended being much close with her, I guess they could both speak Spanish and I could not. They would see each other regularly, and again I thought, she must be nice person. But she look crazy and she since never brush her hair, very strange.

After a few months Mariely told me that her friend didn't have any place to stay and the reason was because of something. Mariely asked her to stay with us, but I only rented a two bedroom flat and in the contract only allowed two people to stay in the flat. But Mariely suggests her to stay in the living room. Nothing much that I could say except to agree with whatever she do. Because I am her friend but if my landlord found out about it, I would be the one who got into trouble because the contract was under my name.

After a week the problems began to start. That Spanish woman didn't have money to buy the food. When the three of us went shopping she started taking anything she wanted and put it in my trolley, but then I ended to pay for her food. My friend Mariely was very clever, she ignored her and just paid for her own shopping, but I am a bit naïve, that's why most of the people took advantage of me. Mariely brought toilet paper and she used it a lot, and some of her stuff she used it, Mariely was really not happy, so she told her off. From that moment their friendship got worse until the arguments started, I didn't get involved with anything. That Spanish woman started screaming, shouting madly to Mariely and said the word, "I kill you". Soon as Mariely heard those words, she became so scared and the whole night she was in my room. She brought a knife and all the sharp things into my room; she tried to hide from her. I could see her face getting so pale because of worry that she thought the Spanish woman was really going to kill her, it was hilarious. I told Mariely that she didn't mean it that way; she just said it because she was angry, but Mariely still took it wrongly. The next day when Mariely wanted to come home from work, she would call me and asked me to take her home. It was like this for almost a week and I still ended up buying food for the Spanish woman.

Then one day the Spanish woman came forward to talk about my plan to write a book. I started to ask her about her background as a writer. Se has told me something that she had write which very intersting but I never heard about that. Than after she told me that she very interesting to write a book about my life storey. I was so happy and just couldn't wait to get started even though at that point is I entrusted her mission of writing my book which at that time was a priority in my life. Without thinking twice and without asking anyone is opinion I had agreed for her to write it. The following day she began to write and began to find out a little about me. With a pen in her hand, she wrote it down in a notebook. We started having interview during which she would ask me questions about my past and life in Malaysia. One night after I had been out with Mariely and another friend, we back home and the Spanish woman not there. We got hold of her notebook and checked out whether she was making any progress in the book. She'd already been interviewing me for 2 week. As Mareily understand Spanish so we did find stuff in it that I had been telling her so I thought to myself, ok, she's weird but she's writing the book at least. At the point I was hooked with the idea of getting the book to print that I was ready to put up with strange stuff and compromise on important things such as living in peace and with sane people…when we realised she was a bit mental, it was too late for me.

Not long after, she moved out from our flat and stayed by herself. We were so pleased as her ways were impossible to live with. Then she told me that I had to pay her £500 a week. But if I didn't pay her she would stop writing and she might go back to Spain. Also she told me, if she has to go, she would not give me whatever she wrote. Because of that it made me very worried especially she had almost got my life story, so I agreed to pay her with the amount of money that she wanted. It was a rip off as I had to pay her money, plus pay her keep – lodging and food. She ate a lot and I had to pay for all of that. Anyway I had decided I would carry on paying her accommodation even if it was not my own house as long as she wrote my book. As time go on, she even meets a few friends of mine to interview and that made me more confident. Once a week, she would read it through to me the content that she had written in the laptop in front of me. She did show me what she wrote but I couldn't understand any word because she writes in Spanish. She had explain to me that her English was not very good but when the book was finished, she promise that her brother in law would translate it to English and I didn't need to pay anything, all included. I found it a little strange but I put my trust in her and I told myself everything going to be fine and my dream was almost coming true.

In the next few months, she had told me that she needed to interview the rest of my family especially my mother. I could understand that but it put me under so much pressure because I had no money to take her to Malaysia. It cost me a lot of money because I had to pay all her expenses. She told me, if I didn't do that the book was not going be finished. Give me so much worried because I wanted my book to happen and for all I knew it was almost there. This put me under a lot of pressure because I didn't know from where I was going to get the money, but out of the blue I thought about the bank, only the bank can lend me money. Without wasting any time, the next day I went to the bank to make an appointment. And the following day I was interviewed by the bank manager. I was so nervous but at the same time I was so worried that they wouldn't approve my loan. My heart stopped beating and my eyes just went blank when the bank manager said, "Your loan has been approved; the money will be in at any moment."

I couldn't believe what I was hearing and I thought that easy, he must be joking but I said, "Really! Thank you, so I check any time at the cash point?"

He agreed and I left the bank with word "WOW" and big smile on my face; I just couldn't wait to tell the Spanish woman that we were going to Malaysia. That all I focus at this time.

The next day I checked my bank account, gosh! A lot of numbers and I missed counting because I had never had such a lot of money in my account, I double checked again, WOW! £10,000 I still couldn't believe it but I was on top of the world, so I could do what I wanted to do. At that time I never thought how to pay it back, the only thoughts in my mind was what the hell I care as long with this money I can do a lot of things.

I told her the news that we are going to Malaysia with so much happiness and the following week we took our journey. I paid her return flight, her hotel and everything.

We stayed at New World hotel, right in the central of Kuala Lumpur, so it was very convenient for both of us. Then I took her to a few places in town and took her to where I used to work as an aerobics instructor. I took her out at night, to see how night life in Malaysia was. But I was very disappointed about her behaviour when she was in the clubs. She so different, she chased over men and left me alone, she was behaving badly towards me. If she didn't get what she wanted, she wouldn't move her ass from the club. I got pissed off with her behaviour and told her off. But then she didn't want to go back to the hotel. I had to put myself down and come forward to her and beg her to go back to the hotel with me. The reason I did that was because, this was her first time in this country, and she is a woman so I didn't want anything to happen to her. I feel like my respondbelity to look after her. And she wanted to go out to clubs every night, until one night she followed one man to go somewhere and she didn't get back to the hotel until almost five in the morning. I didn't care whatever she wants to do, but I thought she came to Malaysia to do what she had told me; instead I have to suffer with her behaviour. After five days in capital city than I brought her back to see the rest of my family and went around to see most of my relatives.

We spent two weeks in Malaysia and I hoped she had all the information that she wanted. We returned to London. A few days later, she told me that the book was done but she needed more money which I had to give her. After she received the money she asked me to return the next day to get the book. I did what she said, return to her place the next day as promised, but she was not in her flat. I tried to call her but the phone was switched off. I returned the next day with two friends of mine surprisingly her neighbour said, "She's already moved out." I started to worry, panicking because I didn't know how to find her; I didn't know any of her friends. I tried to call her many times and I left many messages on her voicemail but she did not even return my call. Already been a week since she had promised to hand me the book and I started to think that I had been cheated, but surprisingly, I received her call said, "I have your book, so we can meet in the café, and I will give it to you." Soon as I heard that my whole body got lighter and I feel so relieved, thank god, she still have a heart.

When I met her, she totally became a different person. Before she handed the book to me, she expected more money from me. She thought that I was stupid, but anyway I had to promise her with my good word until I got my book. Soon as the book was in my hand, I told her sorry there is no money for you. I have given her £6, 0000 and did not include all her expenses to Malaysia.

She handed me the book but it was written in Spanish, which I couldn't even understand. I looked at her and said, "It's in Spanish?"

She replied, "Well! You have to find the translator."

I said again, "But you told me before that your brother was going to translate."

Then she said, "Sorry! He can't do it."

I was devastated as soon as she told me that I had to do it myself but nothing I could do. I got back home full of frustration thinking, people sometimes can be very nasty and bad hearted with evil character. Whatever happens I will survive. Looking back now, I can't understand why I did that. I guess I was fixated with the idea of the book and this clouded my mind. Things escalated from there and it become more and more obvious that she was not meeting my expectations in terms of her writing and in term of her availability, her treatment of me, etc. She took my computer and did not comply with our agreement of her getting the book translated into English. But I just wanted her to finish the book and give me what she had done.

I had the book but I couldn't read it. To find the translator cost me £3,000, hell! That's a lot of money. I worked everyday and saved the money that I had just to get the book translated so I could read the content inside the story. After a few months, I had managed to pay for the book to be translated. I was so happy when I got the whole book finished. As soon as I finish read the book, I not jumping happily that she wrote incredibly well. I feel a bit sad because she didn't put much storey and a lot more things she hasn't written as I wanted. My friend came to visit me, to see how upset I was than she introduced me to her famous friend who knew more knowledge about the book. It was very nice of him to read my book and give me a very genuine opinion and he suggested to me, to rewrite it all over again because the story of my book was like a child's story. I was so embarrassed, then I asked a few more people to get more opinion, sadly they all said them same. My heart sank and I got really emotionally, mentally and physically broke down when I look at the content of the book. My mind was lost completely thinking that I had lost all the money and I didn't get what I wanted.

At the same time I was getting so depressed because my life was in a bad situation. I worked hard trying to pay everything off but still it was not enough. I had loads of bills that I could not settle; I missed paying my rent for a few months and I missed paying monthly loan that I borrowed from the bank just for that bloody Spanish woman who told me she was a writer. The loan interests were getting higher and the bank started chasing me. Credit card statements kept coming, but the worst thing was the bailiffs kept sending me scary letters and came knocking in my door. I ended up in a lot of debt. I was really depressed, I felt scared for my life; scared to go out from the house, scared in case the bailiffs were waiting outside. At that moment I am living in a scared life. It came to a stage where I just wanted to end my life, solve all my problems, but luckily someone who I was not expecting walked into my life and took me away from the life of hell and settled all the problems. Since that day, my life got better, and I can never thank this person enough.

As soon as my life recovered I thought, I should have looked for another writer but from the experience that I have teach me a good lesson to learn about life. I was so scared to trust people. But instead I decided to write all over again with my own words and my own writing. With the help of a great friend of mine Paul, he has given me so much encouragement and help from Giovanni who always with me and go through with it together. No words can describe how appreciated I am to Giovanni and Paul for what they have done. Without them I never have been at this stage.

I happily rewrote the book and life got so much easier. I had to fly back to Malaysia to get more information that I needed.

CHAPTER 20

My Brothers

In a flood of tears, alone in the house, I could not stop crying. I had been talking to my mother in Malaysia, telling her about my decision to write a book. Her response was a surprising revelation. I thought my mother would want me to be silent and keep the family violence a secret, but instead she was very supportive. She thought the telling of my story was a good idea.

This was not going to be easy. As I began to recall the long suppressed memories, I began to feel depressed. I kept thinking, I have escaped but my mother and brothers are still in Malaysia with no hope of ever seeing another side of life. I had always been very concerned with the well – being of my family. What hurt me most in life, then and now, was to see them suffer. My mother's problems and those of my brothers were and are a source of great distress.

My mother suffers from depression, which makes life very difficult for my brothers. They must pay the price of her illness. She has been unable to give them affection; she had said terrible things to them and they have ended up doing terrible things themselves.

Zamberi, my second brother; has run away from the house because of my mother's anger. He had many arguments with her when he started smoking and experimenting with drugs. Because of all that goes with that lifestyle, he jeopardized his health enormously. He was arrested by the police and spent time in jail. When my mother called me to tell me what had happened, it was a great shock to me and I took it hard. I couldn't believe that my poor little brother was in prison. Why did this have to happen to him?

Life had dealt our family a low blow. I cried a lot about it, but soon Zamberi was bailed out with money my mother had made working selling her food at the roadside. He told us that the police had beaten him, hitting him on his head and back. I listened with tears in my eyes. All I wanted to do was give him a big hug, but I couldn't do that. I was in London with a broken heart, and he was in Malaysia with a broken spirit.

The good news is that now Zamberi is married and has settled down with a respectable business on his own. He is off drugs and doing better for his wife. I am very happy for him because that is what he wants for his life.

Redzwan, too, has been the cause of much worry and heartache. Though, he has always been concerned about my failure to marry. I have been even more concerned about his situation. My brother was drinking from time to time and he did some experimenting with something. This later was what I was most worried about. I prayed for him daily. It seems that the situation may improve, because he has recognised the error of his ways and get married to the girl that he likes. He is talking about getting married. I wish everything would fall into place and my brother could achieve a little normality life. I will be so relieved when Redzwan settles down and finds some happiness in his life.

Nazeri my younger brother who lived with me in Kuala Lumpur so long ago, whom the family called Adik, but when he stayed with me, I called him Nas, until this day that name has stuck forever; I am very pleased for that. He soon disappeared after I went off to London. I can't get the idea out of my head that it was my fault for having left him by himself in Kuala Lumpur. He just disappeared, never communicating with any of the family. We do not know anything about him to this day. I would love to see him again and help him if he needs help. He was my sweet little brother and I loved him dearly. He was such a gentle boy and always had a smile on his face. He remains always in my heart and I miss him very much. I have shed many tears whenever I think about my little brother. I know he is somewhere in this world, I will find him one day and he would be forever in my life.

My younger sister Nurul, had been living with my mother at first, but then she got so upset because my mother put her under a lot of pressure. She got lonely then gave an excuse to my mother that she had to move out because of her work. She rented the house and work at the café, that is what we had been told but no one know where she lived. Because she is the only sister that I have, so I had been spoiling her and did the best I could for her. I even wanted to take her to London for study. I hope she will be a good girl and do the right thing in her life.

All this misfortune is the consequence of our parents and the childhood each of us had. I feel great sadness for my family. I love them all and they have good hearts in spite of the enormous problems they've encountered. It makes my head hurt to think about all the suffering, and after I spend time remembering, I become weary and curl up on the sofa in my living room. I sleep like a child, weary from so much weeping.

It was my hope that this book would put things in their place and bring some closure to my grief. Therefore, I knew it was very important that I remember all the things that happened to me and my family. I wanted to share my experience with others – I could not keep my feelings hidden in my heart any longer.

I pray for my whole family everyday. I love them with all my heart and I want to feel that better times must lie ahead from them. As I made my way through writing my book, I began to feel more optimistic and less depressed. The pain began to ease a little.

CHAPTER 21

Trip to Malaysia

March 2006. It was a good reason to return to Malaysia. I left my house early having made sure everything was ready the night before and purchased gifts for my family and friends. I was travelling by Malaysia Airlines and it would be a thirteen – hour flight. At last I arrived at the Kuala Lumpur airport. Thank goodness Malaysia Airlines didn't lose any of my bags!

A sign wrote, "Selamat Datang," which means "Welcome". I was back in Malaysia, the country of my birth.

I got a taxi to the Flamingo hotel, a place that would be sure to bring back memories. Kuala Lumpur airport is quite a way from the city; it takes more than an hour to get to the Flamingo hotel.

I was surprised that the hotel staff still remembered me from before. And they put me in Room 221, one of the rooms I had stayed in so many years ago. Did they remember, or was it just coincidence? I felt a little strange. The room had a terrace, and from there I could see the swimming pool, the lake, the swan, a few flamingos and the sunset. It is not a five - star hotel, but it was comfortable and was in a peaceful setting. It's perfect far a relaxing break. The nicest thing about the Flamingo hotel is the lake with the swans gliding across its surface, truly calming and beautiful. When I used to stay there before, I would sit near the pond every morning after breakfast with bread and feed the ducks, wondering if I would ever get back to London.

I didn't sleep too well that first night. The journey affected my body clock and I had jet lag. In the morning, I decided to go to another hotel for lunch and order fresh shellfish and other fresh Malaysian foods. The lunch is excellent at the Renaissance Hotel, where I use to work as an aerobics instructor.

After lunch I gathered up my courage and started looking around for friends to see if I could find some of them still working there. Walking into the gym, I instantly saw a familiar face. She saw me too and said, "Hey Gina! What are you dong here?"

I smiled and explained to my friend Getta that I lived in London now and I was back for holiday. Getta, who is Indian, looked slim and very sweet. We embraced and started to talk. It had been a long time since my departure and nobody knew where I was. I just disappeared for a long time and now I suddenly showed up with a new image. Well! That's me, Gina!

I was delighted to see her. Next, I telephoned Sanajan, another old friend of mine, and we met up. I was so delighted to see her again. We had so many shared experiences and much to catch up on. It was a joy to come across old friends and remember some good times.

It wasn't necessary for me to ring Kazmin. He called me often in London and knew that I was returning to Kuala Lumpur. He called me on my mobile and wanted to see me, but I wasn't sure how I felt about seeing him again. It had been many years since we had last seen each other. When I left for London the last time, I was convinced that I would never see Kazmin again – but I agreed to meet him while I was in town.

So there I was, waiting for him to arrive. Ding, dong! The door bell rang – it must be Kazmin. I looked through the spy hole and sure enough, there he was.

I opened the door and we both said hello. That was it; there was no kiss and not even a hug.

He made himself comfortable on the sofa. I felt like we were strangers, and I found the feeling I used to have for him was completely gone. He looked so depressed and I could see that something was wrong, but he was cool and tried to show no emotion.

I sat on the corner of the bed thinking how strange it was to see him again. We had what felt like the usual normal and boring conversation. I answered his questions but I did not ask anything about his life. I could see in his eyes that he was not happy. It was a strange sensation to have absolutely no feelings for the man sitting in front of me. After an hour or so, he excused himself and left, strangely I was so relieved.

I had become friends with the woman in charge of the maids at the Flamingo hotel when I lived there so many years ago. She had confided in me a lot her problems. Her husband had died a long time ago, and she had raised her three children without anyone's help, and that reminded me of my mother, except my father didn't die. She had come to my room whenever she has a time, and we would chat. I liked to listen to her talk about her life. She had tuff time without her husband. I was very fond of her because she was so kind and sweet and always had a warm smile.

She realised I was staying at the hotel and popped in just as Kazmin was leaving. She looked middle – aged but had the same warm smile. We talked longer then we should have; she had much work to do, and I was tired and a sinus infection was irritating me. I gave her some money and we parted and agreed to meet again. I thought, she really is a sweetheart.

I rested a little and then got dressed and decided to go out for dinner at a nice restaurant. I'm very fond of my country's food. I love the spicy dishes with their hot flavour. My favourite meat dish in Kuala Lumpur is the T-bone chilli steak at my favourite restaurant called, Victorian Station.

On my way there, I remembered something that happened the first time when I was in London. I was really missing my favourite meat dish, so I jumped into a cab and asked the driver to take me to Victorian Station. I thought that city of London must have a Victorian Station, especially foreigner; they love to eat steak, so off we went. After a while he pulled over and said, "Here you are, in Victoria Station."

I looked out but a lot of people walking pass so I said, "Victorian Station, the steak house."

He looks at me with strange face and said, "This is Victorian Station, is not a steak house, is a train station."

As I a bit embarrass I respond with very simple word, "Ok!" then I keep my mouth sharp. I was very disappointed and went back home in his taxi.

The next day I woke up refreshed in my bed at the Flamingo hotel and decided that since I had never been to a museum in Malaysia, I would go to one today. I took a taxi and went past some of the places where I used to work and live. The streets were always full of people walking, and because of the heat, most of the women were trying to protect themselves from the sun with parasols. I use to do that as well when I was in Malaysia, because I was scared my skin would tan.

This reminded me of something else that had happened in London. My first summer there, I carried a parasol to protect myself from the sun. I looked around, and I was the only person carrying a parasol, and I found it strange that people walked in the sun without protecting themselves from the sun. It seemed they all wanted to get a tan, whereas I wanted to lose mine. It occurred to me that no one is happy with their situation. We all seem to want some sort of change.

After my excursion to the museum, I had to rest and prepare for the next part of my journey: home to Penang and Kedah.

CHAPTER 22

Penang and Kedah

Penang is in the northern part of Malaysia. It has several high – tech industries and many wonderful resorts. My family stayed at Kulim which is not very far from Penang Island. Because where my family lives is just a small city so there is no airport and never will be. The airport that I have to go to is called Bayam Lepas in Penang Island. Even though I had never visited any places in Penang Island but I did study about Penang Island when I was at secondary school and I can describe a little bit about Penang Island.' Pulau Penang'is the Malay name for Penang. Literally translated Pulau Penang means 'Island of the Betel Nut Tree' the island is the fourth – largest in the country, it is also the most populated Island in the country. The Island is connected with the mainland by the Penang Bridge. The Bridge begins at Gelugor in the Island and ends in Perai on the mainland. The mainland portions of the Penang state is known as Seberang Perai (Province Wellesley) and together with Penang Islands and other smaller Island, from the state of Penang.

I arrived in the evening; it was a flight of only forty five minutes from Kuala Lumpur.

My brother Zambri, his wife Ina, and my sister Nurul were waiting for me at the airport. We exchanged the Muslim greeting, Assalamualaikum which means peace be upon you and gave each other the traditional handshake, followed by a warm embrace.

We made our way to a resort hotel on an island where we would stay. It was the first time my brother and his wife would eat in the hotel restaurant, and they were excited. I wanted to stay in a nice resort hotel because I wanted to treat my mother to a comfortable and relaxing time and give her a break from her difficult life.

Life Behind the Silence

After a good meal with a lot of traditional Malaysian food, we left by car to see my mother. She lived in another world, completely separated from the comfort of the hotel resorts in Penang Island. We had two choices either crosses by ferry or take Penang Bridge motorway that connects Penang Island to the main peninsula region of Kedah. Also Penang Bridge is a vital link connecting Penang Island and Perai ion the mainland of West Malaysia. The Penang Bridge is no doubt one of many architecture wonders of Penang. It marks the new milestone that brings Penang closer to the world's attention. The dreams of having a bridge finally triumph when Dr Mahathir took over as Malaysia prime minister. Because I hate sea and I very scared with ferry or boat so we decided to go trough the Penang Bridge to the city where my mother lives called, Kulim.

Kulim is located at the South East of Kedah state, in Malaysia. Kulim is a district that consists of fifteen smaller sub districts also known as 'Mukin'. Kulim town has grown from a small residential area back in the 1950's into one of Malaysia's top industrial park area is. Kulim got its name from a tree and that particular tree is valued for its wood usage during 1997, the value for Kulim tree per m was about RM270. The Scientific name for Kulim tree is Scorodocarpus borneensis.

My brother was driving and every time we stopped at a traffic light, he locked his fingers together and made his knuckles crack.

Zambri and I look a lot alike. My sister Nurul and I do not look alike, because she has a different father. I love her enormously. Nurul is very thin; she is a kind and gentle soul with a warm smile. She would do anything for me, and she is a very clever girl.

My sister – in – law Ina seemed to be a sweet and gentle young lady. She had dedicated herself to the role of the traditional housewife. She did not go outside the house for work; my brother did not allow her. They don't have any children yet. They got married in September of 2000. My mother was not happy with them, because Zambri married without my mother's knowledge, but then he took our father to the wedding.

Once we arrived at mother's house; I could see my mother Harisun, standing in the front waiting for us. She greeted me with hugs and kisses, telling me she has been worried like the mothers are and she asked me, why didn't you call? It was late, so many questions that she handed to me, but I could see her happiness in her eyes. I didn't say anything just looked at her and smiled. She didn't know the plan that I had made for her.

My mother had prepared a delicious dinner of chicken korma, fish, and sweetmeats. There was one particular fish that would help control my sinus infection. As we were having dinner, my brother Redzwan turned up to say hello. He lived alone in a house close to my mother. After the meal, as she cooked a big dinner, a long – lost family member returned, we left my mother's home to go out into the community and deliver sweets to the neighbours.

My mother was shocked and surprised when we told her that she was to pack a bag and that we were going to stay in a resort hotel in Penang Island. My mothers never want to spend much, thought this would be a waste of money. She had a perfectly good house to sleep in! This would be the first time my mother and Ina would visit – never mind stay in – a resort hotel, and I wanted them to enjoy the experience. My brothers Zambri and Redzwan would stay behind in the village.

It was late when we arrived in Penang. The journey from my mother's house to Penang took about two hours. Everyone was too tired to be excited and just wanted to sleep. We arranged to meet early the next morning for breakfast. Then we would go back into the surrounding countryside to meet some of my family; aunts, uncles, and cousins. Some I had never met, and others I had not seen in years.

The next morning, like a dream I heard a woman's voice, very tender and smoothly called, "Chek, wake up!" (It was my mother calling me by my nickname "chek". My mother called me chek since I was a little girl.

I opened my eyes slightly; looked at the time, dear lord! It was six o'clock in the morning; my mother was up – as she always was – in order to say the morning prayers. But why she has to disturbed me, I could not get up that early. Then I could see my mother sitting nicely on the chair, she was already dressed beautifully ready to go. Oh god, please help me! My mother thought the day was wasting away and that it would soon be too hot, some need to be up and going!

Give me no choice I had to get up and wake Nurul in the other room. My mother watched me with big smile as I dressed. When everyone was ready, we went down for breakfast. I was proud that I could treat my mother. There was much laughter at the table, and I enjoyed this moment immensely.

We began our journey. It would take four hours to drive to the village where my uncle lived. As we travelled through the villages we stopped at a house that served as a store for the neighbourhood, where they sold food and some drinks. Some dry fish sat outside on a stand, buzzing with flies and

Life Behind the Silence 141

smelling horrible. The conditions around the house were miserable as well. There were flies, mosquitoes, and cockroaches. Musty air and the smell of sweat wafted out of the house.

After driving for a long time in the intense heat, along a dirt trail rather than a proper road, we made for the interior in search of our relative. My mother was very happy to have a chance to visit her brothers and sisters. Ina knew the area well and acted as our guide, showing us which trail to take.

We finally arrived at the house of Abdul Halim, my mother's younger brother. He had married a Thai woman and they had twelve children. I had never met his wife and children. Twelve was a lot of children for my uncle to maintain, but their life was very simple and happy. He is a very good father, and he knows his responsibilities to his family. He tries his best to make sure his children receive a good education and has been a good husband to his wife. Halim always work hard for his family and no matter how tired he was, he always had a smile on his face.

It had been a long time since I had last seen my uncle and it had not been a pleasant experience for me. It was obvious that he either chose to ignore that time or did not remember it. But I had decided I was going to make the best of this visit; I wanted them to see I had survived.

As we all gathered together, my uncle had his usual ever – present smile on his face. When I looked deep into his eyes, I remember what had happen so many years ago, I could see from his face that he knew and remembered too.

I would never forgive him and also I would never forget. That awful memory would always be in my mind. It will be there forever.

As I approached inside his house amid chickens running about, I saw a half – naked child asleep in the doorway. The children were sweet and I played with them a little. I do love children and I hope one day to have my own. These children might have been dirty, but they were delightful. Before we left them, I gave some t-shirts in all sizes for the children. I also gave them some fresh fruit and a little money for them to spend.

In a any moment, we were ready to go home. As I felt sorry for my uncle's life, I gave him some money for him to spend for his family and asked him to accompany me to a nearby mosque because I wanted to make a donation. As we were leaving, a woman came to get some milk from my uncle's shop. She had brought her two sons to see us. News of our visit in the area had spread fast and we were considered quite a novelty.

My uncle served them a drink and my uncle said to my mother if she wanted to see where my grandfather was buried, he pointed to a nearby place. She looked at me whether I want to go or not. But I explained that we did not have time to pay our respects, because we needed to go soon and she seemed puzzled. But she could not know that I had no desire to pay respects to the grandfather who had tried to violate me so many years ago.

My uncle accompanied me to the mosque, and I gave some money to the person who was in charge at the mosque, so they can do some small offering. We all shook hands, and then we all said good bye.

As we continued our journey, a typical Malaysian Summer storm began and it rained heavily for a while. As a driver I had to think about my passenger, my mother, my sister and my sister in law, I have to drive very careful. We decided to go to the house of Zainol, my favourite uncle and it took me another two hours to drive to be at his place. I am a fast driver, so when the rain stopped, I began to take my speed, everyone was silent but I can see my mother's mouth mumbling something and I know she started to pray. But she didn't dare to say anything to me because if she did I would drive even faster. Every time I make a corner, I really take some speed she held the seatbelt tight, it was so funny.

On the way there, we passed the house that I was born in, but we didn't stop because everything had changed. It was surrounded by the beautiful country that I remembered as a child with green mountains everywhere. I could see the river and cows, goats, and buffalo. Many people planting rice even in the rain. It was very peaceful. This road also reminded me of when I was thirteen years old; I use to cycle all the way from home for almost two hours to be at school and cycle back another two hours home. All this still fresh in my memory, feel like yesterday.

Soon we arrived at Zainol's home, the same house I lived in with my mother when I was a child. Zainol and his wife were very kind and showed that they were very fond of me. As soon as we arrived, his wife prepared some tea and served it to us in lovely cups decorated with gold and silver. These cups were for special occasions only.

We sat on the floor, first taking off our shoes, as is the custom. Zainol teased me, saying that my skin was getting paler from spending so much time in London. We stretched out our arms to compare our colour and laughter.

Around his house were many rubber trees that now belonged to my uncle. They had belonged to my mother once when she was young, before she ran away from my father and left them unattended. Uncle Zainol showed me how to cut the bark of the tree so the sap would flow out to be collected and sold. This is the place where my mother used to work as a rubber tree tapped when she was young. I never learned how to cut the bark of the rubber trees. I thought the air was dirty and smelly. My uncle showed me some of the potato – like roots that my mother would collect and mix with the local mushroom. This was the very food that kept me alive as a young girl. I remembered that we had nothing else to eat because my father never worked to provide his family with any necessities. I remember, We drew water from a small well close by, but now all gone completely, I can't even go there because full of jungle and now every house in the country there has running water. While before, there was only a river that I fished and swam in as a young girl. This all brought back so many memories, both good and bad.

After a wonderful visit with my uncle Zainol, we continued on our journey. We had still more relatives to visit, but we decided to go home because it was too far to go and the time was limited for us to go there. After driving a while, we stopped at a roadside stand to purchase some fried bananas, similar to banana fritters, which we ate in the car. Fried banana is a traditional tea time food in Malaysia. They are everywhere and are very inexpensive. But I found that in London one can only get them in nice restaurants.

We arrived at Zambri's home and dropped Ina off. We took a break before continuing our drive; we lay in a hammock tied between two trees. My brother had lit bonfire to keep the mosquitoes away.

On our way back to the hotel, we stopped at Jamilah's house. This was my mother's sister and she lived very close to my mother's home with her five children. She made some tea, as is the custom. At every house we go to, they make tea. But I don't drink tea especially coffee, it gives me stomach problems. She was very pleased to see me and teased me non stop with so many things included asking me about my love life. We had a pleasant time, but we didn't stay long. We had to go back to hotel in Penang, and it was already late. Tomorrow we would be back to the countryside to visit more relatives.

CHAPTER 23

Meeting My Father

The following morning, my mother woke early, as she had done the first morning. That was her job during our trip. She felt everyone should be up before daylight, because there was a lot to do. I was very happy to see my mother really enjoying her stay at the hotel. She had never stayed at a hotel before and she didn't even know how to turn on the water in the shower. The first time she took a shower, I heard screaming and shouting in the bathroom because she had run the shower with hot water. I rushed to the bathroom as soon as I heard her loud voice, as I thought something had happened to her. She was standing in the bathtub soaking wet. I burst out laughing, it was so funny. The fact that my mother had never experienced something as simple as a hot water seemed foreign to me.

We went over to our Auntie Ramlah's house. I'm very fond of my auntie. I remembered living with her for a while when I was little. It was during a time when my father didn't want me at home, so my mother sent me to auntie Ramlah's house for safety.

It was a long journey. They lived quite far away and it was very hot day. We stopped at a roadside stall to get a cold drink. Nurul bought us a local drink called Sugar Cane. It is a very common drink in Malaysia. The locals didn't have cans, so they gave it to us in a small plastic bag tied with an elastic band with a straw sticking out of the top and a lot of ice. It's rather rustic, but it does the job. The drink was very refreshing and sufficient to quench our thirst, even in the hot weather. At almost every roadside stop, one can see motorbikes with an umbrella and a machine for making the sugar cane drink.

Half an hour before reaching my auntie's house, we passed the road where

Life Behind the Silence 145

I used to walk in the hot sun every day to school because my father would never give me a ride. We passed my school, a source of many memories. It looked the same and had had only a few minor modifications. We passed the river where I used to swim with a friend after school and where I would catch some fish or prawns to eat raw for lunch. I remembered times when, on my way back from school, I would go into the jungle and pick a kind of fruit that is dark blue in colour called 'Buah Keluduk'. In English 'Buah' mean fruit. When I ate the fruit, all my teeth would turn black. My mother always made a big deal out of this, and was angry with me about it. I felt a kind of peace at the thought of these simple pleasures as we drove.

Finally we arrived at Auntie Ramlah's place. She is my mother's older sister, very small and thin, with the face of a child. Her expression reflects an inner calm, and she is very sweet and affectionate, but she also has an intelligent look about her. She was dressed in bright colours and wore a knitted cap on her head in order to cover her hair. She has seven children; her husband died some time ago.

All her children are married now except Kamal, who was very close with me. We had a lot in common. Kamal is a very honest and kind person but a bit stingy and he was a very sweet boy, I adored him. His older brother, Sudin, was who his father wanted me to marry him when I was just a girl. He just lives around the corner of his mother's house. As soon as he saw me, he came around and talked to me. He asked me so many questions. And he even said that he still loved me, and he still kept my picture in his purse but it had almost run out of colour. He looked so messy and fat. Soon after, his wife came with his children, then he stopped flirting with me and was serious. I looked at him and smiled. His wife was very young but was losing all her front teeth. She wore a sarong with slippers and looked old for her age. Thank God I did not marry him!

Kamal lives with his mother and they have a plot of land where they grow a few crops for their own consumption. He also raises cocks and hens. There are several fruits trees. The farm is in a very remote area and it feels like a small paradise, calm and peaceful. They have everything they need because they work the land well and keep it productive.

My mother and my auntie could not stop talking. It had been a long time since they had seen each other and they had many things to catch up on. Meanwhile, my cousin and I went to pick some vegetables to eat for lunch, and walk alongside the river, just next to my auntie's house. It reminded me of when I stayed with them; I used to swim and play with my friends in this river. Every time I got back from school, my auntie would put my meal on a plate and I would eat on my own on top of a rock, my heart very peaceful at this time without my father around. This river used to be wider and deeper, but now it was getting smaller and the water not as clean as it use to be. Anyway, we had a delicious lunch. My mother cooked and I ate like a pig.

After lunch Kamal served us fresh coconut that he had just harvested from a tree outside the house. We spent a good while at my auntie's place. She gave me a beautiful cushion that she had embroidered herself. But then we had to say goodbye. I gave her a big hug, and as with all the other relatives, I gave Kamal money for the local mosque. I gave a big, warm hug to my cousin Kamal, I tried to kiss him on the cheek to say goodbye, but he was not used to a woman kissing him and was a little shy. I could see the sadness between my mother and my auntie when we departed.

Our next stop was my father's house. My mother was not happy about that, but I explained to her that if I was going to write the book, this was a necessary trip. Besides, I wanted to see how my mother would now react to my father and his family.

It had been many years since my mother had seen Abdul Wahab, her ex-husband and my father. What my mother did not know, and will not know until she reads this book, is that I had secretly met my father a few years before on a previous trip to Malaysia. It had happened almost by accident. I flew into Penang from Kuala Lumpur. My brother Zambri was waiting for me at the airport and, after greetings, my brother announced that he was going to take me to my father's house. He said that my father was getting old and asked about me all the time. I was nervous when Zambri mentioned his name, wondering why he wanted to see me. But I told Zambri, as much as I would love too, I was not ready yet. But then, Zambri begged me to go with him. I told him that our mother was waiting for us at home so we had to go back. My mother had told me before to never see Abdul Wahab again after what he had done to me. If she knew, she would kill me for going to see him. Anyway my brother went quiet and his face looked very sad because I turned his offer down. I felt for my brother but he didn't know that our father abused me badly. It was so painful and so hard for me, but I did it for my brother. As a deal I told him to keep this secret and he agreed never tell to our mother.

It took about an hour to drive to where my father lived. Zambri drove quite fast on the dark, narrow roads. He knew where our father lived; he had

Life Behind the Silence

kept in touch with him through the years. Zambri assured me that our father had become a better man. He had become an Iman and was quite important in the local mosque. He was the leader of prayers and the person in charge of calling all to pray. Abdul Wahab had been married three times; first to my mother, which of course was a complete disaster. Then, he married another woman, with whom he had two daughters. And he was now with his third wife, they had five children, three daughters and two sons. Now, I supposed, I would meet some of my sisters and brothers that I hadn't meet before.

I was afraid. The only thing I could think about was about my mother waiting for me at home and I felt so guilty for what I had done without her knowing. And what was I going to say to this man who had never took me as his daughter, and wanted me dead?

We arrived at last at his house. Zambri parked the car just in front of the house, and he suggested we didn't tell him who I was at first. He suggested that I should pretend I was nis girlfriend. I thought this was crazy. I saw a man come out but I could hardly see in the dark, so I asked Zamberi, "Who is that man?"

Zambri said, "That is our father."

We were inside the car. As he moved closer, all I could think was dear Lord, he's getting old. He looked so different from my memory of him, and he did not look as good as he did before.

Suddenly, I heard my father voice say, "Is that you, Zambri?"

I watched him approach and I thought, this man used to hit me, and now I am going to see him, after twenty-two years. I don't know how I feel towards him now.

Zambri said, "Yes, it's me."

My father asked, "Who is with you?"

Zambri said, "My girlfriend."

My father said, "So bring her in."

I told Zambri that I didn't want to get out from the car, but he told me to just relax. That was easy for him to say. I was going to be face-to-face with the man who had abused me and damaged my entire life.

Once were inside the house, Zambri introduced me to him, we shook hands and he asked me to please sit down. I thanked him, smiled and sat down. I looked at him, and all I could think of was all the misery he had caused our family. The little girl he wanted to kill had survived and had grown up into a beautiful lady, and I was proud to stand in front of him right then.

After ten minutes, Zambri asked my father if he knew who this girl really was. My heart sunk when he said, "I don't know, but you said she was your girlfriend."

Zambri laughed a little laugh and shook his head. Then he said, "She is not my girlfriend, she is my sister, and your daughter, Kakak." (Zambri called me Kakak, which means sister.)

We looked at each other and his face was shocked. Suddenly he hugged me and started crying like a baby. I didn't feel anything, and did not know whether I wanted to hug him back. I could not even cry, no tears came out of my eyes. Inside me, I could still feel the pain, the awful pain he had given me that, until today, was still fresh in my heart. As I stood there, it seemed like yesterday.

Then I knew that I would never recover. I couldn't explain to him how hurt I was. I kept asking myself, why was he hugging me? Why was he crying? Was it guilt? Or was he pretending?

To this day I am not sure. That was first time in my life I ever got a hug from the man I called my father, but still I didn't feel any love from him. In fact I hated him touching me, it was something he should have done a long time ago.

I rubbed his back, telling him it was OK and that he shouldn't worry, all the while feeling most uncomfortable. I was able to relax only when he let go of me. His face was so sad and he kept looking down. He wouldn't look at me. Every time I looked at him I felt pain and I just could not stop thinking about it.

He introduced me to all five of his children and my young stepmother, his wife. She seemed very nice, but not as nice as my mother. I looked around the house, no comparison to my mother's house, which was so tidy. My youngest step-brother was three years old and could have been my son.

My father had three daughters now. I remembered one time when he told me that he would marry again to have a daughter, because I was not his daughter. So – good for him, now he has three daughters and two daughters from the second wife. I have to admit it hurt me to see how he talked to his daughter now, he was very loving. He did seem to be a kinder and more gentle person. I couldn't believe that this ws the same evil person who used to become so insane. He got what he wanted so good for him and I was very happy for his daughter because they would not have to suffer like I did.

I was late and we had to say goodbye. I gave him a big smile and kissed him on the hand, as was the custom. This is meant to show respect, but it meant nothing to me. Seeing him felt like a horror film or a terrible dream - I was not sure which.

I went back to see him again, this time I was with my mother and not

Zambri. She had expressed no desire to seem him. I had convinced her that I was going to tell the truth about our lives. What I did tell her was that I wanted her to see him. I also wanted to see how they interacted, because it had been many years since they had seen each other. They were, after all, my parents.

The trip to my father's home took a long time and my mother said nothing the entire journey. She just sat in the back seat, deep in thought. She seemed preoccupied and I was sure that she was OK, so I just left her alone in peace.

We arrived at the place where Abdul Wahab lived, and this time I was very nervous because I was not sure what was going to happen. My mother did have a bad temper and was capable of anything. I greeted the house with Assalamualaikum, but no one answered.

The door was open, so we left our shoes by the door and entered the house. There we found my father sleeping on the floor. He was not wearing a shirt but was wrapped in a sarong. Most old men in the countryside wore a sarong when they were at home. He quietly woke up and ran to the room to find his shirt. As soon as he came out, he sat up on the sofa looking straight into the corner where my mother had decided to sit. He looked shocked and looked at my mother again full of surprise; he was not expecting her to come. I just gave him a big smile. My mother had anger on her face and did not even glance at him.

His third wife was very nice and prepared some orange for us to drink.

My father and I talked a little, but not much as my mother sat and watched us. A few times I laughed but my mother seemed not too happy, her face would change and she would give us an angry look. My father tried to make conversation, he even said that he had kept some photos of my mother and he fetched the photo album. That still didn't make my mother happy, in fact it made things worse and she demanded to know why he still had photos of her.

My mother looked very young in the photos. She was beautiful. She looked like Claudia Cardinale, the famous actress. I tried to make conversation with my father by asking how long it been since they had seen each other and I said, "Dad, don't you want to say hello to Mum?" But my father just laughed and said nothing.

My mother became so angry at seeing him being so nice to his new wife and children, knowing that he had made her life miserable, that she nearly exploded. Suddenly she got up and poured the orangeade back into the pitcher, a big insult. I knew it was time to go before anything worse happened. We had been there for twenty minutes, but it was more than my mother could tolerate to see me appearing to talk happily with my father. They were both very stubborn, and it was time to go.

As we said say goodbye, I noticed my mother was already in the car. Twice my father put his hand on my shoulder as we walked to the car. I experienced a strange sensation; I felt the need to embrace him, and for him to embrace me. I felt the need to be loved, but it did not happen. I handed my father money for the mosque and said goodbye.

On the drive back, everyone was quiet. I said that seeing my father again moved me. Suddenly, my mother broke down and began weeping inconsolably, unable to control herself any longer. I stopped the car and helped her get out. She almost fainted and kept sobbing bitterly.

We sat down together beside the road. I kept telling her that she had to be strong and that I felt the same way she did when I saw him. I said we must not let the past get us down. I told her to look at herself and the daughter that you have and look at him. He still has to work hard, but you are able to relax. You even have your own car and a nice place to live, and who has done it for you? The daughter that he said was a bastard. You should be proud to show him the girl that he hated has now grown into a beautiful, successful woman.

My mother said the only thing she remembered when she saw him was the beatings he gave to both of us. She kept crying. I tried to calm her down by telling her I felt the same way as she did, and that we needed to be consoled by the possibility that he was a better man than he was with us. I was crying inside to see my mother so hurt.

When she had calmed down a little, I took her back into the car and we continued our journey. She sat in silence, her thoughts far away. She said she wanted to see her oldest brother, who did not live far from there.

CHAPTER 24

The Visionary

The last time I had seen my uncle I was ten years old. That was twenty-nine years ago. My God! I couldn't even remember what he looked like now, but surely he would be getting old.

We arrived at our destination. My uncle and his wife and some of her children were at home. I did not recognise anyone; only my uncle, whose face I still remembered. My mother recovered from her sadness and happily talked and joked with her brother and sister-in-law. Seeing that gave me a feeling of peace. I became the centre of attention since I was the prodigal daughter, living overseas and unmarried. They all asked me so many questions. The main one, of course, was when I might get married, and to this question I said nothing. Mustafa, my older brother, and his wife had ten children and twenty-seven grandchildren. They were a very big family and they all lived close to each other. After some time, it was time to say goodbye. Everyone exchanged farewells and I gave my uncle some money for the local mosque. We started our journey back to Penang.

It had been a long day and when we arrived back, it was dark. We were hungry, so we went to a Chinese restaurant where they had a good selection of fish and seafood in a live fish tank. You could choose the fish you wanted to eat and they prepared it for you. We chose a very large fish; we needed to restore our energy from the exhausting day.

Our stomachs full, we took a walk through the night market and saw many interesting things for sale. I was too tired and wanted to go back to the hotel, but my mother wanted to continue shopping. I left and told her not to wake me early, as we were only going to rest and relax on the beach tomorrow. She agreed and thank God for that.

The next day, even though I had slept all night, I was still tired, I couldn't even lift my body up from the bed, and couldn't open my eyes. I looked at the corner of the bed, there was my mother sitting, already dressed beautifully, waiting for me to get up with a big smile on her face. As soon as she saw me open my eyes she asked, "What time is it now?"

I said, "Don't know."

But I knew what she meant, so I quickly jumped in the shower and got ready to go for breakfast. There were many kinds of traditional Malaysian breakfast, but that I liked. I prefer Western breakfasts. As usual my mother had coconut rice. In Malaysia we have coconut rice for breakfast. My mother is a busybody, always looking at people trying to find something bad so she can make a comment. Suddenly, her eyes spotted a Westerner sitting alone, and she urged me to move the table and sit near him. I could see she liked that man, because she commented that the stranger was tall, blonde, and handsome, and she even can see he had blue eyes. I knew she had always wanted me to get married to that kind of man, I have no idea for what reason. She was always scheming to find a husband for me. I assured my mother that Prince Charming was in my future, but I did not think this stranger was him. My mother was quite disappointed and just could not understand, mumbling something about being a hundred years old and using a cane to walk. I am sure it was me she was talking about. I looked at her and winked with smile and said, "Mum! Don't worry, one day Prince Charming will find his Cinderella."

She replied, "Whatever."

One of the reasons I love London and the UK weather is that I do not have to worry about the hot sun tanning my dark skin. But I did here, and now my mother wanted to go sit by the sea and relax near the beach. It was very hot, and I knew my skin would burn.

We walked along the beach while I complained every minute about the heat, then my mother found a large rock in the shade that we could sit on and she could dangle her feet in the sea surf, and she sat there lost in thought. I had not seen my mother so happy and peaceful in all my life.

In a soft voice, as if recalling a dream, she started talking about her life. She talked about how she met my father and Nurul's father. She always talked about her first lover, Omar. She told me that she was really in love with Omar. If she had known where Omar lived, she would have gone to Omar and left my father. Omar was always in her mind, and she always listened to the song,

"Kenapa Kau Tinggalkan Aku" which means "Why have you left me?", and she feels so sad thinking about him. Her love story really touched my heart and I could understand how heartbroken and frustrated she felt at not seeing him again. I would love to find out about this person and bring him to my mother. I am sure there is something behind the story between them because, almost fifty years on, my mother still never stops talking about him, just him and nobody else. I can see very clearly that Omar was very special to my mother's life. After the story of her lover finished, she kept silent and looked at the lonely sea and the sky, and listened to the wind's song. I left her alone with her thoughts, but I sat the other corner of the rock and look at a grey mist on the sea's face and I totally understand how she felt, because I had been through it myself, I had been heartbroken; I shared her feelings in silence. I felt enormously sorry for my mother. She never received love from my father. And then I remembered the time she fell in love with my boyfriend Johari. As I am now mature enough and have learnt enough about life to understand her relationship with Johari, I can understand her feelings at that time. She was lonely, she needed love and she needed a man, especially while she was still young. When I think back I hate myself for my stupid behaviour toward my mother, but I was too young to understand at that stage. And now, deep down in my soul, I am deeply sorry for my selfishness and wish I could find someone to make her life happier.

As the day was getting windy with the white clouds closing in, I felt a little cold. Suddenly she shocked me, pretending to push me down into the sea. I screamed loudly, scared to death, but she burst out laughing. Then she continued talking about all the details of her life, about the birth of her children and how they survived. All this was being recalled, not with anger, but as if she could not believe that it had all happened to her. She seemed at peace, as if the events with my father the day before had not happened, or were just a distant memory. I could not recall ever seeing my mother so at peace, and I was so happy for her.

As we talked, the pauses in her conversation grew longer and longer, and soon she was fast asleep in the shade on top of the rock. The light ocean breeze ever so slightly blew across her.

I went to sleep as well. I don't know how long we fall asleep for; I was awakened by my mother, and she had a sense of urgency in her voice. She said she wanted to visit a person who practised witchcraft so she could ask him about my missing brother, and she also wanted another opinion about my love affair with Kazmin, but she didn't know that I was no longer in love with Kazmin. I was startled because I do not believe in such things as witchcraft, but people in Asia, and in particular Indonesia, Thailand and Malaysia, believe in this form of fortune telling and also in magic spells. I decided to go with her because she always does this to look for my brother, and I thought it might be fun to see, so I went along with her.

Nurul, my mother and I drove for miles and finally arrived at the house of the man who would perform this black magic. I remember Kazmin telling me how his wife Rosnah would use witchcraft on him in order to control him. Well! Good for him because he also used witchcraft to do a lot of things so they deserved each other. I thought the only real magic was when I disappeared and then reappeared in London. Now that was some real magic.

The man greeted us, said some prayers, and told my mother she needed to purchase some items necessary to perform the magic from a shop down the road. We went there and purchased a bottle of mineral water, a small bottle of oil, two candles, some kind of a leaf called Sireh, and some wax stones called Kemiyan.

I wondered, what the hell is this? Now I could hardly wait to see. I had seen witchcraft every time I visited my mother. My mother would ask me to drive to the place house of the person who performed the black magic. This was the only way she knew how to find my brother Nazeri. She had gone to almost all the black magicians in that area but none of them successful. She would ask everyone she met if they knew anyone who knew witchcraft, then she would go to visit them by herself. She didn't care about the journey. Both of my brothers didn't care about my missing little brother, so they didn't bother to help. My poor mother sometimes had to pay someone to help her, and then they would take her to the place that does witchcraft. Every time I went home, it would be my job to be her driver.

I recalled one time when I was in Malaysia visiting my mother, and I was there for a month. One evening my mother had told me that her friend had told her about a new witch in that area, and that he was very good. So that evening she wanted to go and, of course, I had to drive her there. For me it was fine and I loved to see the way witchcraft performed. Sometimes it could be very scary and the person's voice could change and they would sound like a different person. I never believed such things; I found it so funny and weird. Of course, my mother believed in these things because she lived in the countryside and she had been following these practices for a very long time.

On the way to the black magic place, I could hear my mother talking to herself as she always did. I interrupted her and said, "What are you talking about?"

She replied, "I have been going to hundreds of witches to try to get your brother home, but still no news, I hope he is in good health."

I told her, "Don't worry Mum one day he will come home. Just pray for him. I promise, I will do whatever it takes to find him and bring him back to you safely."

But in the back of my mind I was wondering why my brother hadn't come home? I was sure something bad had happened somewhere, especially as he was so scared of my two brothers. We had arrived at the house. The light inside the house was so bright and, from the outside, I could see a few people in the house. I was sure that these people had come to see the black magic as well. We walked a few steps, then entered the house. As a custom, we had to leave our shoes outside the house. There was a queue, so we joined the queue by sitting on the floor, gathering with the strangers and waiting for our turn. As soon as I sat down, all the men looked at me like they had never seen women in their life. And the women looked at me as though they were jealous, maybe because I was dressed so differently to them. City girls look after themselves better than the country girls, which made me different from the others. When I started talking to them they all stared at me and they could tell straight away I was an outsider. As all my life was spent in the city, I didn't know the local dialect. The slang that I speak now comes from the city so I can be a bit arrogant sometime, just for fun.

The person who performs the witchcraft was sat in a room. Whoever goes to see him has to go in the room and tells him the problems that they have. As soon as someone finishes, the next person jumped up. I couldn't wait to go in to see the performance. It was our turn next, soon my mother saw that the person before us had come out from the room so she quickly stood and walked straight in, where the witch was waiting for the next customer. We sit in front of the him. The room was dark, lit only by a few candles, and I could hardly see his face especially as he had very dark skin but I managed to look at him. He was quite a young guy and he had someone to help him. Suddenly his voice borke the silent, asking us, "Where do you come from? And what is your problem?"

WOW! I was getting excited now. My mother introduced herself as a mammy, that special name everyone calls my mother. No matter where we are, she will always introduce herself as mammy. Then my mother said, "Mammy has come from not very far from here and mammy wants to see you about my son, he never came back home very long time go so could you please see and tell me what is happening to him?"

He asked my brother's name, and for his shirt and pictures, which my mother had already prepared from home. My mother became so familiar with such things, so she already knew what the witch would want. My mother handed all the stuff that he wanted to him. He grabbed it and put it on the floor in front of him, then he picked up my brother's picture. He asked the person who worked for him to bring a bowl of water and some candles. The bowl of water was put in front of him and he lit the two candles by his side. The performance had begun. He held my brother's pictures on the top of the candle with care so the pictures did not burn, and he mumbled some words which we didn't understand at all. Suddenly he shook his head and my mother, so anxious to know, asked him, "What happened to my son?"

He said, "I am sorry is a bad news."

I started to worry and asked him, "What happened to him?"

He was still shaking his head and told us, "Just wait, I will tell you in a minute."

Then he put my brother's picture on the floor and he looked straight at the water inside the bowl in front of him. He closed his eyes and again mumbled something, then he blew into the water. Than he look at the water and he looked at my mother and said, "Bad, bad news."

When he said that my mother got very worried and looked at me with big eyes. I tried to make myself serious so my mother wouldn't get mad with me. He looked at the water, shook his head, and said, "Your son has died, and I can see his body in the water."

As soon as my mother heard that, she looked at me with her eyes open wide open, then she burst into tears. I tried to comfort her and said, "Don't cry mum, just relax, we can talk later."

At the same time I looked at the stupid witch full of anger. I really didn't want to stay at this place any longer and look at these nasty people. It was bullshit. How could he say my brother was dead. The guy who had performed the witchcraft was getting very worried, but I before we left my mother asked me give some money to him. I was not very happy at all to give money to someone who tried to hurt people like my mother but I had no choice. My mother excused herself and left, and I gave him one last angry look before leaving as well.

Life Behind the Silence 157

In the car on the way back home, my mother was still crying. I tried to calm her down and I said, "Mum! Please don't believe him, he's not a god! He does this just for the money. He was so happy when he saw you cry, that meant his performance was working to make people like you believe him. Come on! Adik has not died Mum. (My brother Nazeri was the youngest and we called him Adik.) Just believe it yourself and pray for him that he is in good health and he will come home one day. That is what I always do Mum. You can go to see witches but don't trust something stupid because their job is to make people believe them, so forget about what he said earlier, it is untrue. I promise as soon I get back to London, I will try another way to find him and will bring him back to you."

I could see my mother stop crying and I know she felt a bit better after I had said that. Then she started telling me about her experiences with witchcraft since my brother went missing. She said, for all the witches that she had been seeing, this was the first time someone had told her very nasty news about my brother. The rest of the witches had told her almost the same story – don't worry he is well and happy. He is enjoying his life and he has a family. He is staying quite far from Malaysia. He wants to come home but he has some problems, but don't worry he will come back one day.

I told her that I was sure that many of the witches were very honest and were truly trying to help people, and of course there would be many who aren't, who were just taking people's money and conning people around, for example the fucker who said my brother was dead.

I did not hear any words from my mother, I looked over and saw she was sound asleep. I wondered if she had just heard what I had said, or if I had been talking to myself. While I was driving I had many thoughts in my mind. It was almost midnight, there weren't many cars on the road and only a few lampposts, which made me a bit scared especially as my mother was soundly asleep. It was a very peaceful drive in the countryside and finally we arrived home. As I lay in bed, I remembered another time when I experienced the work of a witch.

This time, it was a man and his wife who were performing the ritual. They arranged his utensils, and then the magic began. Everyone sat on the floor, shoes had been left at the entrance to the house.

The man wore a white hat. He placed an open newspaper on the floor, and, on the top of newspaper, he placed a plate. On top of the plate, he placed a small pot containing a piece of dry, burning coconut which he had previously cut with a knife. He lit three candles, added a few small pebbles to the pot and then tied a red handkerchief around his head.

Oh dear! I was ready for anything to happen. My mother was very familiar with witchcraft so she helped adding more stones to the pot. The man rubbed his hands and his arms. He murmured a few words to encourage the vision. I started to smell something like incense. His wife worked with him and started to speak, and at that moment they indicated that the spirit had appeared.

They greeted the spirit. I also welcomed it, as did, but inside I was thinking this ws just madness. In truth, I was scared. My feet and hands were getting cold and I just wanted to run from that house.

At that moment, the man took some sort of tree leaf and asked a question. We all answered. Then he took a plastic bottle with a white substance in it that looked like a paint and rubbed some on the leaf. He continued speaking with his eyes closed.

Then he folded the leaf, making a little packet, and gave it to my mother. He opened the bottle of mineral water and passed it over the pot. My mother put the cap back on the bottle.

The man took two long, thin, white candles and asked me to repeat after him by saying, "Jude."

I thought, who the hell is Jude?

My mother was watching me very closely, so I repeated the name, Jude, and at the moment the man took the candles and gave them to my mother. She instantly started coughing. He opened a bag of little stones that Nurul had purchased and gave her some instructions. With that, my mother threw a few of the pebbles into the pot while the flame inside still burned. The rest of the stones she left on the plate as instructed.

The man gave some instructions, and Nurul started writing down every word so as not to forget anything. The visionary's wife uttered a few words as her husband waved some perfume over his face and body.

Suddenly, for some reason unknown to me, I blurted out Kazmin's name. The visionary asked me some question about where this Kazmin lived. I responded that he lived in Kuala Lumpur, at the same time my mother added some stones to the pot. I was surprised that my mother knew what to do – she must have been experienced at this particular ritual.

The visionary told us it was a spirit from Indonesia speaking. He then slapped the floor and told us not to go to Indonesia. My mother asked about

Life Behind the Silence

Nazeri, my missing brother. The visionary said he believed my brother was in Indonesia. I thought, Indonesian spirit? This is bullshit.

We picked up the little leaf packets with the pebble inside, the candles, and the mineral water. My mother wrapped it all very careful in newspaper, as if it were a special gift. Then she put it all in a plastic bag and gave it to Nurul for safekeeping.

The session now over, the man told me that this Kazmin loved me but he was under a strong spell and could not move. He told me to eat the leaf that he had prepared and Kazmin would return to me in a week. All I could think was that I was not going to eat my leaf and I certainly did not want Kazmin to return to me.

The visionary asked my mother to come back another day with a photo of my brother, Nazeri, and something that belonged to him, such as a shirt. Only then would he be able to tell her something about my brother. I was ready to leave. I had seen enough of this witchcraft. We said goodbye after my mother and Nurul had given him some money. We all decided not to tell my brother about this part of our journey, he would be very angry with us because he did not believe in this sort of thing.

We set off for my brother's house.

CHAPTER 25

End of This Trip

My brother Redzwan's girlfriend, Ani, was a small girl with short hair. She had been divorced and had three children from her last marriage. I was not very happy that my brother chose this girl to be his future wife. I wanted my brother to be happy and not to end up like Kazmin, with a dominating wife and no life of his own.

I wanted to meet this woman, because I had heard much gossip, and thought a face-to-face meeting was appropriate before I left Malaysia. I decided to visit Ani at her salon and get a haircut and some one-on-one time with my future sister-in-law.

After a brief greeting, I sat in the chair for my haircut. She started talking non-stop while doing my haircut, maybe she was trying to impress me by being friendly and nice to me. She told me about my brother's past homosexual experimentation, which I never known about. I'm not sure that I believed her and I had never heard such a thing from anyone in my family. I decided I would find out myself from my brother. She talked about his drinking and his careless spending of money. She assured me that she loved him very much and, since they had met, he had changed a lot. She said would turn him into a better person, and she would be a good wife to him. I thought yeah, whatever, just finish my haircut quickly, I want to get my ass out of here. I had had enough, and I felt like I was being fed a bunch of bull, so as soon as the haircut was finished all I said was, "Thankyou, very nice haircut, you are good." In fact it looked terrible!

And before I left her I said, "Nice to see you and look after my brother."

What could I have said? If I had said how I truly felt it could have ended in violence. So I left her happy in her own mind. I really wanted to go back to the hotel. I had a million things on my mind and I needed to rest after long day, because tomorrow I was going back to Kuala Lumpur, the big city, and my real life. It was time to say goodbye to everyone.

Back to the hotel, something was not right with my mother. Whenever I spent any time with her, she always had something to bring up. This time, for no apparent reason, she got angry with Nurul. I was really tired and had a bad headache, and I lost my temper, shouting to my mother, "Shut up Mum! What is your problem? I have done everything for you and you don't appreciate any of it, you don't even know how tired I am." Then I turned to Nurul and said, "Yes! Nurul you have a different father to me, so what?"

My mother stopped her ranting and ran to another room sleep with my sister-in-law, leaving me and my sister alone. My sister was very upset and crying. I went to her and said, "Sorry for saying that, but I don't mean it, I just said it to stop Mum's anger. She has no reason to be upset with you."

I gave her a big hug and kisses. This was the last night I was going to spend with them before I left but my mother behaved like a kid. She couldn't bear to see me and my sister being too close, if she did then she would always cause an argument. That night I tried to find out why my mother's behaved with this jealously towards me and my sister. I didn't get the answer, but I would one day.

The trip was starting to wear everyone down, seeing my father and all our other relatives had stirred up so many raw emotions that had been pushed away for many years. The fact that I was leaving in the morning made my mother angry, and Nurul was on the receiving end of outburst.

The next morning all was fine. My mother, Nurul, and my sister-in-law took me to airport, and I left Penang for Kuala Lumpur. I was sad to be leaving my mother and my sister, but at the same time I was also relieved to be leaving the countryside behind. After all, I had become a city girl so I was eager to get to Kuala Lumpur and even more keen to get to London.

On the plane I reflected on my visit to Kedah. I felt intensely satisfied I had seen so many relatives – including taking my mother to see my father after such a long time. It was almost unimaginable that we could sit in the same room after so much time and have almost a normal father-daughter conversation. It seemed like a dream. It was good to think that my father might have changed for the better. After all, it had been twenty six years, but it was hard for me to forgive and to accept him back into my life.

I arrived in Kuala Lumpur and checked into the Renaissance Hotel. The weather was hot, humid and sticky.

I called my friend of many years, Sanajan, to see if she could have dinner with me. She had known about my relationship with Kazmin, and she too had had a rough upbringing and a bad marriage, so we had a lot to talk about and could empathise with each other. After dinner I went back to my room. As I entered the room, the phone started ringing; it was Nurul reminding me to eat the leaf the visionary had given me.

I had forgotten about his instructions and would never have thought about this again – and certainly would never have eaten the leaf – but here was my sister calling to remind me, so I thought what the hell? I decided to try it to see whether this magic was real or not. My intention was to not get Kazmin back, but to know about witchcraft for myself.

I ate the leaf and nearly vomited. What a horrible taste. I hoped the spirit from Indonesia would not come to see me.

To clear my mind of all this shit, I went to the hotel gym and started working out. Surprisingly, my old friend Ramesh appeared. I didn't know he was working as a gym instructor for the hotel, and it happened that he had late shift. Ramesh and I had known each for other a very long time, we had worked together previously as co-instructors when I worked at Universal Gym in Kuala Lumpur. He also used to be my part-time lover.

Ramesh invited me to go out for a drink after he had finished work. I said OK; these would be my last two nights in Kuala Lumpur for a long time so I wanted to let my hair down.

That night Kazmin called my mobile asking me where I was. Without thinking, I told him that I was at the Hotel Renaissance, Kuala Lumpur. After I hung up the phone I realised, if I didn't want to see him, why had I just told him where I was? What would happen if he came to my room? Stupid me! Because of that I went to a club and ended up getting back to my room at two in the morning. When I opened to the door, I noticed a strange, smoky smell in the room. I recognised it as the smell of Kazmin's cigarettes, but that was impossible! How could he have entered my room, how did he have the key?

Just then the doorbell rang. I hoped it was not Remash waiting to see me.

I looked through the peep hole, damn, it was Kazmin! What should I do? Should I not open the door? But I was sure he knew that I was in the room, so I decided to open it. Once he was in my room, I asked if he had come by earlier. He seemed surprised and asked how I knew, so I told him that I recognised the smell of his cigarettes. He smiled about that.

Life Behind the Silence

I asked him how he got in and was stunned when he said he told reception that he was my husband and had lost his key card – and they just gave him another one. I thought that was very clever of him, but I was furious with the hotel, how could they be so stupid?

Kazmin was a bit tipsy. He had come by earlier and found that I was not in the room. He decided to go to a pub and have a few drinks – and then he had taken some tablets to get even more high. He looked miserable and I wondered where his wife was. He explained that he and he wife had had an argument, and now he wanted to spend some time with me. My heart started racing. That was not going to happen but at the same time I started to feel nervous, what should I do? Should I kick him out of my room? Could I do that? That was the question.

But I did not say a word. I just sat on the chair as he lay on the bed. Kazmin started talking non-stop about how he loved me and wanted to marry me because he was not happy with his wife.

Suddenly I remembered the leaf, I had eaten that leaf and the visionary told me that Kazmin would come to see me. WOW! It was really happening… or he could just be drunk and not know what he was talking about.

Kazmin fell asleep on the bed and I tried to sleep in the chair. At day break I woke and went down for breakfast. I called my mother and sister to tell them that I ate the leaf and Kazmin had come to see me. They were very pleased, but not for me. I was tired and in no mood to share in their excitement. I had an uninvited drunk asleep in my room, and my whole body ached from trying to sleep in a chair.

At breakfast I became even more angry about the fact that this five star hotel had given my room key to a stranger. It could have been anyone and I could have ended up dead in the room. I decided to file a complaint to the hotel manager, and they apologised and issued me with another key.

Back in my room, Kazmin had woken up and ordered some food for himself. While he ate and smoked, I just sat and looked at him without speaking. He looked at me and said, "You know I love you, my heart has never been with my wife and all that I have done in my life has been for you."

I just sat and looked at him and smiled without any reply. All I was thinking was why is he saying this now? After all the years I waited for him? Maybe it was because now he could see my life was getting better, and I could afford to stay in five star hotels. I knew Kazmin very well, he always went for the money. I thought, don't you try me Kazmin. It's too late and all those words that you have just said didn't mean anything to me. I wanted a normal life without fear and the problems that life with Kazmin would bring. Our story was a sad one with no future.

After a while he excused himself and went to his office. We said goodbye and he said he would see me tonight back at the hotel. All I could think was, "No you won't, not again."

To cheer me up, I went down to the swimming pool and relaxed. I love to swim but not in the hot weather because I am scared my skin will go dark. I just lay by the pool and wondered what I should do about Kazmin. I needed an excuse for him not to come to my room.

I finally thought, this is bloody ridiculous. Why should I be worried? I should just be myself and not give a damn.

My body was so tired and I ended up spending the whole evening in my room by myself. Kazmin called and wanted to take me out for the evening, and I told him NO – several times. I explained that I was tired and had an early flight the next day; therefore, I needed some sleep.

He was very upset and told me that he would come over to the hotel later that evening and I thought good luck with your key. I packed and went to bed, but it was difficult to sleep because Kazmin kept calling me every minute. Each time I would tell him to call me later, but then I decided to take the phone off the hook. Let him think whatever he wanted to think, I didn't give a damn.

I thought I had some peace at last, but in the early hours the doorbell rang. It was Kazmin, drunkenly protesting because the key had been changed and I refused to go out partying with him. I let him come in. He said all his (married) friends were out with their girlfriends, and he did not have a girlfriend. And then he spoke the truth, "You're like a stranger to me." Within a few second he dropped off to sleep on my bed.

I thought, get a life Kazmin, you should think before you hurt me. My heart hurt badly and I couldn't ever take him back into my life. After I finished my last minute packing, I sat in the chair and looked at the sad figure lay in my bed. Even as he slept, his face contorted with the stress he was under.

The time to depart for the airport had arrived. I tried to wake Kazmin in order to tell him goodbye, but he was so drunk that he could not even open his eyes.

So I whispered "I'm leaving now"' and kissed him on the forehead. It was sad to leave him in this state but I was sure he was going to be fine. I felt sorry for him so when I checked out of the hotel, I paid for an extra day so Kazmin could stay and relax for a while. I took a taxi from the hotel to the airport. After I checked my luggage and while waiting for boarding, I tried a few times to call Kazmin to make sure he was OK, I wanted to tell him about the extra day he had at the hotel, but there was no answer. He must have been dead to the world.

I was feeling stressed and was so tired that I was looking forward to the thirteen hour flight back to London. The flight was made uncomfortable because of turbulence, but in spite of this I slept the entire journey. The plane landed in London and all I could think of was getting home and resting in my own bed.

I tried again to call Kazmin from the airport. He answered at last, fifteen hours after I had left him that morning. He was shocked to hear that I was in London already. I explained that I had tried to wake him up before I left, but he was too drunk. I told him about the extra day he had at the hotel.

Then I told him to enjoy the room and said goodbye. There was no response, he was probably fast asleep again, so I hung up and made my way back to my home sweet home.

CHAPTER 26

Frozen Eggs

I prefer to live in safety and feel secure, especially in these times. I protect my privacy; I do not get involved in other people's lives, and I do not like others prying into my affairs. I use to live in an area of London known as St John's Wood. The area had a discreet atmosphere, and people tended to leave you alone. But now I have moved out and live on Baker Street, which was close to the centre of the city, and that was very convenient for a single lady like me.

As I was addicted to exercise, I decided to live near Regent Park where I could run everyday and that made my life so much easier. My life is very personal and I like my privacy so I chose to live on my own.

In June of 2005, I was walking home after a jogging session when a young man passed me, he said, "Hello."

I looked at him and replied in kind. I didn't think anything of it until he turned around and started walking with me. He started a conversation, and I was in the mood to talk, so it seemed natural to exchange phone numbers as I got close to my home. His name was Giovanni.

One week later, he called me and asked me out for dinner. I was going to meet him at the tube station at seven in the evening for our first date. It had been a long time since I last went on a date.

I waited for him at the tube station for over fifteen minutes. I hate waiting and fifteen minutes is too long for me. I decided to call him and it went directly to voicemail, so I left a message and went back home. I didn't get too upset that he didn't turn up because, as it was a first date, I always expecting that anything could happen. So I decided to go out with my friends for dinner when the phone rang. It was him, and he said he was sorry for being late and that he was waiting for me. I felt rejuvenated and told him I would be there in twenty minutes, even though I could have been there in five, just to have a little bit of revenge for him making me wait for him.

When I met him, he was a little shy at first. I hoped he wasn't going to take me by train. If he did, he was not going to make me happy because I was all dressed up. He hailed a taxi so we could be on our way, thank God! Anyway once we were in the taxi he was a different person. He wasn't shy after all. He was friendly and funny, which made me feel comfortable around him.

Our first date went very well. I liked his company. He sat next to me, holding my hand all night without letting go, and always looked at my face while saying all sorts of lovely words. He took me to a posh Thai restaurant and I love Thai food. Impressive, I thought! I couldn't wait to find out what he did for a living. The food was divine but I lost my appetite because of his caring and romantic nature and I felt like a princess for a few hours. I just hoped he was genuine, not just out to impress me with his charm.

After dinner he politely took me home and said, "Goodnight, see you again."

I asked him to call me when he got home so I would know that he got home safely, and he did. But the truth was I just wanted to have a conversation with him. Sadly he just said, "Yes! I am home, good night." That was it.

I was still holding the phone and I wondered where he had gone, I didn't expect him to hang up just like that but yes, hand up he did. WOW! That was bloody rude. I was a bit disappointed and it really put me off seeing him again. That night I decided to kick him out of my head.

Over the next few days I got bored and lonely. Giovanni kept calling and wanted to take me for dinner again. So I decided to see him for our second date. After that, we ended up seeing each other three times a week, and soon it felt like we had spent the whole summer together. In fact he gave all his time to me, and showed me that he didn't have anyone else in his life, it was wonderful. I was feeling very close with him – and I was starting to think that he really liked me.

September 23, my 40th birthday. We had been seeing each other for four months. For the week before my birthday, he came to see me every day with one rose in his hand. I thought, how sweet! Then the day of my birthday, he surprised me early in the morning with a bouquet of roses and wished me happy birthday. That was beautiful and at that moment I felt so wonderful.

I was so happy and when I looked at him standing in front of me with bouquet of roses, straight away I could feel love coming into my heart. Then he said, "Tonight I am taking you out for dinner so get ready, I am coming at 7pm."

I responded happily, "Yes please!"

I just couldn't wait to see where he was taking me for my 40th birthday dinner, and I was eager to see more of his charm; I adored this kind of man and I hoped his charm became something more real.

He called me exactly the time that he promised and he asked me to come out because he was waiting outside. As I was ready, I quickly ran outside the house and looked around but he was not there. I thought, where the hell he is? Is he playing games with me or what? Then my eyes spotted the limousine parked just round the corner of my house. I wondered why a limousine would be parked here? Surely waiting for someone famous or someone rich, I wished that the limousine was waiting for me. Maybe one day. Suddenly my daydreaming was cut short when I saw my Italian date come out from that limousine and call me, "Gina! I am here."

When I heard his voice called my name, I couldn't move. I stood for a few seconds carefully looking at him to make sure that it was really him. And yes! It was him. The only word that I can say was, WOW! I was not expecting this to happen to me. Then, slowly, I took a step toward him. I couldn't walk properly and I couldn't even get into the limousine properly. This was the first time I had ever sat in a limousine. Soon I was in, and he poured me a glass of champagne and said, "Happy Birthday, cheers!"

I tried to hold my nerve and pull myself together, and said, "Thank you, cheers!"

Then he handed me a small box and asked me to open it right now. I was so excited I wanted to tear off the wrapping but I thought, as I was sat in a limousine, I had to act like a posh lady. So I gently opened my present because my Prince Charming was watching. As I saw the shine of the stone, I was speechless. It was a white gold necklace with a heart-shaped pendant full of diamonds round the heart. Giovanni took the necklace and put it around my neck. I felt my life change. I had found a man who respected me and treated me like a lady in a way I had never been treated before. He made me feel so good about myself. The heart pendant full of diamond that he gave me was just like his own heart, precious.

He took me to dinner at an expensive restaurant in town, Italian food of course. As soon as we arrived at the table I saw one rose waiting for me. It was a very romantic candle light dinner. After dinner, he took me to a very exclusive club. I felt so elegant that night. It all went smoothly, my body close to his body and dancing all night with his fingers running all over my body. It was a sensational feeling, my heart was beating happily and my soul whispered, 'He is the one.'

I still didn't know what he did for a living but he spent a lot of money on expensive restaurants and bought expensive gifts for me. He looked very plain and for some reason he didn't look like a millionaire. I felt like something was not quite right with him but whoever he was as long he made my life happy, I was fine. One day I would find out he was not a millionaire.

One afternoon he called me from the hospital where his father had been for some time, and during this conversation he said "I love you" for the first time.

I drew a breath and responded that, "I love you too."

I felt the tone of the conversation change when he asked me to have dinner with him that evening, telling me he had something that he needed to tell me. I was a bit worried.

That evening he picked me up as planned, but he seemed different. As we drove to the restaurant, he looked so guilty and had a sad look on his face. I looked at him and said, "Are you OK?"

He looked at me, held my hand and said, "I tell you later"

As we arrived at the restaurant, he asked me to sit on a bench just outside the restaurant, because he had something to tell me. So we sat. I just couldn't wait to hear what he was going to tell me. Maybe he was going to surprise me and propose, that would be my dream. He looked so nervous and it took him a few minutes to start the conversation. He said that he loved me, and I told him that I loved him too. He looked at me with his big eyes and paused, without a single blink, then he told me again that he loved me – but that he was married.

As soon as I heard the word married my whole body dropped onto that bench, my heart sunk. I wondered why he hadn't told me at the beginning? I bought back the memories of my father who lied to my mother, Kazmin who lied to me, and now Giovanni had lied to me! I just sat there and cried, but not for him. I cried because I didn't know why this kept happening to me. I cried because I was so stupid.

I asked him why he had not told me this before. He explained that he wanted to but he did not want to lose me. He told me that he was just going through the motions with his wife, and they had decided to get divorced five months before he met me. I told him that was not right and he have told me at the beginning that he was married, but now this was too complicated. The evening ended on that bench – we went home without our meal.

The next day I went for a walk at Regents Park just to clear my mind. It was summer time and the weather was beautiful. I lay in the grass, hopelessly thinking about how I had given my heart away. I was annoyed with myself, after all the lessons life had taught me I still hadn't learned.

But as with the writing of this book, I have decided to continue our relationship for many reasons. He saved my life at one stage, when my life was almost torn apart, and no words can describe how appreciative I am of him. The day he walked into my life, he made my life better than ever, with his caring ways, which is what I love about him. Our relationship got better as we went along. We started to understand more of each other and we had a lot in common, which made us closer and made us love each other even more. At the beginning I never planned our relationship to go in this direction. I was learning about happiness and what it means to be truly in love with someone who cares about me. Love is blind. I know this as a fact now as I found myself in love with a married man; even though I tried not to get into relationship with a married man. Because that is the one thing that I didn't want to happen in my life. I wish he had told me at the beginning that he was married as I would not have got involved. But he played his game very well; he broke the news after I fell in love with him. Anyway, from then on I was happy with him, because he is a man who knows how to look after his woman. He would surprise me early in the morning with bunches of roses, and magnificent presents on my birthday and Valentine's Day. He would always do things to surprise me, which I loved him for. He was such a wonderful guy, I couldn't ask for more, and I hoped it was going to last forever. But it might not, who knows? He might just have been trying to impress me at the beginning. If that happened, it would be another disastrous experience in my life. Surely at that time I would be hurt but put a smile on my face, because I would have been stupid to fall for his charms. But then there would be nothing I could do about it, life still has to go on.

A year later he talked about marriage and children. WOW! Straight away I was thinking that I was going to be a wife soon, have a husband, have children of my own and be a mum, that is what I wished for. Since he mentioned that, I dreamt almost every day, for weeks, months and years, but nothing happened. After all his millions of wonderful words, he made me wait five years for him to secure his divorce, and still my life was hanging without strings. The arguments began. The only arguments we would have was when I asked, "When will your divorce be filed? And be final?" All he would say was, "Soon, just wait, it will be any day now." Five years I had waited and still he gave me no DAY. I knew now that my life had been messed up again by someone who I had put my entire trust in, and that he had destroyed my dream. So I had to make my own way and my own decisions.

I was getting so worried about my age, and my worrying put me under a lot of pressure. Because I wanted to have my own baby so much and in the next few months I was going to be forty-five. I started to suffer with my loneliness; I was broken hearted and depressed because I wanted to believe that I still had a chance to have a baby. I spent time on my own thinking, what should I do? Then I thought, seeing friends and talking about this is a good idea. But, sadly, since I had been with him I had lost almost all of my friends, there were just a few that I still had contact with. I made a phone call to my dear friend Mariam and she agreed to meet up with me. I was really surprised with myself because I am not the sort of person who likes to discuss my personal life with someone, I always keep things to myself. But at this stage I needed friends. And thank God! I have good friends and good friends always give such good advice. Mariam suggested that I see a doctor and that really helped me. I didn't wait any longer, within a few days I had made an appointment to see my doctor. Now I knew how important it is to have friends in life.

I am an independent person but I wasn't in this situation, because I was too emotional to do it myself. I needed someone to be with me, so obviously Giovanni had to come along with me to the clinic, because we were still in a relationship. We were at the clinic on time and I waited impatiently for my name to be called. A few minutes later, I heard a woman's voice call my name. I jumped up straight away and my heart started to thump as I wondered what news I was going to get. Slowly I pushed the door and walked in, and then I saw a pregnant doctor. I thought, why do I have to see a pregnant woman at this moment? I sat in front of her and my mind just focused on her pregnancy. I couldn't stop thinking, why can't I be pregnant? Suddenly her voice interrupted my thoughts. She looked at me and asked me a few questions. My answers told her everything she needed to know. Then she came to the serious matter that made me burst into tears in front of her. I was too weak to handle it at that moment and I got too emotional. If what she had told me was true, I couldn't accept it. Giovanni knew how upset I was so he asked the doctor a few questions and she suggested taking me to see a gynaecologist.

Before we left, the only words that I managed to say were thank you and bye.

We both stepped out from the clinic but my whole body felt weak. I got really upset, emotional and angry at the same time when I looked at him; I just wanted to kick his face for wasting my life all this time. My anger was really going to blow up at any moment, just like a volcano about to erupt, but I held my patience and didn't explode at him. At the same time though, the relationship never get any better.

At home, I waited for the right time to call my mother. I called my mother almost every day and we would chat for hours and hours about many things in life. But today I was going to talk about something different that she had not expected. I really didn't know how my mother would respond when I told her about my decision. And I was very worried but I had to do it, because it was so important.

I picked up the phone and dialled her number. It didn't ring for long before she answered the phone. As she knew that I always called her at this hour, she had surely been expecting my call. I tried to keep myself as calm as possible. As usual we started with casual conversation and I told her something funny that had happened to me just to make her laugh, but at the same time my brain was working very hard to find the right way to discuss the matter. As I come from a Muslim family, I was very concerned about her anger and rejection. But I kept myself strong and decided that, whatever my mother said, I would stick to my decision. Then I mentioned to her that I had missed my period for three months. She sounded worried, as all mothers would, especially at that stage of my life. She had really wanted me to get married and have children for a very long time but it had never happened. From my tone of voice she knew that I was upset and worried. Then she tried to comfort me by saying, "Don't worry, Insaallah," (Insaallah means god willing) "it is just a warning, you still have a chance to have a baby but it will have to be soon."

Before she started asking about marriage, I quickly mentioned to her that I wanted to have my eggs frozen. She was silent for a few seconds but then she said, "Just wait! You never know, maybe you're going to meet someone and get married."

As soon as I started talking about my treatment, I suddenly heard someone's voice calling my mother so she had to excuse herself and asked me to call her later to talk about the issue. As soon as she hung up the phone, I felt so down because I needed her at that stage, to share my worries, even

Life Behind the Silence 173

though she was a thousand miles away from me. I lay on my sofa with sadness in my heart and kept asking myself, why has this happened to me?

It was the 22nd May, around 2.30 in the afternoon, and the temperature was about 27 degrees. It was really sunny and too hot for me. Most people take advantage of the nice weather and go out and enjoy the sun but not me; I prefer to stay indoors, away from the sun. Even though I come from a hot country, my skin is very sensitive, and I hate sun. I sat by the window, just looking at the beautiful sunshine and thinking, I wish I had a life as beautiful as the sunshine. At that moment my life became so cloudy and I felt so sad. I worried and cried when I was alone, I needed to put my head on someone's shoulder but there was no one to lend me their shoulder at that time. I was hurt and depressed and needed someone to talk to, someone to comfort me, but there was no one beside me. I couldn't stop thinking and talking to myself, and my mind always whispered, if I don't get what I wish for, this world will mean nothing to me and I will need to go from here. At night I couldn't sleep and during the day I couldn't focus on my life. I tried to hold myself together as much as I could but I still needed HELP!

It was still summertime in London and the hottest day of the year. As I sat alone on my sofa facing the window, the sun burst in towards me. I was sweating, I was so hot. I couldn't bear the heat so I switched on the fan and directed it right at my face. Yes! That's better, I thought. I decided to call my mother and discuss the things that I wanted to be done. I was sure she would be waiting for my phone call at this time of day. I just couldn't wait to hear her opinion and suggestions, whether she agreed or disagreed, so that I could live in peace!

I dialled her number and the phone rang. As usual she answered within a second. With her lovely tone of voice she said, "Assalamualaikum!" (This means peace be upon you.)

I answered, "Mualaikumsalam!" But I don't know the meaning of that.

As always our conversations started with our daily lives. Thirty minutes later, she asked me about the subject that I had wanted to discuss with her the day before. I started to get a bit upset because I really didn't want to hurt my mother but I had no choice so I said, "Mum, Remember yesterday I told you that I had missed my period for three months?"

She answered, "Yes! Of course I remember."

Then I said, "Mum, I'm not too sure if you like my idea or not but I hope you do. Originally it was not my intention to do this but now I have no choice,

I have to do it before it is too late."

I waited for her to say something but she just kept silent. I guess she was waiting to hear what I was going to say. So I continued and said to her, "Mum, I am going to search for a fertility clinic. I have made the decision to have IVF treatment to freeze my eggs."

She straightaway said, "NO!"

She almost started her lecture but I quickly cut her off and said, "Mum, I know you want me to get married and have the wedding that you always wished for. As you know, I wanted so much to make your wish come true and it was my dream too, but I can't wait to be married before my life becomes a disaster because I really don't know when marriage is going to happen, it may be never, and I need children of my own. As you know, I am going to be forty-five years old soon and anything could go wrong, you know what I mean. At the moment I am so depressed, with a million questions in my head, and day by day my life is suffering, Mum. I wish I had someone who I could talk to and who could give me the support that I need at the moment. I hope you understand why I have made this decision. Please, Mum!"

She still kept silent. In the meantime I just hoped she understood that I was doing something for my own future. My heart beat faster, waiting for her answer. All mothers want to see their daughter happy and I was sure my mother wanted to see me happy.

Suddenly her voice broke the silence. She said, "As you know, from day one I wanted so much for you to get married and have a baby in the proper way. Of course I am devastated that you have decided to do it this way. But there is nothing much that I can do, it is your decision and I respect that. As a woman, and also as a mother, I do understand how important it is for you to have a baby in your life so please go on with your plan. I am behind you all the way and will pray day and night for your success. I just want to see you get pregnant soon and bring out the little one into this beautiful world, with the happiness that you always wanted. It doesn't matter if it is with a father or without a father, we will give the child a life full of love. What can we do, things do not always happen the way we plan. Remember, God is always with you!"

My heart stopped beating. I was really shocked to hear these words come out from my mother's mouth – I had never expected this at all. This wasn't my mother, the mother that I knew before always followed the religious way, especially as she lived in the countryside. She wouldn't have wanted people to talk badly about me if I had a baby without a father. Well! She really surprised me; my mother was now starting to understand that we were now in a new generation. She talked freely about her opinions, which I was really proud of her for and I was very happy with the way she was thinking. I had a smile on my face as I was so full of happiness because of her support. I can't tell her how appreciative I was for her encouragement.

Suddenly her voice sounded a bit disappointed and she said, "How about Giovanni?"

My mum adored Giovanni as he had done so many good things for her. I had explained about Giovanni to my mother, I had told her that he was such a kind person and that he had such a good heart. He looked after my life very well but he didn't care about my heart. And that didn't make me happy. He cared about his situation and his wife more than he cared about the person who he shared his life with. If he had cared, I'd have never suffered like that. For many years I had been waiting for him and at the end he still hadn't given me what I wanted. I didn't think he cared, because he already had two children of his own. If he cared for and loved me, he would have given me the things that I asked for to make me happy. Every day I screamed for help. I had so much pain inside, I would cry without tears and every day I asked myself, Why has he put me through all this? Mentally and physically I was really hurt! My mother is my best friend and I talked to her about everything in my life, including my love life. Any boyfriend who I have been with, I have always introduced to her on the phone, but I have had to be an interpreter because my mother can't speak English other than a few words, which are 'Yes', 'No', 'By'e and 'How are you?' But she likes the words 'I love you' the most. Surprise! Surprise! She understands the meaning and she is very flirty when she says those words to my boyfriends, bless her!

Any personal things in life, I will ask my mother's opinion and she is the first person who I go to, to discuss these with. Sometimes she agrees, sometimes she doesn't and sometimes we have arguments on the phone because we both have very strong characters.

I really felt for her and I said, "Mum, I am so sorry but I have to do it this way and if you don't want to tell your two sons and our relatives the truth, you can make up a story."

Then my mother said, "NO! I am not going to lie, I will tell the truth, all the truth. There is nothing wrong with what you are going to do so don't worry about that."

I was so happy, my mother was becoming more understanding about life now, and that was amazing. Before I hung up the phone I said to her, "Mum, I hope – no, I am sure – that one day I will married. I can still make your dreams and my dreams come true, and I will never give up hope, Mum."

My mother said only a few words: "Insaallah! And I pray for you as I always did."

I am a forgiving person and always accept people's apologies, even when I am hurt. I needed someone to be around and to share what I was going through in life. I am a very independent person but wasn't in this situation; I couldn't take it. So for that reason, and also the fact that I still cared about him, I accepted Giovanni back into my life. It wasn't easy and I hoped he knew how much he had hurt me. Because of all the damage that he had done to our relationship, I was left in so much pain. On the other hand, he was the only person I had who I could share my situation with. I knew that I could rely on him for anything because he was the person who could always help me, whatever I needed. He loved me and wanted to be with me, but he was also married and had children, and that wasn't fair on me.

With my mother's blessing, and with Giovanni around, I had a lot more confidence to go through with it. Giovanni helped me search for fertility clinics on the internet and get all the information that we needed. At that time I just focused on starting the treatment as quickly as possible, without wasting any more time. The appointment was made to see the doctor a few days later, on the 8th June 2010. My first appointment was at eleven thirty in the morning. As I needed someone at that time, of course Giovanni came along with me. He was willing to do everything for me except have a baby in the natural way. It hurt me a lot because I had waited for five years, and at the end he had brought me to this place. We were in the waiting room with a few other patients. In my head were a million questions and at the same time I was so worried about what was going to happen after the test. Giovanni sat in front of me with his eyes sticking out like a frog, his curly hair like spaghetti and his face flat like a pancake. I hate him so much, I thought, for what he has put me through. Suddenly a tall, white-skinned nurse walked into the room and called my name: "Gina Abdul Wahab!"

As soon as I heard my name, my nerves started to move in every part of my body, and then I looked at her and said, "Yes! That is me."

Then she said, "Follow me, the doctor is waiting for you."

I followed her, climbing the steps to the room where the doctor was waiting for us. She was very friendly and chatted with me a bit, which calmed my nerves, and she was very funny, which put a smile on my face. As soon as she pushed the door, I saw a lovely middle-aged man, who stood to welcome us with a friendly smile on his face that made me less worried. He shook hands with me and Giovanni then politely asked us to sit. He looked like a very nice man. The conversation began with a few questions and then we came to my age and of course he was honest. But I became so sensitive and emotional that I burst into tears in front of him. I looked at Giovanni. Hell! Only God knows how mad I was, I just wanted to kill him. Because of him I was at this place. The doctor tried to calm me down and handed me a glass of water, then after a few minutes I managed to speak.

He started to examine me. He looked at me with a smile and said, "Good news! Everything is fine so you still have a chance to get pregnant, but we still need to take your blood."

Even though he had given me good news, I was still not confident. I kept asking myself, Why has my period not come for three months? Anyway, after having the blood test, I told the doctor that I had decided to have IVF treatment and freeze my eggs for the future. I was so happy when he told me that I could start the treatments straight away, if that's what I wanted. So my next appointment was made for a few days' time.

Three days later I was at the clinic at five in the evening. I waited just ten minutes then in came the nurse who had entertained me on my first visit. With a smile, she asked me to follow her as the doctor was ready to see me.

When I entered the room he was already standing with a smile on his face. He said, "Hello! How are you, madam?"

I replied, "I am fine, thank you."

He said, "Well! Have a seat. I have good news for you."

My heart started thumping, I just couldn't wait for him to tell me what the good news was about.

Then he said, "I have your blood test results and they show that your hormone levels are very high. For your age, this is very good, I am very happy."

I was very happy to hear about my blood test. Then he explained to me how the treatment worked, which is why I was not looking forward to it. Before I started the treatment I had to be admitted to hospital for a day for further tests and the results would come a week after. I knew for sure that I wanted to do it but at the same time I was so stressed. I hated waiting, it made it more painful inside and sometimes I couldn't be myself. I was all alone at home. I cried, I laughed, I screamed and I talked to myself. Sometimes I just wanted to end my life. But I am a strong person, and that is the character I have had all my life. While my head was a mess, suddenly, out of the blue, my period came after three months. WOW! I was over the moon with relief, I felt like I had won the lottery.

The time had come; I had to be at the hospital at nine in the morning. Luckily the hospital was not very far from where I lived. Giovanni took me, of course. I hate hospitals and I hate needles. Funnily enough, the more I hate these two things, the more I get them. Brilliant! We were in the waiting area, waiting for the nurse to come to take me to the room where I was going to stay for a day. Not long after, I saw a male nurse walking towards us. He asked a few questions then took us to the room and left us alone. I sat in bed and looked at every corner of the room. I thought, what am I doing here? Then I looked straight at Giovanni and all of a sudden my mind went blank. Without reason, I lost my temper and became so aggressive towards him. I could feel my heart bleeding. He had hurt me badly; I couldn't even stand on my own two feet. He had no idea how I felt at that moment. I wished I could do it on my own so I didn't have to see his face. I just couldn't stop asking myself, what have I done so wrong that would make him willing to see me go through with all this? I almost exploded but I tried to hold myself together as much as I could, and tried to be nice as I could. He is here with me and I am not on my own, I thought, and I do appreciate all that he has done for me. Well! So he should have anyway. We were in the room for more than two hours. It was such a long wait and I hate waiting. Suddenly someone knocked on the door and I said, "Come in."

Despite the fact that we had been waiting two hours, in walked my doctor with a big smile on his face. He said, "Sorry I am a bit late! Are you ready?"

I thought, yep! You are very late! Anyway, I replied, "Yes! I am!"

Then he said, "So see you in theatre."

After thirty minutes the nurse came and took me to theatre. I didn't say anything to Giovanni before I left and didn't even look at him, I was just too angry. When we got to theatre my stomach started feeling sick with all the worry. So many questions were spinning round my head. I just hoped everything was going to be OK. They were ready to start. There were a few people around me and the doctor and nurse tried to talk to me. They asked me a few questions while giving me an injection of anaesthetic. Slowly I began to feel drowsy.

I could hear a few women's voices and one of them mentioned my room number. I tried to open my eyes but I was feeling so drowsy, but I knew I was not still in my room. I could feel someone pushing my bed and I knew they were taking me to my room. Soon they made sure everything was OK and then left me on my own. A few minutes later I saw Giovanni walk in towards me. Surprisingly I was feeling OK, and feeling hungry. Soon after I had eaten I just wanted to go home, I couldn't stay in the hospital any longer. I thought resting in my own bed would be much better.

Two weeks after the operation I had go back to the clinic for my results. On my way to the clinic, I was so worried. It could be good news, and that would make me very happy. But if it was bad news, I wasn't prepared to hear that. When we were in the room with the doctor, he decided to give me the bad news first, which made me so frustrated. But the good news was, I could still go for IVF treatment, and that brought me so much happiness. The doctor explained to us how the treatment worked and gave me the pill to start straight away. To begin with, I had to take the pill for a week then the injections started – every day in my ass – to produce the eggs. I hate needles, so Giovanni helped me to do it. He injected me every day in my ass. I thought, thank you for your kindness, Giovanni! Why can't you do better than this, rather than sticking a needle in my ass? This is really sick. After a week of injections, the scans started every day, which I also hated. This treatment really made my hormones change and it made me become so aggressive sometimes. I couldn't focus on anything and my brain became crazy, and my mind kept changing every single minute. I couldn't be myself at all, and sometimes I did stupid things. I thought, come on, Gina, be strong, you're almost there. After three weeks of treatment, my eggs were ready for collection. I was so happy, I just couldn't wait for it all to be over.

23rd August 2010. The moment that I had been waiting for had come. I had to be at the hospital by seven in the morning. All the way to the hospital my mind just prayed and hoped that I could produce at least three eggs, but if there were more it would be much better. I tried to block out what the doctor had said about my age, which was that if I was very lucky I would produce three eggs, but if I could produce one or two he would be very happy. I know that my thoughts were negative, but he had left me very worried.

We were at the hospital on time and of course Giovanni came with me. I had been to the hospital many times and I still hated hospitals, but this time was the worst. I was worried and scared; I had never felt like this before in my entire life. At this stage I wanted my sister, Nurul, to be with me because she is the person who can give me so much confidence. We were waiting for someone to call us. I could see the gentleman walking towards me; I was sure he was the person who would call me. Yes! I was right. He smiled and introduced himself to us and asked a couple of questions. Then he took us to the room where I was going to stay and get ready for the moment of truth. While I was waiting, a few different nurses entered the room and asked me a few different questions. They were followed by a doctor, who was going to collect my eggs. Then they left me and Giovanni alone in the room. They would be back in an hour's time to take me to theatre. After fifteen minutes the phone in my room rang. I let Giovanni answer. I was sure he was talking with someone from the hospital, but I had no idea what they were talking about.

As soon as he hung up the phone, he excused himself because the doctor wanted to see him. I asked him, "Why?"

He smiled and said, "To give them what they need."

I looked at him and smiled. I smiled not because I was happy, but because I couldn't believe that he would choose do it behind the curtain. How could he? I was shocked and didn't say a word, I just looked at him when he left. I was on my own in the room feeling so hurt and so confused, thinking, why does he make my life so difficult? Why does he never feel sorry for me? I really couldn't understand. However, I was really thankful for him giving me something that I needed. I wished he would do it in the proper way. Why had he always worn protection when we were together so I would not get pregnant, when this would be his child anyway. Why hadn't he discussed with me in the first place that he wanted my child in that way? I thought I just wanted to freeze my eggs for the future. And he also never talked about his personal life and that is something which I was not very happy about.

I could hear someone trying to open the door and I knew it was Giovanni. I tried to keep myself as cool as possible and I tried to have a conversation with him but every single word just made me mad. I tried not to cause an argument but when I looked at him, I just keep asking myself the same question: why doesn't he give me a baby in the natural way rather then putting me through such a lot of pain, and wasting such large amount of money? WHY? WHY? WHY? I really couldn't get the answer. The only answer that he kept giving me was about his wife and his children, but now he was giving me his baby. It was something I couldn't understand and I never will.

Life Behind the Silence

Suddenly someone pushed my door open without knocking. It was a nurse and she asked me, "Are you ready, Gina?"

I thought, that was rude, entering my room without my permission, but I replied, "Yes!"

She said, "Follow me."

I said, "OK! But can I go to the bathroom first?"

She allowed me to do so. It was just an excuse because I was pissed off with her for making me wait so long so now I would let her wait for me. When I came out she was standing right near the door like a soldier, her face ruddy. I was sure she was either having a period or problems with her boyfriend; mad woman. Didn't she know that I had more problems than her? That is the reason I hate hospitals, so many people have mental illnesses. The sooner I got out of there, the better. So before she exploded I quickly followed her and left Giovanni without saying a word, it was just too painful at that moment. On the way to theatre, I started to feel sick and my body became weak because I was so worried about the amount of eggs I had produced. Yet again I was spending the day in the place which I hated so much but it was my decision. As usual a few people were around me, asking me a little bit about my life, then within a few seconds I was in a different world. The next thing, I opened my eyes and I was in a different room. Without doubt I knew things had been done. I just wanted to be sent back to my room. I was tired laying there listening to the nurses talking and laughing around me. I needed to rest in peace. Thank God, someone eventually took me to my room. After a few minutes Giovanni walked in, but I couldn't even open my eyes or say a word. I felt so weak, but I was disturbed by his phone text tones. As soon as I opened my eyes he quickly put the phone away and that made me so annoyed. How could he do this? I lay in bed in pain. Why doesn't he focus on me rather than his phone, I thought. I didn't trust him at all because he had lied to me hundreds of times and he would do it again. I was so paranoid and an argument began straight away and continued without stopping.

Someone knocked on the door while we were in the middle of our argument. I said, "Come in!"

We quietly pretended nothing was happening between us. The doctor introduced himself then said, "Gina, we managed to collect three eggs but one of the eggs is destroyed so there are two eggs now. What you want to do with the eggs?"

As it had been my decision from the beginning, of course my answer was to freeze it. But we had a slight problem. The doctor wanted to inject both of my eggs then put them back in my womb the same day. I was shocked because Giovanni hadn't discussed anything about that with me. Yes, I did want to have a baby but not like this. Frankly, at that moment I was so confused. The doctor tried to explain the situation to me, he told me that it was for my own good because of my age, but I kept to my decision to freeze both of my eggs. I did understand that he was trying to help me but he didn't know anything about our relationship. For sure he was wondering why I didn't want to do it now rather than later. Twenty minutes he was with us but I was still sticking to my decision. Then he left us and asked someone to come and talk to me.

Not long after, someone knocked on my door. I said, "Come in!"

As the door opened, I saw a young blonde woman with a lovely smile walk towards me. She started to ask me questions. She was so lovely, so much easier to talk to than the doctor and she understood the decision that I had made. But then there was another problem, she had to go and check whether both of my eggs were healthy or not. After she left, I had a talk with Giovanni. To make it fair, I decided one of the eggs would be injected with his sperm, and that I was going to have both eggs frozen, and then I would have them transferred to my womb when he had discussed it with me properly. Suddenly someone knocked on my door again. I said, "Come in!"

It was the young woman who had come earlier; she was bringing news about my eggs. I was very nervous about the results, but then with a big smile she said, "I have good news for you, both of your eggs are healthy. So what you want to do?"

Phew! I was so relieved and so happy when she told me that, and I told her right away what I planned to do. She was very happy and said, "That is fine."

Then she left us in peace. As soon as the door closed we carried on arguing and continued all the way out of the clinic. I thought, what a fucking life I have had. Sorry for my language, but I was very upset with my life. On the other hand, I was the happiest person in the world because I could be a mother soon. I just wished I could share my happiness with someone. I know Giovanni was with me but for some reason I just couldn't share my happiness with him, especially as he never talked about our relationship. It was always me who would bring up the conversation about our life. But now I had had enough, I was too tired to talk to someone who didn't care about our life and who never thought about the future. I would make my own decisions about my life. I thought that was for the best.

Life Behind the Silence

A few days after they had removed my eggs, I had to go back to see my gynaecologist. On the way to the clinic I just hoped this was the last time I would have to go. Giovanni took me there but the relationship had not got any better. We arrived at the clinic, and he parked the car right in front. But before I jumped out of the car he stopped me and said, "Can we talk?"

I look at him and said, "What do you want to talk about?"

He said, "I am sorry for what I have done to you all this time. I want to start our relationship all over again."

As soon as I heard those words, that was it. I said, "What else have you lied about?"

I waited for him to tell me but he didn't say a word, instead he just looked at me like he was stupid. Anyway, I really had given up, I couldn't take any more so I told him that we had to go because the doctor was waiting for us. This time we had to wait a little longer than usual. I was sitting right in front of him and it made me so angry just looking at his face. I could have exploded at any time if he had opened his mouth and started asking me silly questions again. Thank God, he kept his mouth shut the whole time. After almost half an hour's wait, the doctor still hadn't arrived! The blonde nurse that we knew came to have a chat with us while we waited for the doctor to arrive, which was very kind of her and kept my brain occupied. Suddenly I saw the doctor walk in so I knew that any minute he would see me.

The nurse excused herself and went upstairs to the doctor's office. After a few minutes she came back and took us to see the doctor. As usual, when I walked in, he was already standing to welcome us, with a big smile on his face. "Congratulations," he said, "I am so happy about the news. Are you?"

Of course I said, "Yes! I am very happy too."

He asked me to sit and Giovanni too. He just couldn't wait to know what I had done with my eggs and I told him, "I have had them frozen."

He was really not happy with that. He asked, "Why did you freeze them? Why didn't you have them transferred into your womb? That is for the best if you want to get pregnant now rather than later."

I said, "Yes! I know but not now."

He looked at me in a strange way and asked, "Why?"

I explained to him a little bit about what was happening, but he still thought that Giovanni was right, which made my anger blow up. Without warning, I expressed my feelings with floods of tears. Then he shut his mouth, sat quietly in his chair and listened to my explanations. For once I felt so relieved because someone was really paying attention and listening to what I was going through. Giovanni didn't say a word but my doctor was so caring, he ran like a yoyo and got me a box of tissues and a glass of water. It was so funny the way he acted, it made me laugh even in the middle of my sadness. Then he sat and continued to listen to my explanation, like a counsellor, and he said, "If that is your choice I do understand but everyone makes mistakes, and so has Giovanni."

I answered, "Yes! Everyone makes mistakes but he has made a thousand mistakes and keeps lying to me. That's not a healthy relationship. I do love him, that's why I am here with him but where is my life, and happiness? That's all that I need."

I started to realise how much of his time I had taken, but he was very polite and didn't ask me to go, instead he listened and agreed with what I said. Before I went I apologised for taking up his time and I thanked him for understanding. He wished me all the best and said he hoped I made the right decision. I left the clinic feeling so happy because I had met someone who was so generous and who had given up so much of his time to listen and comfort me, even though he was a doctor. God bless him!

CHAPTER 27

Facebook

My holiday in Malaysia had come to an end so it was time to go back to where I belonged: London. My mother came along to the airport with her friend to say goodbye to me. I was sad to leave my mother behind but at the same time I was relieved because I didn't have to argue with her anymore. Before I left her I made sure she had enough money, food and everything for the whole year until my next visit. Even though I live a thousand miles away from her, she is still looked after. As long as I am alive, I will make sure that she has a good life. She never had a good life when she was young, even when she was married. So I will do everything in my power to make sure that she is happy. I know she doesn't love me as much as she loves her other children but I am just doing my job as a daughter to a single mother. There are loads of things that she has done to hurt me but I have kept silent about it all, because she is my mother and I would not do anything to upset her.

I had arrived in London and was looking forward to being back at my own place. I could do whatever I liked. Going back home to see my mother and the rest of family is not a holiday for me. There are too many things that I have to do for my mother. I was really exhausted when I got on the plane, I slept all the way to London. My body was drained as soon as I got home, it took me weeks to get back to my normal life.

1st January 2010: I had a few wishes for this year that I really hoped would come true. To have my brother back in my life, which would be everything that I could wish for, to have my book published and to have a husband and children, which had always been my dream. I hoped 2010 would give me the happiness that I had searched for all my life and that my dreams would come true. If I received all that, I would be the happiest person in the world. No words can describe how this happiness would feel. Every day I waited and hoped my wishes would become a reality. Waiting is one of the hardest things in life and I had been waiting all my life, but I was sure one day the waiting would be over and I would finally get what I wanted. I believed in myself and I believed in God.

My heart, my soul and my mind had always been with my brother Nazeri. I thought of him all the time and he always came to me in my dreams. In my dreams, we talked, we joked, we laughed and we cried; it seemed so real. I knew he was still in this world and that one day I would see him again, but only time would tell. I left him when he was sixteen but of course he would no longer be a young boy. He was such a good boy with such a big heart, but I couldn't even imagine how he would look now. I was always wondering, where is he? But I knew he was somewhere in this world. I could feel warm tears run down my cheeks. I had tried so many ways to find him but I had never had any succcess.

Whenever I thought about him, it would always ends in tears. I felt so guilty for leaving him on his own and now it was my responsibility to find him and bring him back to my mother. I knew I was wrong for taking him from my mother but at the time I just felt sorry for him. He was only ten years old but he worked harder than his two brothers. It hurt me to see him doing things that he was not supposed to be doing at his age. Because of that reason I took him away from my mother. After I left him, my brother didn't go home to visit the family. Of course both of my other brothers blamed me for him going missing. My mother missed him badly, she cried every time she talked about him. To see my mother crying hurts me a lot and my heart bleeds but I keep my feelings to myself and try to be strong.

There was one stage where I started searching for my brother on the internet almost every day. Then one day someone told me to join Facebook. I didn't believe in such things because you hear so much bad news about it. I thought it was impossible that Facebook could find my brother, who had been missing for seventeen years. I might have been a little bit old fashioned then, but eventually I thought, why not give it try? So without wasting anymore time I signed up to Facebook, added all my details then straight away searched for my brother's name but I couldn't find him. I tried over and over but it kept coming up with a picture of a different person. But I could imagine that my brother would be on Facebook. For what reason I'm not sure; did he even know how to use a computer? These questions were buzzing around my mind all the time. My brain still pictured him as a little boy. But seventeen years is such a long time, he should be a grown-up man now and he could have changed to be a different person, but I hoped not. I still remembered the tone of his voice, especially when he laughed, always with a sweet smile on his face.

But one day I received a message from someone on Facebook. It said: *Hey Gina! My name is Axel, how did you find me?*

I thought, this is very strange, why has he asked me this? When I looked at his picture... um! He came from Australia! I did not even know him, so why should I respond to him? Surely someone from facebook was trying to play me around. I ignored his message because I don't trust anyone.

The next day, I again received a message from Axel. *Gina! Do you know Nasir?*

My heart started thumping at the mention of my brother's name. But at the same time I thought, ummm... he is trying to be clever because I have a friend named Nasir, and of course he is Kazmin's friend. At that stage I didn't trust Kazmin. He was upset with me because I hadn't lent him money, so I was very suspicious about him. Also, I had friend who lived in Australia so all this made me very suspicious. If it's really true that he knows my brother, I thought, why doesn't he tell my brother and let him get connected with me? Why does Axel keep pestering me? This is really weird!

Once again I ignored his message but he didn't give up. Then he said, *If you are Gina, Nasir has been trying to find you for a very long time.*

Ummm...! Maybe I should find out who the hell this Axel is, I thought. I responded to his message. *Who are you?* I asked.

He replied, *I am Axel, his stepson.*

This really confused me but made me think twice; could I trust him? My question was, how could my brother have a stepson? Well! At that moment I couldn't get my head together. This is bullshit, I thought, I have no time to play games. For two days I ignored his message and I made up my mind to delete him from facebook the next day.

But then I received this shocking message: *Gina! Were you living in Kuala Lumpur, Malaysia before? Nas' mother's name is Harisun. He lived in Kulim and has two brothers, named Zambri and Redzwan.*

As soon as he mentioned the name Nas, my heart stopped and my whole body started shaking because I was the person who started to call my brother Nas. My heart couldn't stop thumping and at the same time I asked myself, is this real? At that moment my mind went blank and I couldn't focus properly. I tried to keep myself together but I desperately wanted to know about my brother so I replied, *Yes! I was living in Kuala Lumpur before but now I live in London. Anyway, how is my brother? And where he is? I've been searching for him all this time and missing him terribly so please can I talk to him now?*

Axel responded, *He is asleep now but you can phone him on this number and I will wake him up.*

I replied, *Thank you so much, I really appreciate what you have done.*

It was 11th February 2010 at 19.45, a cold, damp evening. I was very nervous but excited at the same time as I impatiently tried to call him. I had tried a few times but hadn't got through. I started to grow suspicious but then I realised it was my mistake; because I was so excited, I had been dialling the wrong code. I tried again and this time the phone rang. My heart started jumping as hard as the ringing phone, my mind tried to focus and and I whispered, God, please help me. I hope that it is truly my brother, please don't disappoint me. My hand was sweating, my nerves completely out of control and I couldn't even stand.

Suddenly someone picked up the phone and a male voice answered. I didn't know who it was but he said that he was Nas. I was not too sure as I didn't recognise his voice because it been such a long time. I just couldn't wait for the moment of truth so I started asking him many questions to make sure that he truly was my brother. To all my questions, he gave me the correct answer. I thought, yes, he is my brother but my question was, why has he spoken in English with me all along, why doesn't he speak Malay? Ummm...! That was a bit strange! To put my mind at rest I asked, "Can you speak Malay?"

He answered, "NO!"

On hearing that my heartbeat dropped. I was very disappointed because I thought, that's it, he's not my brother. I was so frustrated because I had started to believe that I had found him, but I obviously hadn't. But something told me that I should ask one more question so I said, "How come you can't speak your own language? You were born in Malaysia and you were sixteen years old when I left you. I have been living in London for a very long time but I have never forgotten our language."

Without hesitation he answered, "Well! I didn't speak Malay for a very long time."

I thought, come on! Don't give me that bullshit; you should know where you come from. He really pissed me off and I almost slammed the phone down but suddenly he laughed at something I had said.

Life Behind the Silence

Hearing his laugh made my heart jump high and I was suddenly screaming, saying, "Yes! You are my brother, I remember your laugh now, it is you!"

The more he laughed, the more it brought my memory back. I burst into tears and I just couldn't stop screaming. I couldn't believe that I had been speaking to my brother for the first time in seventeen years; it was a miracle. We talked and asked each other about our lives over the past seventeen years, there were so many things that we needed to catch up on. But because of the big time difference I had to let him go to bed even though I wanted to talk more. But we arranged that we would speak again in the next few days, on his day off.

After I hung up the phone, I sat like a statue for a minute, my mind still in shock; I couldn't think anything at this stage. I was full of happiness and had a big smile on my face as I tried to make myself believe it. I kept asking myself, is it really happening? Or I am dreaming? I pinched every part of my body; it was pain and it was real. My head felt crazy and all night I thought only of him so that I was barely able to sleep. The next morning I felt so alive, like a new person with a new life, and I felt like I was walking in the air; the feeling of shock was still in my body.

Before I started to do anything, I had to call my mother to let her know that I had found my brother. When I told her she screamed and cried hysterically. She asked me how I had found him, and I had to explain to her about Facebook. Obviously she didn't understand but she couldn't stop asking me when I would bring my brother back home. She asked many more questions and I had to explain everything to her in detail to put her mind at rest. My mother couldn't wait to see my brother and every day she put me under a lot of pressure. But I couldn't force my brother, he had grown up, I could only talk to him; the decision was his.

The day came when he was going to add me on Facebook so I could see his pictures. I just couldn't wait to see what he looked like. Before I started my day, I went straight on my computer and checked Facebook. As soon as I saw his picture, my heart started beating faster. God! It was him. His face hadn't changed much, although he had of course grown into a man. Gosh! His face was so chubby and the high cheekbones that he used to have had disappeared. My dreams had come true, thanks to Facebook and to Axel. No words can describe how happy I was to have my brother back in my life.

I called him once a week, on a Tuesday, which was his day off work. We had so many things to catch up on after seventeen years. For the first week our conversation focused on our lives and family. Of course some emotional stories ended with tears and happy stories ended with laughter, it was wonderful. We talked for hours as we have a lot in common. Our relationship hadn't changed, he was still the person who I could talk to and share a lot of things with. As well as phone calls, we also sent each other messages on Facebook almost every day. We talked about our good and bad days and he always reminded me to eat and told me not to work too hard. WOW! That was so wonderful and new for me because none of my other family members care about me; my other two brothers have never said anything like that to me. To hear my brother say something like that made me feel strong and gave me so much more confidence about life.

I found out my brother lived with his partner, and that he had been in a happy relationship for many years. His partner had one son, Axel, and one daughter, named Samantha. My brother had gone home a couple of years before but hadn't found my mother. As my mother rents her houses she had moved around a lot, then after that he didn't go home again because he had a problem with his visa. Of course I didn't tell my mother about my brother's personal life. As we come from a Muslim family, my mother would have been really upset if she had found out that my brother was living with a woman without being married. I didn't want to lie to my mother but I did it for a good reason. In fact, now I remember that some of the witchcraft said about my brother was true.

He has his own restaurant call Locked Grill and he is the chef. I never knew that he liked to cook. The Nas that I knew was so laidback, especially with cooking, which he knew nothing about, but now he is a chef. I couldn't believe it. But as we talked I found that something was wrong with him, because sometimes he became so grumpy, like an old man. He was always moaning about his work, telling me that every day he had to go shopping on his own, then prepare the food and cook on his own. He was doing that routine on his own for almost four years without any break. It was bloody hard work. He worked hard, from late morning until the early hours and on the weekend from seven in the morning. He managed to sleep only a few hours. He was doing that just for his partner and her children and at the end of the day he had nothing in his life. I felt so sorry for him, he had no life and no future. My brother is a very nice person, which is why someone could easily take advantage of him. But I couldn't get involved and tell him what to

Life Behind the Silence 191

do because they had been together as a family for many years. His partner had looked after him more than me so I should be grateful for that.

I knew my brother was a hard worker, he had been since he was a little boy. When he lived with my mother, he had to wake up at five in the morning and cycle from house to house selling cakes and sweets to help my mother buy daily basics for the family. My other two brothers didn't want to help at all. At that time I didn't earn much money so couldn't help my mother much, but I gave what I could. My heart broke to see my brother working like that, so I decided to take him to live with me. At that time I had no idea how big a responsibility it was to look after my brother. I still remember when he found out that I was going to take him to Kuala Lumpur to stay with me, he was over the moon. He couldn't stop smiling, he looked like a monkey who had been given bananas. I had a little car at that time so I drove back to the city. The journey took about seven hours but I had fun driving and seeing my little brother beside me, so happy about his new life, made me happy. I couldn't predict how our life was going to be but I hoped for the best.

Now, hearing about his adventurous life, I was so proud of him. My brother was now a grown-up man, he was very mature and had a good sense of humour. He always talked about his dream. He loved golf, it was his passion. He played very well, in fact he wanted to become a professional golfer one day and play for his country, Malaysia, and the country that he lives in now, Australia. He practised hard, even though he was busy with work. He tried to share his time between work and golf as much as he could. I was so happy for him and willing to give him whatever support he needed. It was amazing to hear my brother dream and I wished him all the best for his career, because I knew how passionate he was about his golf.

My brother had had enough of his work; he was tired, he was not happy and he needed to think about his future. For these reasons he decided to sell the restaurant. That news made me so happy, as it meant he could concentrate on playing golf professionally. My little brother used to have much less of a temper than me and my other two brothers. He never knew how to argue and always had a smile on his face. Well! That was before; I didn't know about now, he might have a worse temper than all of us. But he was still very humble and down to earth. That had always been his character and I hoped he was the same person that I used to know. My mother always used to say nice things about him, and she always mentioned that he never answered her back when she got angry. But Redzwan and Zambri, and me especially, we have really bad tempers. If my mother got angry with me, I would answer her back with hundreds of words and I can be very stubborn. Every time my mother told me that my brother was very clever, because as soon as he saw her hold the stick, he would cry before she hit him, which made her feel sorry for him and then not have the heart to hit him, I thought, what a cheeky boy.

The brother that I had known seventeen years before was a very calm and quiet boy. He was still the same person but with a totally different character, but in a good way. When we had conversations on the phone he could be a very cheeky boy. He loved to tease me all the time, copying the way I talked; for instance, I always said, 'You know what?' Then I would pretend to be upset. He was so happy and had a big laugh. I thought, you little monkey, then he would talk to me nicely. But anyway, I was happy to know that I could make my brother happy. It was like a game; I teased him back – about the way he talks, the way he walks and especially the way he eats. As is the Muslim custom, we used to eat with our hands when we were kids, so I reminded him: "Hey! I still remember when you were a kid, the way you ate like an Indian. Every time single time you put the food inside your mouth, you would always stick your tongue out and point one finger out to nowhere, it was so funny. Who were you pointing at anyway?"

I cracked myself up, then I realised it was only me laughing. He kept silent but then said, "That finger pointing out was a warning, it meant get away from my food, and be careful around my legs because they are very well trained in karate and I have a black belt."

I said, "Woops! Whatever!"

Ee ended up laughing together and I thought, he has no idea how happy I am to have him back in my life.

Thank you to Facebook; what would I have done without it? Thank you to Facebook for making my dreams come true. My life had definitely changed. Thank you for creating a space where I could find my missing brother and thank you for bringing him back into my life. I was now on top of the world; no one can ever imagine how happy I was.

Life Behind the Silence

CHAPTER 28

Waiting

It had been four months since I had found my brother Nazeri on Facebook and we still hadn't seen each other! I was in London and he was in Australia. Well, for me the distance was not a problem. I was missing him badly and wanted to fly out as soon as I had found him. I wanted to surprise him, to fly to Australia without telling him. But what if he didn't want to see me? Or he could be a different person, who knows? Also, he always told me that he was very busy with work and hardly had time for himself. One day when we were on the phone, I said, "Can I come to Australia to visit you?"

He said, "Well! We will see."

I was very disappointed but I completely understood, seventeen years is such a long time. He definitely needed time. But I wondered, doesn't he want to see me after seventeen years? Well! Of course I was very sad but the most important thing was that I had my brother back in my life, so I would wait until he was ready.

I started making my own plan. I thought I could ask him to come to London to see me, then from London we could both go back to Malaysia to see my mother and the rest of the family. Dear Lord! Surprisingly, he agreed to my plan. I was so pleased, I just couldn't wait for him to get to my place. I hate waiting, especially waiting for something that I never imagined would happen to me. At that moment I felt crazy and every day I hoped he would come very soon. I was so worried in case he turned up as a surprise, like I had planned to do to him. So I tidied up the spare room and emptied one of my cupboards, so that he could use it for his clothes.

The most upsetting thing was when he told me about his work problem. For three years he had run the restaurant and in that time he had never taken a break. It really hurt me when I heard that. I decided I would try the best I could to help him.

Every day I would sit in the room that I had prepared for him and imagine that he was already there. As I live in a two bedroom flat there was nothing that I could do to make it more exciting to welcome him. But I did clear things up in the kitchen. I went through some of my special health food and replaced it with some unhealthy food for him. As he was a master chef, I didn't want him to find out about my food, or he would swear like Mr Gordon Ramsay.

22nd of June 2010. It was a bright, sunny Tuesday afternoon but I was indoors. I was suffering with hay fever. I kept sneezing almost every minute, my eyes were itchy and I had a runny nose. I was having an easy day, chilling out on my own watching the France versus South Africa in the World Cup and at the same time changing the channel to see Wimbledon. I was very sad about the football because South Africa were losing I wanted them to win because they are a poor country and were the host nation but hey! That is the game. I love tennis even more. I did used to play sometimes but I wasn't a very good player. My eyes were busy watching tennis on the TV, while my mouth was busy talking to my brother. Our conversation started with the World Cup. Surprisingly he said, "France! France are bad!" Bad! I thought he would support them because his partner is French.

I had waited day after day, week after week and month after month, and I was still waiting for my brother to come to London as he had promised. Every time we had a conversation, I asked him, "When are you going to come?" And his answer was always, "It will be soon, very soon."

I was sure he got fed up with my nagging but I was getting fed up with waiting and I didn't know how much longer I would have to wait. I felt like 'soon' would never come. So with my sisterly powers I forced him to tell me what his problem was. It took quite some time for him to tell me what exactly the problem was but at last he revealed the truth: he had no money for the flight. His business was having problems and he was having a tough time with money. Without question I was willing to help him pay for his ticket. At the beginning he refused but as a sister I had a little bit of power. I was tough with him about my decision and in the end he had no choice but to accept my offer. I was so happy when he agreed to come with me to visit our mother.

Calmly he said, "I am doing this just for you, sis!"

I said, "Thank you, I really appreciate it and I am doing it for you and mum."

He did mention to me that he didn't want to go home on his own, only with me. I wondered why. Surely something had been upsetting him. I know I was forcing him to go home but I had to because my mother was pestering me all the time. I promised her that I would bring him back home on the day we had celebrated. My mother had been missing him for a long time and of course he missed my mother too. Our family had been torn apart when we were so young. As everyone was getting older, my heart wanted so much to see our family together. As we had never had that experience in our lives, I would like to see all of us gathering together, having a meal, laughing and having a fun time. That is what I had been missing and that was my big wish.

I transferred the money for my brother so he could return with me to our family. Within a week he received the money. September 9th; it was a perfect time to go home because it is when Muslims celebrate Eid (in Malaysian we call it Hari Raya but in Arabic they call it Eid), and for him to be with the family on that special day would be wonderful. I would do whatever it took to see my family happy, especially my mother. I was so happy my brother would celebrate with us.

It was a month until Muslims would celebrate Eid, so every Muslim around the world was busy preparing to go home to be with their family. To be safe I had booked my ticket in advance. I knew my brother's character, he is very careless, so I had to remind him every time I spoke to him to book his ticket. I was just so worried about him. Soon he told me that he already had his ticket, so then I stopped worrying.

I was so excited and couldn't wait to see him and because of that I packed my luggage one month before my departure to Malaysia. I packed all his clothes and the golf set that I had bought for him. Unfortunately I couldn't take his stuff with me but Giovanni was willing to help me. Giovanni would arrive in Malaysia two weeks after me. I am thankful to him for his generosity, he gave me so much moral support, which I really needed. Every day a million questions were in my head. I thought that me and my brother would have a million things to ask each other after seventeen years. I still couldn't believe this was happening to me. Life can sometimes be really wonderful. Some people are lucky and some people are not and I am one of the lucky people, thank God!

I decided to fly one week before he arrived; just because my journey would take longer than his. I would stay at the hotel in Kuala Lumpur and wait until he arrived.

It had been almost seven months since we had found each other and for seven months we had chatted on the phone almost every week. But now the time had come. It was 2nd September 2010, my flight to Malaysia was at ten in the evening and it took thirteen hours. My mother and the rest of my family didn't know that I was bringing my brother back home, it was going to be a surprise!

I remember one time I was in Malaysia for four days but still continued phoning my mother as usual. As she only knows how to answer the call but not to find out where the call is coming from, she thought I was calling her from London. Exactly a week I was in Malaysia before I went to visit her. I arranged for my cousin Kamal to wait for me at the airport and take me to my mother. I arrived and stood right in front of the gate then I gave her a call. Within minutes she picked up the phone and I said, "Mum! What do you have for dinner?"

She told me that she was cooking a very simple dish that night. Then I asked her, "Do you have enough food for me? Because I am very hungry."

Her voice sounded a bit suspicious and she said, "Where are you?"

I said, "I am in front of the house so open the door, I want to come in."

She started shouting and saying, "You don't play with me."

I said, "I am not playing, just open the door."

Then I saw her rush to open the door. I was standing right in front of the gate. As soon as she saw me, she started to scream and said, "It is a ghost."

Her phone was still at her ear. I cracked up when I saw her reaction; she thought I was a ghost! In fact, I could really have been a ghost because it was already midnight. Anyway, it was hilarious and I loved it, and now I always do it to whenI return home. Well! She should know me better by now.

Anyway I was boarding the plane and making myself comfortable. The first thing that I do when I get on a flight is to pray that I have a safe journey. The truth is, I only pray when I am on a plane because I am really scared of flying. My seat was in the middle and either side of me the seats were empty. I hoped a smelly person would not sit beside me. Then I saw an old woman walking towards me. She took her seat beside me on the right, which I was very pleased about. A minute later she was followed by a man in his late forties, who tokk his seat on the left. I looked at him, ummm...! Not bad. I was very pleased because he looked tidy and clean.

As soon as he took his seat he said, "If I fall asleep and my head falls on you, please push me away."

I smiled and agreed and thought, he's funny, he must be the sort of person who sleeps deeply, I just hope he doesn't start snoring. If he does, I will wake him. Suddenly the woman sitting beside me started chatting to me and asking me a few things. I thought, well, I have some company, but she talked a lot, she was non stop. She didn't even shut her mouth for a second and she didn't let me rest for a minute. But she was so funny, she made me laugh all the way. She had a good sense of humour. When I fell asleep, she covered me with a blanket so I did not catch a cold. I thought, hello! I am not a baby. But really I felt wonderful. She made me so comfortable; I felt that I had known her for a long time. She was so friendly and liked to talk but then it got too much for me and in the end I fell asleep and left her on her own.

I don't know how long I slept for but as soon as I opened my eyes, I saw that she was still awake and that now she was chatting with her husband on the next aisle. Quietly I asked her, "You don't sleep?"

She said, "NO! I never sleep on the plane; if I want to sleep, I need my own bed."

I thought, gosh! You have so much energy. As soon as I started talking, she immediately stopped talking to her husband and started chatting to me. That was funny. She was such a wonderful woman with a wonderful heart.

When the steward came around and gave us the menu for breakfast she asked me, "What are you going to have for breakfast?"

I looked at her and whispered, "Sorry I can't eat."

She raised her eyebrow and asked me, "Why?"

I told her it was the month of Ramadan so I had to fast, even though I wasn't actually fasting, it was just to give respect to the steward and the other Muslims who were fasting. She didn't agree with me, she wanted me to eat and she told me that she would ask for the food for me and give it to me to eat. I looked at her and laughed, it was so sweet of her but I couldn't let her do that. I asked for my breakfast myself in the end and she was so happy when I ate, bless her.

I told her that I was having on my period but she misheard and said, "What? You had no time to go to the toilet?"

I wondered why she said that to me then I told her again, "I am on my period and I have blood all over my trousers."

Then she said, "Ooo…! I thought you had no time to go to toilet and you weed in your trousers."

We both cracked up; that was hilarious. So many things happened and then she ended up talking to the man beside me, who had just woken up from his sleep. I was so relieved when they started talking as I could relax but I was stuck in the middle. They were from London and they both transferred at Kuala Lumpur airport to go to Australia.

The flight landed on time and we said goodbye to each other. I didn't want to end the short relationship that I had had with her and I hoped to see her again in the future. I walked out of the airplane and straight into arrivals. I started to feel the humidity and sweat started dribbling down my back, which I hate. After I had collected my luggage I went straight to book a ticket for myself and my brother to Penang in a week's time. Then I walked outside and jumped in a taxi to the hotel that I was going to stay at. The journey from the airport to the city took about one hour.

I was going to stay at Traders Hotel, my favourite hotel. Traders Hotel, Kuala Lumpur, is located in the heart of the city centre and offers easy access to the wonderful attractions of Kuala Lumpur. It faces the famous Petronas Twin Towers, which are a short distance away and provide the focal point for business and shopping.

I arrived at the hotel and, after paying, I walked into the room; it was about nine in the evening. I unpacked all of my things and hung up all my clothes, then my stomach was full of butterflys, which meant I needed food. I was too tired to go out so I called room service to make my order. I had a plate of chicken and rice, and enjoyed the food that I had missed for quite some time. Before jumping in the shower I stood in front of the window and looked at the wonderful Twin Towers, which were all lit up in the night, and saw how beautiful Malaysia is, apart from the hot weather, which I hate very much. Here I waited for my brother to arrive from Australia for another six days. Every day I kept myself busy with shopping, and of course I pampered myself with beauty treatments. After all, this was me, Gina, who always looks after herself and always wants to look good.

CHAPTER 29

Surprise Call

The day came when my brother would arrive from Australia. The moment that I had been awaiting for many, many years had arrived. My brother would be arriving at ten that night. I was going to wait for him at the airport and take him to the hotel so we could have one day by ourselves before going to see my mother and the rest of the family. Nine more hours and I would meet up with my little brother. At that moment, my nerves started to fill my body. To keep myself occupied I went to the gym and had a good workout, which made my body, brain and mind fresh so I could focus and give myself confidence.

I went back to my room and was feeling hungry. I wanted to order some food but instead I just grabbed some snacks because I was looking forward to having a good dinner with my brother that night. I still had plenty of time, so I slowly dropped my body on to the bed and had a little nap. When I woke up I checked the time; another five hours to go. I thought I should get up and start to get ready. I walked straight into the bathroom and suddenly my phone rang while I was brushing my teeth. I thought, who the hell is calling me at this time, shall I answer the call or not? Well! I grabbed the phone while my other hand was holding my toothbrush and my mouth was full of toothpaste. I answered, "Hello!"

My heartbeat stopped when I heard my brother's voice. "Hi, sis!"

I accidentally swallowed the toothpaste. Yuk! Then I jumped in and asked him, "Where are you? Are you going to surprise me or what? I was just going to get ready to go to the airport."

Then I heard him laughing. He said, "Sorry, sis, I missed my flight."

I still didn't believe it until he started to talk seriously. He said, "Sis, maybe this happened for a good reason but I will be there tomorrow night, we will arrive at the same time."

Well! Whatever his excuse was, it didn't surprise me at all, because that is him. Since he was a little boy he has been such a careless person, he is always late and forgets everything. He always made me angry when he was a little boy but he never cared less when people were angry with him, he would ignore them and walk away. And his character was exactly the same as before. I almost screamed at him when he told me that he had missed the plane. But because I hadn't seen him for seventeen years, I held my anger in; he was lucky. I had already booked a flight back to my mother for the next night, so I suggested he came a bit earlier so as not to miss our flight. But there was nothing he could do because that was the only flight he could take. Again I reminded him that he had to be there the next day night because it was our Eid celebration.

Before ending our conversation I teased him, saying, "Hey! For the past two weeks almost every day you kept reminding me to be at the airport on time and to not be late, so who is the worst?"

We both laughed and I said, "See you tomorrow night."

As soon as I hung up the phone I quickly got ready to go to the ticketing agency to change our tickets to the next day. I jumped in the taxi at the hotel and asked the driver to take me to the station to change the ticket. September is the month I was born, and it is also when Zamri and Nazeri's birthdays are, so we have a lot of celebrations. September is also the month of the rainy season in Malaysia. Every day it will rain and it lasts maybe one or two hours. That night it rained heavily and there was strong thunder and lightning every minute. I don't mind rain but I am very scared of thunder. Heavy rain makes the road full of traffic. I hate traffic as it makes it take such a long time to get to my destination. I was getting worried in case thete was no ticket available for the next day. Because of our celebration a lot of people were rushing back to every part of the city to be with their loved ones. I prayed everything was going to be fine. At that moment I was really mad with my brother. He doesn't worry about anything. All the pressure was on me, I worried about the ticket, about him and about my mother. It usually takes only fifteen minutes to get from the hotel to the ticketing agency but because of the traffic it took almost one hour.

At last I arrived at the station. I jumped out quickly but I asked the driver to wait for me so he could take me back to the hotel. I ran around trying to find the ticketing office. Soon I found it and queued for five minutes. Luckily it didn't take long because I had booked business class tickets. My brother is really spoiled by me. Thank God! Everything was fine and because they were business class they didn't charge me for the cancellation. My brother would arrive from Australia at ten twenty the following evening so I had to take the last flight, which was at five to midnight; the next flight was the next day so I had no choice. The flight would take about forty-five minutes then it would be another hour's drive to my mother's house. We should arrive at my mother's around three in the morning. The next day was Eid so I was pretty sure my mother would still be awake at that time. Usually on that night she will cook cake and some of her special dishes for the celebration.

As soon as I had finished I rushed to the taxi, which was luckily still there. He no doubt waited because I hadn't paid the fare yet. On the way back to the hotel I gave my brother a quick call. The phone rang and his partner answered. Well! Surprisingly his partner told me different story about why he missed the flight. Well, whatever the reason was, that is my brother. As I was calling from my mobile phone I tried to cut the conversation short. I was worried about my credit because I use pay as you go. I know his partner talks a lot so I found a good excuse to speak to my brother.

My brother said, "Hello, sis! How are you?"

I wanted to say, "No! I am not fine, you have given me a lot of hassle" but instead I said, "I am fine, thank you."

As I know that he can sometimes really take his time when he walks, and can be very slow, I told him, "As soon as you walk out of the plane, please walk quickly because we have to jump on the next plane to Penang. If we miss that flight, we'll end up sleeping at the airport because the next flight will be six in the morning."

He was not very happy about that and said, "Ah…! Sis! That is too rushed for me, can we stay one day at the hotel so I can spend time with you before we go back to see the family?"

I said, "That was my plan but now, NO! We have to go back because the next day is our Eid celebration so we have to catch the last flight tomorrow night otherwise we'll end up sleeping at the airport. You don't want to sleep at the airport, do you?

Then, unhappily, he said, "OK, sis! I will try."

What he didn't know was that I had made a plan for him so I said, "But not to worry, a week after the celebration we will return to the capital city and spend some time together before you go back to Australia."

As I know my brother's character very well, for the last time I reminded him again and said, "Please don't be late! When you get to the airport, please don't take your time walking around, make your steps bigger because we have to jump on another flight,"

Then I said, "See you tomorrow." I couldn't imagine the next night, as soon as his flight landed he must run like a rat. That was funny, especially with his leg, poor him!

When I arrived back at the hotel I went straight to my room. I just wanted to have a good night's sleep to clear my mind. As it was already programmed in my brain that I was going to see my brother that night, I was a bit disappointed. But hey! One day would not make any difference, I could deal with my emotions and another night of waiting for him, that is what life is about.

I hope the waiting will soon be over, I thought, you better get here, Nas.

CHAPTER 30

Meet Up After Seventeen Years

I had been staying at the hotel for one week waiting for my brother. I hoped he was not going to call me and tell me that he had missed the flight again, but I knew deep down that he would definitely would be there. I was feeling very fresh that morning after having a good night's sleep. Exercise is like a routine to me, so before I started my day I went to the gym to do my workout. I spent a good hour in the gym, which made me feel like a new person, and then I was ready to start the rest of my day. I went back to my room and started packing all my stuff. Hell! There were so many things that I had to pack, it looked like I had a family. I began to grow nervous, thinking that I was going to meet up with my brother that evening for the first time after seventeen years. I couldn't imagine what my reaction would be when I saw him. From then on my mind couldn't stop flying and my nerves couldn't stop jumping. I kept going to the toilet and drank many glasses of water to keep myself calm. I was all alone, wishing I had someone with me that could keep my mind busy. I kept breathing in and out; that was all I could do at that moment. I looked at myself in the mirror, smiled and thought yes! I'll be fine.

It was the time for me to check out and settle all my hotel bills. I took a hotel taxi to the airport; the journey took about one hour. My brain started feeling a bit tired and I fell into a deep sleep all the way, but suddenly my eyes automatically opened and there I was at the airport. As I had so much luggage, it was too heavy for me to carry so I let the taxi driver put it on the trolley. I thanked him and handed him a tip. He look at me and gave me a big smile. I wasn't really sure about that smile, he could have been smiling because he was happy to receive the tip or it could have been because he had seen how big and heavy my luggage was. He must have thought that I had filled up my luggage with rocks. In five hours' time my brother would arrive. I killed time walking around and did some shopping. I was so hungry but I couldn't simply order some food and eat because it was the month of Ramadan, when all healthy Muslims fast from sunrise to sunset. During this time they must refrain from all food, drink, chewing gum, any kind of tobacco use and any kind of sexual contact. Ramadan is the ninth month of the Islamic lunar calendar. Every day during this month Muslims around the world spend the daylight hours fasting. Malaysia has two seasons, the rainy season and summer, so in Malaysia Muslims have to fast for twelve hours a day for a month.

I love the month of Ramadan. Honestly, I hate to fast but somehow I managed to do it for one day at the beginning to welcome the fasting month and another day at the end of Ramadan to say goodbye to the fasting month. My mother would kill me if she knew about it. I still remember when I was very young, my mother always asked me to fast, which I did in front of her, but what she didn't know was that I was cheating behind her back; for the whole month I didn't fast. We have to start practising fasting at the age of eight or ten, or maybe even younger. I never fasted, especially when I had to walk an hour and a half to and from school in the hot weather. So when I was at home, I would make excuses to my mother, like every half hour I would go to the well to have a shower. My mother wondered why I had a shower so often. What she didn't know was that I was going to the shop to buy biscuits and then eating them at the well. I ate quickly before anyone came then I had a shower and at the same time drank the water. Sometimes I ate some food in the kitchen that my mother had cooked, then I made the food very messy so I could blame the cat.

As I grew older my character still never changed. At the time I worked as an aerobic instructor it was really hard for me to fast, as if I did I had no energy left to teach. Out of respect for Ramadan, even if someone can't fast for some reason, they can't eat in public. But I did something very naughty. As I looked like an Indian, I asked my Indian friend to give me a red dot. Then I put the red dot in the middle of my forehead so I looked like an Indian girl, and I went outside to have lunch freely in public without anyone noticing. Lucky me!

That was before but now, at the age of forty-four, I still haven't changed much. One day I had just arrived in Malaysia airport from London, and I went straight to the ticketing counter to book a ticket to Penang. They asked me to have a seat while they were issuing my ticket, which I did. I felt so thirsty so I got a drink. Without thinking about the fasting month, I drank straight in front of the staff and most of them were Muslim. I wondered why they were looking at me in a bad way. Soon I realised it was the fasting month and I slowly put the drink away, but it was too late. Obviously they knew I was Muslim because they had my passport. Well! There was nothing much I could do apart from ignore them, and as soon as they had finished I walked out quickly.

Anyway, I thought it may be time to break the fast at about seven fifteen, so I had no choice but to wait another fifteen minutes. I wish I was in London, where no one bothers about the fasting month, and I can eat anywhere I want without worrying. I sat in the café waiting for the time to go by even though I was not fasting. Out of respect for other Muslims, I wouldn't eat in public.

I really didn't know exactly what time the fast breaks in Malaysia so I walked towards one of the Malay guys who was working at the café and asked him, "Excuse me! At what time do we break the fast?"

He said, "Sorry, I don't really know but you can check at the office over there."

I gave him a look and said, "Well! OK!"

This really surprised me. He is Muslim, I thought, and he doesn't know what time we break the fast. He was definitely not fasting.

At seven nineteen the announcement was made that we could now break the fast. Straight away I jumped up to queue and I was the first one to make an order. I was very happy because I had my favourite dish, which is oxtail soup, chicken rice and rojak. Rojak is mixed fresh fruit with special spiced gravy; I love it. If I see these dishes, I never say no, I can eat them over and over and never get bored. I was so hungry I ate like a pig and cleared everything on my plate. After my meal I walked around to digest my food. There were another three hours to go until my brother's flight would be landing. I stood at Arrivals watching people passing by, feeling so nervous. I couldn't even stand still because my knees had started shaking, as I couldn't control my nerves. I whispered to myself, "Come on, Nas, where are you?" I just couldn't stop looking at the time, I looked almost every fifteen minutes. I can't explain how nervous I was and I have know idea how many times I went to toilet, even though I hadn't drunk a lot of water. Every time I looked at the time, it made my heart thump even harder. With one hour to go my feet were getting tired as I had been walking a lot, so I sat in one of the cafés just in front of Arrivals. I knew his flight had not landed yet, but I watched every single person who walked past. I had to have a lollipop to calm my nerves. With half an hour to go, I started to imagine him walking out of Arrivals with a big smile on his face. Man, this was weird! The time was getting even closer, any moment the flight would land.

I looked at the screen and saw that the flight from Perth had landed and my heart started jumping. My hands, my feet and my whole body felt cold, I was just too excited. I warmed myself up wandering around like a tiger in a cage. There were many people at Arrivals; of course they were waiting for their friends, family and lover sto arrive. But nobody knew the girl standing in a corner all alone, full of happiness and nervousness, waiting to welcome her brother who she hadn't seen for seventeen years. I saw people start coming out. They walked straight to their loved ones and hugged and kissed, and some of them were in tears. I watched them with happiness, I just couldn't wait for my turn. My brother would walk through this entrance any moment now. I kept looking at the time and after almost half an hour he still wasn't out. I really hoped he had not missed the flight this time, if he had I would not have known because I had checked out of the hotel and he didn't know my Malaysian phone number. I just prayed that he would turn up. I am not a patient person and I hate waiting. "Come on, Nas! Where are you? Hurry up! Bring your ass here; you should know that I am waiting for you." This made me even more nervous.

Suddenly I saw a young guy and straight away I knew that he was my brother but I hid myself in the crowd. I was pretty sure it was him because his face hadn't changed at all, but he had grown up into a good-looking young man, so different to when he was a little boy. My Lord! His face was very chubby and his belly looked like that of a woman who is five month's pregnant. His hair was in dreadlocks but I knew about that because he had told me before he came. He walked around trying to find me. I knew he would come my way so I readied myself. I stood right in the middle of the room and within a second he was walking towards me with a big smile on his face. This is him, I thought, as he was always smiling. We hugged and kissed each other and I just couldn't stop kissing his lips because I had missed him so much. People nearby were looking at us, they must have been thinking we were a couple because he was speaking with his Australian accent and me with my English accent. Well, not really an English accent, probably more a broken English accent. I touched his face and pinched his chubby cheek just to make sure it was really happening. At that stage my mind went blank, there are no words to describe how happy I was. I just wanted to scream to tell the whole world that I was a winner. My brother was there in the flesh; I had kept the promise that I had made to my mother. I was over the moon and so proud of myself.

We both checked our luggage in and I told the person working at the check-in desk, "This is my brother, we have just met up for the first time in seventeen years. I found him on Facebook." She just looked at me then turned to my brother with shock on her face. I just couldn't stop to telling everyone, that is how happy I was. On the way to the gate I just couldn't stop pinching his cheek and hugging him because I had missed him for such a long time. He just laughed and said, "Stop it! I am not a little boy anymore."

We only waited for a few minutes before boarding.

He smiled when he saw the seat that I had booked for him and said, "WOW! Nice seat."

I said, "Of course business class is a treat for you, and at the moment it is just for a short distance, but maybe one day I will be a millionaire then I can treat you to business class for a long distance flight."

Flights to Penang take forty-five minutes but we still managed to have a conversation. In business class they serve only a small sandwich and juice, but my brother asked for beer. With a smile the beautiful stewardess told my brother politely, "Sorry! We do not serve beer on short distance flights." The three of us started laughing.

I jokingly said to my brother, "G'day, mate. Sorry, no Fosters, mate!" We both laughed then the announcement was made that we would be landing soon.

At the airport my mother's friend was waiting to pick us up and take us back to my mother's house. But my mother still didn't know anything about our visit. Before my mother's friend came to the airport, I warned him not to tell my mother. I am not a bad person, I just wanted to surprise my mother and see her reaction when she found out that the person in front of her was the son she hadn't seen for the past seventeen years. My mother's friend is a lovely guy and very kind. He was there on time waiting for us. He is from Pakistan but had lived in Malaysia for quite some time. At one in the morning, he drove us to my mother's. The funny thing is, he can't speak English but he can speak my language. My brother can't really understand our own language, which I found very weird, but anyway I had to translate for both of them. If I was quiet, both of them were also quiet so I ended up having to talk and trying to make some jokes so they would laugh. Now I know it is not easy to be a comedian, it is a lot of work trying to make people laugh.

In ten minutes we would be arriving at my mother's home. I looked at the time; it was almost two thirty in the morning. I asked him to call my mother and say that he wanted to take something round now for the Eid celebration. He agreed and gave my mother a call. When she answered he said, "Assalamualaikum, Mammy! It's Omar here, are you still awake?"

I don't know what my mother told him but then he said, "OK! I am coming now to bring the curtain for you."

He hung up the phone then he explained to me that my mother was still awake and that she was now waiting for him. When we arrived in front of the house, Omar called again to let her know that he was there.

My mother switched the front lights on and I could see her trying to open the front door. I was very naughty, planning this with my brother and Omar. I told Omar to introduce my brother as his friend, and I told my brother to keep his mouth shut. Then I told them not to tell her that I was in the car. I just wanted to see what would happen.

I was sure my mother would believe Omar because my brother has dark skin and almost looks Pakistani. Anyway, both of them agreed to follow my plan. As soon as they got out of the car, I hid myself so my mother couldn't see me.

My mother walked towards the gate. While she tried to open the gate she looked straight at my brother then asked Omar, "Who is he?"

Omar said, "He is my friend."

As soon the gate opened my brother walked straight up to my mother and said, "Mum!"

My mother walk backwards trying to avoid my brother because he had come so close. She looked at my brother but still didn't recognise him, then she said, "Who are you?"

My brother said, "It's me, Adik."

When I heard that I was really disappointed and I thought, fuck! What is he doing? I jumped from the car and shouted, "MUM! That is Adik! Your son. I have brought him back to you like I promised."

She burst into tears like a baby and could hardly stand. My brother helped her to sit and calmed her down, hugging and kissing her. I was so happy and I kept asking her, "Why are you crying? You wanted him back and now I have brought him back to you so be happy." I said that just to make her stop crying.

My mother looked at me and shook her head then said, "You're always doing that to me, one day I will have a heart attack." I gave her a smile like a little girl.

Life Behind the Silence

We all went inside the house and had a long conversation. I told my mother how I found my brother and about my entire plan. My mother asked my brother a lot of questions: Why this? Why that? So many questions, all starting with 'why'? She told him how hard she had tried to find him and how worried she had been. There were a lot more things to talk about but time didn't allow us to continue, it was too late. It was five in the morning and everyone was tired. There would be plenty more days to talk about those past seventeen years, so my mother showed us to our rooms. As this was a new house, not even I knew where my room was. I had bought this house for my mother a year before but when I bought it, it wasn't ready to move into yet. I paid for the house outright so I don't have to worry about monthly mortgage payments. I gave my mother the keys and then I flew back to London. I was so happy that I could buy my mother a house because that is what she had wanted for so long. There was a smile on my face as I saw how happy she was, with the new house and with my brother. I thought, I am doing my job very well, I hope my mother appreciates all that I have done for her.

I could see my brother soundly asleep in the other room; he was surely very tired. I lay on my bed with my mother beside me, trying to answer a few of her questions, then my eyes slowly began to close and my mind began to fly away to a different world, I was so knackered. My mother was no doubt pissed off with me leaving her to talk on her own. If she was, sorry, madam! The night was over and tomorrow was another day.

CHAPTER 31

Celebration Day

My mother chose this house because it's surrounded and it is a corner house so it has more space than the other houses on the road. I could hear a few birds singing on the window ledge in front of my bed. As I had only had two hours of sleep, the birds' singing made me really annoyed. I jumped up from my bed, opened the door, stepped out on to the balcony then chased all the stupid birds away. I stood for a few minutes to make sure every single bird had gone then I went straight back to sleep. Suddenly this bloody bird brought a group of friends to the window ledge and they were singing even louder at me and were giving me such a headache that I started to scream. Shut up! No! It didn't work at all, they were getting even louder. I was sure that the first bloody bird that I had chased away went to tell all his friends and brought them all to disturb me, bloody pests. They happily continued singing so I didn't think I could sleep. I looked at the time and it was seven in the morning. Well! I guess it's time to get up then, I thought. I was sure my mother would be in the kitchen cooking all of her dishes for our Eid celebration that day. I went downstairs to find her and WOW! Surprisingly, my brother was already in the kitchen helping my mother with the cooking; of course, I thought, he is a chef. I had forgotten about that. I helped my mother too but I just chopped some onions, which makes me cry first thing in the morning. I usually wear sunglasses when I chop onions to stop myself crying but I worried my brother would laugh at me. I thought, I hate this. It wasn't in the kitchen long before I excused myself to go upstairs and dress up myself in the traditional Malay dress for our celebration day before anyone came. A few minutes later I could hear my brother's footsteps go into his room and then I heard him close the door. I thought he must also be getting ready before anyone came to see him.

Then someone knocked on my door. I said, "Come in."

My brother walked in and said, "Can I have a shower in your bathroom?"

I said, "Yes! Sure."

He walked into the bathroom. I could hear a few drops of water then I saw him walk out.

I looked at him and wondered what he had been doing in the bathroom. So I asked, "Did you have a shower?"

He said, "Yes!"

I said, "OK, but I only heard a few drops of water."

And he said, "Yes!"

I replied, "Ummm…! Are you sure you've had a shower?"

He looked at me and smiled and said, "Yeeeah!"

And he went off to his room but I thought, he just washed his face, lazy boy.

One hour later and I still hadn't finished getting myself ready and I could hear someone's voice from downstairs. Well! It didn't bother me, I just continued doing my own thing. Suddenly someone knocked at my door and I said, "Come in!"

There I saw my brother Zambri, who hadn't talked to me for more than three years. He came towards me and gave me a big hug and kisses and said, "Sorry."

Because of our Eid celebration, and also because my brother Nazeri had come home, I thought, apology accepted, even though my heart hurt for what he had done, but then he is my brother. I burst into tears for a moment but then I tried to hold my sadness in my heart on this important day. We exchanged a few words then he left me alone to finish getting ready. I promised myself if I brought my brother Nas back to our family, I would put a smile on my face and be happy as much as I could. I would do everything that my mother asked and I would bear my sadness in silence. I would try to be a wonderful daughter to my mother and a lovely sister to my brothers and sister, especially to my brother Nas. He didn't know about the family situation so I would try to make this happy time the best I could for him.

In a year we celebrate New Year twice. The festival most grandly celebrated by Muslims the world over is Aidiladha. In Malaysia, it is more commonly known as Hari Raya Korban or Hari Raya Haji and a public holiday is observed. Every year millions of Muslims make the journey to the Holy Land of Mecca in Saudi Arabia to perform the haj, a requirement in Islam, as long as someone has the means to do so and is in good health, as it makes up one of the five tenets of the religion. But that day we celebrated Hari Raya Puasa, which is also known as Hari Raya Aidilfitri. In Malay the words Hari Raya mean 'A Day of Celebration' and Puasa derives from Sanskrit and means 'fasting' or 'Abstention'. Hari Raya Puasa means 'Great day of fasting' or 'the festival marking the end of a period of fasting'. Hari Raya Puasa is popularly known as Eid Ul Fitr. Hari Raya Puasa marks the end of Ramadan, the holy month of fasting.

In my traditional Malay dress I walked slowly downstairs, feeling so beautiful, like a princess, and straight into the kitchen expecting all the food to be ready. But as soon my mother saw me she said, "Could you help me peel the onion, potato and garlic?"

I thought, shit! I had tried to take a long time getting ready so that by the time I came downsairs she would have finished her cooking. But it didn't work, I still had to help her.

It was ten in the morning and I was already feeling so hot in the heat of the kitchen. It made me sweat like hell. My brother Nas looked very handsome in his traditional Malay suit, which my mother had bought especially for our celebration day. But I could see that his top was all wet because of the heat. He was so busy around the kitchen, helping my mother stir the chicken and tomato sauce with one hand while the other was busy with his camera, snapping my mother's dishes. He tried to snap my mother but she ran around, screaming, "Don't you dare take my picture, I look so messy." I just laughed as I looked at her messy face and untidy clothes.

My brother Zambri removed his top so as not to get wet as he cracked a fresh coconut. He would grind it then mix the coconut with water and squeeze the ground coconut, which would bring out the milk. My mother would then use the fresh coconut milk in most of her dishes. But I hate coconut milk, so I always have a problem with my mother's food.

I looked at my two brothers, Zambri and Nas, busy helping my mother. Good for them. I thought, but not me, I won't dirty my beautiful dress. So I pretended to make myself busy, walking around the kitchen backward and forward and talking a lot of rubbish but doing nothing. When my mother looked at me I quickly grasped a cloth and cleaned the table or did something else. I would help my mother wash all the dirty plates as long I had a glove. My mother is very clever, she knew this, so she had already brought the glove out ready for me, clever women. I will never wash dishes without gloves.

Life Behind the Silence

All my mother's cooking was done. Her special meals for the day were chicken in tomato sauce, chicken korma, beef cooked in black sauce, tomato rice and noodle soup. For my mother, cooking all of that was easy as she used to be a chef. But now she was getting old, and I could see on her face that she was really tired and that she didn't have as much energy as ten years ago, especially as she has high blood pressure and diabetes (type 2).

A friend of Zambri had come over to wish us happy Eid. They were sitting outside chatting while waiting for my mother's food to be served. My mother never allows me to put the food onto the plates because I will fill up the whole plate. So I had to stay in one corner and watch her and my brothers come to get the food and take it outside to eat it with Zambri's friend. My brother Nas joined them. I was so happy to see my brothers getting along. As soon as my mother had finished her preparations, she rushed to get her pillow and then dropped herself into one corner to have a nap, as she was starting to get a headache. Thanks God she had finished her cooking just in time, otherwise there would have been a problem for me. Because I was the only girl in the house, my mother would surely have asked me to cook something for them. Well! I think I would have been shitting myself if that had happened.

Anyway, they left me all alone in the kitchen. I knew my job; I had to wait for them to bring the dirty plates in. My stomach started feeling hungry, and I took a look at my mother's cooking. Ummm…! Yummy! What a shame I don't like chicken, I don't eat beef and I hate coconut milk. I am a seafood and vegetable eater but sadly on the Eid celebration no one cooks seafood. But I found something else to eat: Durian, king of fruit. Durian is my favourite fruit, I can eat and eat it but the smell is very strong. Some people hate the smell but I love it as much as I love eating it. I was happy now and enjoying eating on my own, thanks God! At least I had something to fill up my stomach.

My brothers started bringing all the empty plates into the kitchen, which meant I had to do some work, great! Zambri took Nas out somewhere; Nas did ask me to go with them but I wanted to let them spend some time together to catch up on the many things that they had missed for seventeen years. Surely they both had a lot of things to talk about. Everyone had gone and left me all alone in the kitchen, but it was a good moment for me to think, about how happy I was to have my family together, and that this was a really happy time in my life. I hoped my family would grow closer and have the happy times that we had never had since we were children.

I started washing up and cleaning around the kitchen while my mother was still snoring. Fuck! What kind of celebration is this? I thought. I hope I do not end up washing up for the whole day. I decided this was the last time I would do the washing up. I wanted to be treated like a princess on our special day but instead I had ended up spending my time in the kitchen. Poor me!

My job was done. I was getting bored on my own and sarted wandering round the house alone, not knowing what to do. I could hear water splashing in the bathroom, which I was sure was my mother having a shower. Thank God she had woken up. At the same time I could hear my brothers' voices from downstairs. Thank the Lord, they were back. I ran straight to them and asked, "Hey, you're back! So where have you guys been?"

Nas told me that Zambri had taken him to his workshop and to his house. I was so happy to hear about that and so happy to see them back together again as brothers, but now as adults. I wished this had happened a long time ago but it's never too late and I hoped things would stay this way forever.

My mother's friends arrived non stop to wish us well for our celebration and of course to eat. I had to be in the kitchen to lend a hand with whatever my mother needed help with, and then my mother served them all her cooking. From the kitchen I could hear everyone telling my mother that her cooking was delicious and I heard my mother say that it was very simple to cook and so easy.

I thought, ummm…! She is really showing off. Her head must be getting bigger now, I hope she can walk trough the door. Well! That is my mother, she has always been proud of her cooking, and she is a very good cook. I thought, well done, Mum! I am very proud of you.

I could see that she was very happy with her friends' comments. I preferred to stay in the kitchen rather than join them because they were not my friends and I had nothing to talk to them about. Another problem was that I was worried to join them because they like to ask about very personal issues and are always gossiping, which I really hate. For them it is normal though, I guess that's just the way people live in the countryside.

Suddenly I could hear one of my mother's friends asking, "Where is your daughter? We'd love to see her."

Within a second my mother called me. "Zah! Come here for a minute."

I thought, here we go. Anyway, without saying a word I took my ass to my mother. Out of respect, I gave my biggest smile, shook hands with everyone and said, "Hello."

Then I took my ass quickly back to the kitchen; I didn't stay with them for long. Instead I stood behind the door and tried to listen to their conversation, because I knew that as soon as I left them, they would start bitching. Everyone gave good comments about me though, which I was very pleased to hear. Soon everyone left, and I was free to move into the living room and lie on the sofa and watch TV.

My eyes slowly closed and I was just dropping off to sleep when suddenly I could hear someone's voice from outside calling a greeting. "Assalam mualaikum" Fuck! What now? I knew it was my mother's friend so I just ignored them and continued to lie on the sofa. But then from upstairs my mother shouted to me, "Zah, someone is outside, could you please open the door?"

I mumbled, "Give me a break", but I said, "Are all of your friends going to come today?"

I still lay on the sofa, thinking, why do these people have to come at this hour, don't they think that people want to have a rest? I took my time getting up, just to let them wait outside a bit longer. But then I had no choice but to get up and open the door.

When I opened the door there were two very young men standing right in front of me. I looked at them and thought, ummm…! Interesting, my mother has very young male friends. Then I said, "Hello."

They both just smiled at me, then I asked them to come in as I had decided to sit in the living room with them. These two young gentlemen were very polite and shy, they faced the floor most of the time. I wondered why they were too scared to look at me. I probably looked like someone who was going to kill them or they might have been shy around women. My mother joined her friends for only fifteen minutes then she excused herself and said, "Sorry, Mammy has some work to do but my daughter is here so you guys can chat with her."

Then she looked at me and said, "Izah! Please keep them company; I am starting to get another headache and need to sleep for a while." Then she left me with her friends. As I was bored of doing nothing for the whole day, I agreed. I thought, please! Go and have a rest and take as much time as you want because these two young guys are quite good-looking.

As soon as my mother left, I tok in charge of her guests. I was sitting right in front of them expecting one of them to have a conversation with me. But neither of them darde look at me. I felt so sorry for them. I said, "Knock knock, anyone here?"

They were both shocked and looked at me with their eyes open wide, but then they smiled as soon as they realised it was me doing that, but still they said nothing. I thought, right! Let me start talking. After that they got so much better and as we went on they grew much more friendly, and soon I started to joke and tease them. They laughed and started asking me a lot about London. It sounded like they very interested in going there. It was eight in the evening and I was starting to wonder when my mother was going to come into the living room because I was starting to get bored. Then I saw her and Nas walking downstairs. Thank God for that.

I was just about to excuse myself but suddenly a little boy walked in and straight away sat on my mother's lap. I immediately knew that the little boy was my sister Nurul's son. Then my sister walked in with her husband and her two year old daughter. As is the custom, out of respect to the older person, she came and kissed my hand then her husband did the same. I couldn't even look at her face at that time; it just made me fucking mad. Then straight away she sat beside Nas and they hugged each other. It made me so emotional to see their happiness. They had both missed each other. My brother had missed her badly because he used to play with her and tease her when she was a little girl. It put a smile on my face to see this happy moment.

As my sister hadn't talked to me for quite some time, I kept myself to my myself. Then I slowly got up and walked to the kitchen to try and hide my sadness and anger at what she had done. But then I promised myself I would be good on this important day, and so I returned to the sitting room to join them, feeling much calmer. I just waited to see what was going to happen. I really tried hard to pull myself together just for the family, especially for my brother Nas, because he didn't know anything about the family and I really didn't want to make him upset and confused. I wanted him to have a good time with them because he hadn't seen them for seventeen years. I could swallow the pain and deal with it. I took myself to the kitchen again to try to hold the tears; I didn't want to cry in front of them. I am a very strong woman but to see my family's happiness, and them loving and caring for each other, was just so wonderful. I am not a romantic person but I can be very sensitive and too emotional and that means I cry easily at a lot of things.

Nurul came to find me in the kitchen. I knew she wanted to talk to me but instead I started giving her a lecture. I had waited for this moment for a long time, the chance to tell her how much she had hurt me. I am very open with my sister, she is not just my sister, she is like my daughter, my buddy and the person who I can share my problems with. I had talked to her again and again, saying the same things over and over every year, telling her not to do it, and yet she had not listened and kept repeating the same mistake, lying and cheating me. But this time she agreed that she had made a mistake and she apologised with her eyes full of tears. Seeing her cry hurt me inside. I am not a cruel person but I wanted her to understand and to stop the bad things that she had been doing. I told her this was the last time I would accept her apology. I said, "If you still want me to be in my life, then please stop now, otherwise you will no longer be my sister. You know that I love you, that's why I stand here in front of you, and I could never hate you, I'm just upset with you. It's not the first time you have done this, you've done it a million times, and I hope this is the last time."

Nas was wondering around behind us like a tiger in a cage, trying to catch some of our conversation. We finally gave each other a warm hug, full of love. She is the only sister I have and she has a lovely heart. I adore her dearly.

It was almost midnight when she excused herself to return to her home. I wanted her to stay the night but she hadn't brought all of her kids' stuff, so I understood. So I let her go and reminded her to come early the next day because we wanted to go to my aunt's house, as I had already promised my aunt.

Nas disappeared to bed very early. His brain must have been very tired after seeing so many things happening around him, and I knew there must be a lot of questions in his head. I chatted with my mother in bed. I hope she wouldn't talk for long because I was knackered. While she talked my eyes were closing and I just agreed with whatever she said: YES! RIGHT! NO! OK! But the truth is I didn't know what she was talking about because my body and soul were flying freely in the air then resting peacefully. As if from a dream I could hear my mother's voice swimming, saying, "You've gone to sleep and left me to talk on my own."

My mind whispered, "Sorry, Mum! See you in the future."

CHAPTER 32

Visiting

It was the second day of Eid and of course the celebration was still going on. This is the day that we visit our relatives that we haven't seen for years, to share this happiest of times together. Myy mother decided to visit her older sister, which I was happy about because I am quite close with Kamal, my cousin. My mother and Nas were ready and, as I am always ready on time, I had been ready for one hour already. The plan was for my sister, Nurul, or as we call her 'Kak Cik', and her husband to come with us. So we had to wait for them. I know my sister very well. She is never on time. She always turns up late; not twenty minutes, not one hour, but a couple of hours. Since she has had children he's been even worse, now she can give us lots of excuses. I had promised my cousin Kamal that we would be at his house by midday, and it was now one o'clock. I know my mother, she hates waiting like I do. Nas wouldn't say a word because he is slower than my sister. My mother started mumbling and asked me, "Do you know what time it is now? Where is Kak Cik?"

My mother kept asking me to call my sister. Before she lost her temper, I quickly called my sister. The phone rang but there was no answer. Well! Of course she wouldn't answer as she knew how late she was. Technology nowadays makes life so much easier, it stops other people going crazy at you. She could just send a text instead of making a call to explain the situation. She's not stupid, this way she didn't need to hear us getting annoyed so she took as much time as she wanted. The problem is my mother put me under a lot of pressure and now she was asking me again, "Did you call her? What time is she coming?"

I said, "Yes I did, but she didn't answer her phone. She sent a text to say that she is on her way."

My mother got really mad and said, " Two hours I have been waiting and she is still on the way. It only takes thirty minutes to get here. We're going now, before I get headache, let her…"

Before my mother could finish her sentence, my sister arrived at last. I thought, lucky you. I had rented a car but I coudn't drive because my licence had expired a very long time ago, but luckily my brother had a licence so he had to be the driver. Without wasting any more time we started our journey. My sister was in one car with her husband and her two kids and me, my brother and my mother were in another car. The journey would usually take about one hour but, with the way my brother drives, it took a bit longer. I know I am a fast driver but my God! My brother drives like an old man, he's so slow. I just wanted to say, "Come on, man! Hurry up." But I couldn't say anything because I had no licence, so I had to keep my big mouth shut. I hated it. On our way I could see my brother really enjoying driving through the countryside; after more than seventeen years, he was back where he was born, bless him!

Finally we arrived at our destination. I could see my cousin and my auntie waiting for us outside the house. As soon as I arrived, all I could think about was the food because I was fucking hungry. They better have a good meal ready for us after we have come such a long way, I thought. The weather was so hot and humid, there was no way that I was going to go inside the house, especially as their house didn't have any air conditioning. I decided to sit outside on the veranda with my sister, my brother and the rest. A few of my other cousins came to join us and we talked about lots of things. I only go to see them about once a year so there were a lot of things they wanted to know, especially as this time I had brought along Nas, who they hadn't seen for more than twenty years. I had to explain to them in detail how I had found him and they asked me so many questions. I sat in the middle, surrounded by them, which was so much fun, I loved it. They didn't ask my brother much because he only speaks English. I thought, you idiot, Nas, I'm going to kill you. But it was so funny when my brother spoke English with them, they would turn to me and ask what he was talking about. I just laughed. So my brother just sat and listened, and agreed with some of the words he could understand. Almost half an hour I had been sitting and chatting with them, but where was the food? My stomach was making a lot of noise because I was very hungry. One hour later, two of my cousins excused themselves and went home. Kamal came out of the house and took a long bamboo stick and tried to hit a few young coconuts. I was resting, enjoying the afternoon wind blowing on my face while chatting with my sister. It is so peaceful in the countryside. My eyes looked around and all that I could see was green plantations, which made my mind feel so fresh and relaxed. I could see Kamal, Zuri (my sister's husband) and Nas chatting and laughing Ummm...! I wondered what they were laughing about. What was so funny?

My aunt came out and asked me, "Zah, are you going to cook lunch for us?"

I looked at her and gave her a big smile and said, "Nope."

Then I turned to my sister and said, "What? She wants me to cook? What is she thinking? I came here to visit, not to cook. That means we're not going to have lunch then, great!"

My sister just smiled but she looked a bit tired. I was sure she was hungry. This really upset me, how could they not have lunch ready for us? They knew we were coming especially for lunch on our celebration day, unbelievable! My cousin, my brother and Nurul's husband came with a few young coconuts in their hands, then peeled the skin and carefully broke them so the coconut juice didn't spill, then carefully they poured the coconut juice inside the container, scooped the young coconut flesh out, mixed it together with coconut juice and added some ice and sugar. They put a few glasses on the table so we could all help ourselves. Without invitation, straight away I got up, grasped a glass and poured coconut juice from a young, fleshy coconut. Because I knew that I was not going to have any lunch, I fdecided to fill up my stomach with young coconut. I asked my sister, "Are you hungry?"

She said, "Yes!"

I told her we were going to eat later at the restaurant or at home. I couldn't believe they had served us only coconut juice for lunch, especially as we were still celebrating Eid. It was fucking shit! Sorry for my language.

My cousin disappeared with my brother, no doubt to show him around as my brother had never been there before. I was very pleased that they were getting along. It made me so happy because I had been worried in case my brother was getting bored. Zuri was doing his own thing with his children. He is a very simple, normal guy and very humble. He will do anything that people require without question. He can be a very nice person and very helpful if you know how to deal with him, but the most important thing is, he is such a good husband to my sister and a good father to his children. He knows his responsibilities and he will do anything for his family, for which I am very proud of him. I am so happy for you, my dear sister.

I looked at the time; it was almost four in the afternoon. I needed to make a move; I had promised to take Nas to see my father. My father really missed his youngest son, but my brother didn't care about my father since my father hadn't taken responsibility for him or cared about him when he was a little boy. But Nas and my other two brothers were very lucky. My father didn't hit them a single time. But I have never been jealous of my brothers or hated them, they will always be dear to me, they are such a special part of my life. Anyway at that moment I just wanted to do the best for everyone. To see my family happy made me more than happy.

Suddenly my brother disappeared with Kamal for a long time. I wondered where the hell they had gone. I walked around the house looking for them. Ummm…! There they were, sitting on the bridge chatting, laughing and smiling. I had no idea what they were talking about. They had never seen each other before and within a couple of hours they looked like they had known each other for a long time. From afar I could see them talking and I was so intrigued about what they were chatting about, I wondered if they were gossiping or bitching.

As I am a very nosy person I walked straight towards them. They stopped chatting as soon as I arrived and looked at me like I was a stranger. I thought, all right! Fine then. So I told my brother the reason I had gone over. Both of them just stared at me but didn't say a word. I thought, Ummm…! OK, I'm off then. I let them continue with their intersting story but I said to my brother, "We have to make a move in five minutes."

As soon as I was a few steps away, I could hear them continuing their conversation. I thought, bastards!

We all said goodbye to everyone and my brother drove the car out of there. As my sister always came with my brother Zambri to my father's house, she knew the area very well. I had been a few times but I am very bad with directions to anywhere, so we followed my sister's car. On our way to my father's house, once again I could see my brother really enjoying his drive in the countryside that he had not been back to for a very long time. But he took so much time with his driving, exactly like a Sunday driver. We talked a lot and I teased him. He spoke English all the time so my poor mother just sat in the back watching us laughing without understand any words. I looked at her; she looked a bit tired and her she was almost falling asleep. I thought she must be hungry so I said, "Mum! Are you hungry?"

Suddenly her eyes opened wide and she said, "I ate rice earlier in the kitchen."

I said, "What? You ate alone? What about us?"

She just smiled; that's why she stayed in the kitchen for a very long time. Then I asked my brother, "Are you hungry?"

He said, "Yes, I am, but I'm OK."

I knew everyone was hungry. I felt so sorry for them and I felt so embarrassed in front of my brother.

We arrived at my father's house at last, after a forty-five minute drive. Before we entered the house, I told my mother not to cause any problems in front of everybody, especially my brother. I told her that both she and my father were getting older and that their children were also getting older and I begged her to do it for me. "I just want to see both of you talking again," I said, "so please put to one side whatever has happened in the past, just this time, for us, for your children on this special day. I want to feel what it's like to have a happy family because I never have before."

Thank God, she agreed. To make her happy, I teased her before she stepped out of the car. "Mum," I said, "you look pretty today and I am sure his wife will be jealous when she sees you."

My mother looked at me and smiled; I knew that smile was not genuine. My heart felt for her. I thought, sorry, Mum! But thank you for your kindness.

Before we got out of the car I could see my father and his wife standing in front of the door to welcome us. I quickly whispered to my mother, "Mum, look at him! He looks so old and his wife is ugly, you're a hundred times better then her so be proud of yourself."

I gave my mother my full support to make her strong. I know my mother is a very strong woman because I am. I let my mother and my brother meet them first while I stayed in the car watching both of my parent's reactions. My mother walked straight past my father without saying a single word to either my father or his third wife, then she disappeared inside the house without asking permission. My father and his wife just looked at her then they looked at each other. I thought, neither of them knows what to do, but then they both walked in to join my mother. My mother can be very rude and very nasty sometimes. That was hilarious, well done, Mum! I wonder what was on my parent's minds and what they were feeling towards each other. It would be good to know. Then I saw my father come out to find my brother. They shook hands and my father gave my brother a hug and burst into tears. From what I could see, my brother didn't care about his sadness and I

Life Behind the Silence

completely understood. It really hurts when I remember what he has done to our lives. It was too late, your tears didn't mean anything to us, Dad. Sorry, Abdul Wahab!

My father looked around then he saw me still inside the car. I quickly pretended to search for something in the car, but then he called me, "Zah! What are doing? Come inside!"

I said, "I will in a minute."

I sneaked a look at him. Fuck, he was still waiting for me. So I stepped out of the car and walked straight towards him and shook his hand with frustration, but I promised myself that I would make the most of it for the rest of the family. I was in pain trying to hold the sadness inside me but I thought, life is too short, I want to see my family happy. Because being together like this had never happened in my entire life, and it would never happen again.

We all gathered together in the living room, including my stepmother and all my stepsisters, brothers and my dad's grandson. He has two daughters with his second wife and both of them were married and had kids so my father was now a grandfather; good for him. He also has five children with his third wife but none of them were married yet.

My mother was a bit quiet and my father didn't say anything to her. I started the conversation by asking everyone a silly question and acting stupid just to make everyone laugh and talk to each other. My mother and my father kept smiling at my behaviour towards my stepsisters and my brother. I could see my father start talking to my mother. Thank God for that. I was so relieved, especially when I saw them smile at each other. I tried my very best to put the family together and to make them comfortable, including my mother, my father and my stepmum. I was overwhelmed to see my parents laughing after so many years. As far as I could remember, this was the first time I had seen genuine happiness between them. I wished this had happened a long time ago. Anyway, my mother started joining in with the rest of my father's family, bless her!

I hoped when I was gone they would keep in touch but that would totally depend on my mother and how she felt about that. But as far as I was concerned, to have a relationship with my father would be impossible! I tried to feel the love from him that I had never have in my entire life but it was hard. I didn't feel like he was my father. He was someone who I hadn't seen for a very long time, he was like a total a stranger to me. I could never take him into my life and he would never be my father. I was very happy without a father because that was what I was used to and that is what he wanted. When I looked at him it brought back all the memories of what he had done to me. It will hurt me for the rest of my life. He might have thought I had forgotten because I pretended; I joked and I laughed with him and with everyone in the house. But what he didn't know was that behind my eyes I was full of sadness about him. I wanted so much for him to say sorry for what he had done and, most of all, I wanted to hear him say that I was his daughter; but he didn't do that, he really was a bastard with an evil heart!

I held in a lot of pain trying to build the family back together, my heart was weeping, but why couldn't he open his eyes and see what was happening at that moment? Why didn't he use his brain and question himself? It was so sad to look at him. Suddenly our happy time was interrupted by my brother Redzwan and his wife. Redzwan is the only relative who hadn't come to see my mother the day of the Eid celebration. Just because of his stupid wife, who is a crazy bitch. She is a control freak; she controls my brother's life. For no reason she won't even talk to my mother and she has even forbidden my brother to talk to his own mother. She really has got a mental illness. They were both shocked when they saw my mother at my father's house.

Redzwan sat beside Nas; he was in shock to see him after seventeen years. My father joined my brothers but he looked a bit sad. I wished I knew what was on his mind. Redzwan's wife walked straight past my mother and I to the kitchen without saying a single word. She didn't even bother to say hello to me or my mother. I felt so sorry for my mother. She should have shown some respect to my mother, even though she is just her daughter-in-law. My father was very upset at her and pissed off with Redzwan because my brother didn't say anything to his wife about her behaviour towards my mother. That's because Redzwan was so scared of his wife. My mother always said that his wife had done witchcraft on him, that's why he became so naïve.

My mother suddenly became very friendly with my stepmother. They went into the kitchen together and then they sat together in the other room too. My eyes were busy looking around at every single corner of the house to see what was happening. I am very nosy so was curious to know what my mother and my stepmother were talking about. I walked past the room where they were sitting and having a conversation. My eyes quickly glanced at them; WOW! They were laughing and slapping each other's bodies, they looked so happy and like they were having so much fun! Anyway, whatever they were sharing I was very happy and very pleased things were working out well. That's all I was hoping for for my family.

It was time to say goodbye to everyone and I left my father's house with peace of mind. In the car on the journey home my whole body just collapsed but I had a big smile on my face because of what I had done for my family. I was sad in my heart and soul though because no one knew how hurt I was and no one knew about my feelings at that time. I gave it my best shot to make everyone happy. I have learned a lot on this journey through my life.

CHAPTER 33

A Moment Changed My Life

Every time I return home to visit my mother, I stay with her about a week and sometimes maybe more. Our relationship as a mother and daughter is a really big problem. I have tried to establish a connection with her but I have never been able to understand her behaviour towards me, and she has never understood me as a person. When we are far apart, we are like best friends. She is the person who I can talk to about everything in life, including my love life and every single boyfriend that I have had I have introduced to her. But when we are together we fight like cat and dog. The arguments always happen after we have been together for five days. She always looks for something to upset me and sometimes she will say something nasty, which makes me lose my temper, and then the argument begins. It has crossed my mind before that I didn't want to visit her anymore, but then she is my mother and I only have one mother in this world. I miss her but I know for sure that she never misses me. I love her but I know for a fact that she only loves me for my money. If I had no money, she wouldn't care about me.

When I was very young – when I saw my father hit my mother because she was protecting me, when she saved my life many times, when I saw her working hard and through all the difficult times in her life – I promised myself that one day, when my life was stable and I had money, the first thing that I would to do was stop my mother working. I would look after her and give her enough money to live on. I would do everything for and give her all the things that she never had before. I would give her everything I could to make her happy. Now I had done what I promised. As a daughter I was so proud of myself. As long as I am still alive, she will be in good hands.

I spoiled my mother a lot because I wanted her to have things and to feel something that she never had before. I had given her more than enough money to live on, I did whatever she wanted and she will always receive anything she asks for. To make her life happy is my biggest desire. But she became a different person. This is because she never had money in her life before. She became so greedy and didn't tell the truth to her own children. When I gave her money, she would tell me that Zambri and Redzwan never did. Then when Zambri gave her money, she would tell him that Redzwan and I never gave her money. When my brother Redzwan visited her, she would tell him that she had no money to buy food. As soon as Redzwan handed over the money, she would him that Zambri and I never gave her any money to her. My sister is the youngest and she didn't have a proper job so of course she had no money, and my mother would tell her that none of us gave her money.

The thing that I am not happy with is that when she wants something, she gets angry with my brothers and my sister. She will say, your sister said this, your sister said that; everything is my fault, which makes me look like a very bad sister. But she cares about herself and covers her naughtiness very well. She had been doing this routine a very long time and none of us knew anything about it. My mother worried that we would find out, so she had to play another game with us. When I spoke with her on the phone, she would tell me bad things that my brother had said about me, which made me very upset. But then she warned me not to tell them. Of course I agreed with my mother because she is my mother and I trust her, but then she would tell my brothers that I had said bad things about them, and she warned them not to tell me, and she would do the same with Nurul. Then we siblings became angry at each other but we had to keep quiet. Soon we were becoming like strangers and starting to hate each other. Because we were holding too much pain inside, we stopped haveing a connection. My mother saw what was happening to her children but did nothing because she was the person who had caused the problems, even though she is our mother.

But it came to the point where God showed us what was happening. To start with I asked my sister why she had said bad things about me to my mother. My sister was shocked because she had never said anything like that to my mother. Then she told me the reason she hadn't been talking to me was because my mother had told her that I had said something bad about her. I asked Zambri and Redzwan if the same had happened to them and they gave me exactly the same answer. I was speechless at my mother's behaviour towards us. So now me, my two brothers and my sister told each everything that my mother had said, none of which was true. Our relationships as brothers and sisters went back to normal. I never thought in a million years she would be able to watch her children suffer because of her.

I couldn't accept what my mother had done to us for all that time so I decided to question her about it. I did not hate my mother, I just wanted to know why she had done this to us. I decided to tell her that we knew everything. I didn't think she would be embarrassed about the things that she had done, but she would be in shock and because of this stop hurting her children's feelings. Day after day I asked her in a diplomatic way. But she gave me loads of reasons which I expected from her. No one can argue with her because she is always right, even thought she was in the wrong. But not me, I would stand up to her and get the truth out of her.

I told her that as a good mother she should make her children closer, not make them hate each other. As a good mother she should teach her children honesty and how to be well behaved. I told her that she had damaged my relationship with my two brothers and my sister so she had to stop. On behalf of my brothers and sister, I told her how upset we were and how frustrated I was. But I was not too sure if she was listening or not because my mother is a very independent person with a strong character; in fact, we both have strong characters and that's why we can't get along. One day she can be such a lovely mother, and we are like friends, then within a minute we are fighting like cat and dog and then we don't talk to each other for a couple of weeks. But thehn when I think back about my mother's behaviour it just makes me laugh. What is good about her is, she has big heart and a wicked sense of humour, but I will never understand her. But I will always love her and will always look after; she is my mother.

My mother has another big problem, which I try to deal with but which is very difficult because I don't live with her. Because she never used to have enough money to buy things for her or for the house, now that I give her the money, she spends it on plates, cups, glasses – anything for the kitchen. The problem is, she buys boxes and boxes of plates, and she puts them in every room. She serves us on the old plates and keeps the new plates in the cupboard, only to look at, not to touch, and the rest she keeps nicely in boxes. Not just that, she buys clothes non stop. All the cupboards in the house are full of her clothes, and there are boxes of them in every room. Every time she visits her friends, especially new friends, she tells them that she doesn't have many clothes. Of course people feel sorry for her and they give her loads of clothes. Once I told her that she had too many clothes and she should give some to charity. My mother explained to me that at one time people looked down on her because she didn't have money to buy clothes, and they spat on her because she was very poor. So now that she is able to buy clothes, she has become obsessed with it. Well! I do understand but it is too much, and most of the clothes she never even wears.

Malaysia is now full of Pakistanis, many of whom sell carpets and other household items door to door. The good deal is, they only collect the payment monthly. This is great for my mother. She stops every single salesperson who passes the house and gets anything she likes. She promises them she will pay every month, which she sometimes does but sometimes when the month ends she can't afford to pay. She gets angry with the Pakistanis who ask her for payment. She tells them that she has no money to pay them and she blames them for forcing her to buy their stuff. Once she told them to come again in ten days when her daughter would be back from London. They came at exactly the time my mother had promised them. After I handed over the money, I walked into the house and had a sneaky look at my mother through the window. She didn't say anything to me; instead, she went up to the man and spoke to him angrily then chased him away. He was so scared of my mother, he drove his motorbike away. I tried to be serious and asked her why she had to spend money on something that she wouldn't use but it was so funny, it just made my day.

My mother's worst problem though, which I can't accept, is when she collects things from people's rubbish. She will pay for a young boy or an unemployed person to bring anything they find to her, for example a TV. She has five TVs that she found in the rubbish. I have never known anyone to have as many TVs as her. She has three fridges full of food, some of which is past the expiry date. I used to clean the fridges and throw all the expired food in the rubbish, but then she would take it and hide it from me. One day I asked my sister to take my mother out because I had made a plan to do something. As soon as they were gone I quickly cleared up the rubbish she had collected and burnt it all. My God! For the first time ever I could see the house without rubbish, it was so much cleaner. Brightening up the inside of the house gave me so much peace. I just couldn't wait for my mother to return home so I could show her how beautiful the house was without rubbish. I hoped she would be happy when she saw it and appreciate what I had done, but sadly she didn't. As soon as she arrived home and saw the fire, she rushed inside the house and asked me what did I had burnt. Of course I was very happy to tell her that I had burnt all the rubbish and I was very proud to show her how pretty the house looked. Well! Sadly, I didn't impress her at all. Instead, she burst into tears and said to herself (although obviously it was meant for me) that as long as she was still alive, no one could touch her belongings. I didn't mean to upset her, I just wanted to help by clearing out her house. I thought it would make her happy. But if that's what she chooses to have in the house, I thought, I can't do anything, and if she is happy to live the way she is, I promised myself, I won't tell her anything from now. But I just hoped that one day she would realise what she was doing. After I had been back in London a few weeks, my sister and brothers started telling me that my mother had started collecting even more things. Well! As long she is happy, that's fine, was all I could say.

Every time I visit my mother, I am so happy I jump like a little girl when I see her, but it makes me sad when my mother thinks only about herself. I don't want anything in return, I just want her to love me and care about my life, but she never has. She loves Redzwan and Zambri more then me. She will give them whatever they need, and she will do anything for them. She was willing to sell some of the land that her father left for her just to help my brother Zambri open a business. She always worries about Zambri's life and is the same with Redzwan. If Redzwan has a problem, she will give him money that I have given to her and she will do the same for Zambri. I have bought a lot of jewellery for her, but it's all gone. Every time Redzwan or Zambri visits her, she cooks a nice meal for them. She never does this for me when I come home. Maybe she will cook on the first and second day, but then she won't cook for me anymore. I have to go out and buy breakfast and lunch, and I then I take her out to dinner. I am happy to take her to a restaurant, but it will be every night for the whole month. Well! If that makes her happy, I am fine with that. But of course it breaks my heart and there are tears in my eyes when I see the way she treats Redzwan and Zambri.

I take my responsibilities very seriously; these are not only to look after my mother but also to help the whole family. I still remember one time I helped my brother Zambri when his business was in trouble. I was in London at the time when he asked for help. I was still studying and worked a few hours a week to get some money for my daily basics. But instead of keeping the money for my needs, I sent it to him and my mother almost every month until one day I had nowhere to live because I couldn't pay the rent. I did everything to help my family, but when I called them, they didn't even bother to ask about my life, they only talked about money. And now I give my mother more than I promise, but I still don't make her happy. I hope that one day she will realise all the things that I have done for her.

Life became very tough after a few years. As much as I liked London, I made the decision to return to Malaysia! For a short while everything was OK. I had some pounds with me, which made me very happy because I could go home to visit my family. They were more than happy to see me because they knew I had money, but what they didn't know was that I had to go back because I had no money to stay in London. I could never tell them about that, because I knew they would laugh and talk about me behind my back, they would never feel sorry for me.

I stayed with my mother only a week then returned to Kuala Lumpur. At that time I didn't have much money, just enough for me to keep going for a short time. I tried to save that money as much as I could, but Zambri came to visit me almost every week. I knew the reason he came was not really to visit me but for the money. Every time he came, he would get 1,000 ringgit. I gave it to him because I was so happy that my brother cared about me enough to come such a long way. I can find money but I can never find happiness. Sooner than later the money that I had managed to save had almost finished and I couldn't give him anymore, so he stopped visiting me. I was getting so depressed because Kazmin's wife was giving me a lot of hassle. That made me decide to return to London but I had no money. I thought, surely Zambri and my mother can help me buy the ticket back to London because I have done a lot for them.

So without wasting any more time I flew back to Kulim, the city where my mother lived. I was so happy, I just couldn't wait to tell her that I was going back to London. I thought that, without doubt, my mother would help me. But I was wrong. As soon as they found out that I didn't have any money, their behaviour completely changed towards me. I had no money to rent a car to drive my mother around. Zambri had a few cars at his workshop but, even though I had helped him a lot with his workshop when he was having a tough time, he didn't lend me one. Every day I was stuck at home and couldn't go anywhere. My mother was not really happy about that and she didn't talk to me much, and when she did she would always put me down. I felt so hurt about the way they treated me. I only had my sister, Nurul, to talk to at that time. Even though she was still a young girl, she really understood my situation, but she was out at work all day. I was at home feeling so hungry. I wanted to cook but I was scared to disturb anything in my mother's kitchen. My mother would get angry with me if i did, especially I as I couldn't buy anything for her at that time. I simply couldn't cook without her; if I did she would ask me a lot of questions so I had to hold my hunger.

One day, when I heard her voice calling to open the door, I was so pleased because I knew I could eat. As soon as she walked in I asked her, "What are we going to eat for lunch?"

She said, "I have eaten already when I was outside. if you want to eat, there are fast noodles you can cook yourself."

My hunger stopped when she told me she had eaten. I thought, how could she do that to me? I knew she had gone to my brother's house to have her lunch. When my sister got home she asked me, "What did you eat today?" She was really upset when I explained what had happened.

Still fresh in my mind is one morning when Zambri came around and told my mother that he was going to have lunch at home today and handed her a carrier bag. I had no idea what was inside the plastic bag. She quickly went to the kitchen and got ready to cook lunch for Zambri. I followed her into the kitchen and offered to help. She opened the plastic bag and in there were about ten, live, king prawns. She said, "Zambri loves prawns."

I said, "Me too!"

Then my mother said, "If you have money, you can buy them."

I didn't say anything but I was really shocked when I heard my mother say those words. But I still helped her by chopping the onions, washing the plates and trying to do whatever I could because I wanted to join them and enjoy the prawns, especially as my mother was cooking them. She cooked lovely sweet and sour prawns. They looked so delicious, I was drooling. Yum yum! I felt so hungry, I just couldn't wait to eat.

As soon as she finished cooking, she took the dish away to one side and covered it then she said, "Zambri bought these with his money so we have to wait for him."

My mind went blank when I heard those words but I just smiled and said, "That's fine! Of course we have to wait for him and eat together."

I couldn't believe my eyes when, as soon as Zambri arrived, my mother quickly brought out the delicious prawns that she had cooked, and then they enjoyed them together without offering me any. I sat in the living room looking at them with sadness in my heart. I thought, this is what I receive after all that I have done for them, thank you so much! It hurt me badly.

The next day I tried my luck and asked my mother for help. She had bought a car for Zambri when her business was doing well, before Zambri opened his workshop, so I begged her to sell the car and lend me the money to buy my ticket to London. I promised her that as soon as I had settled myself in London, I would pay back all the money that I had borrowed.

But sadly neither of them were willing to help me at all. I waited for a few weeks in case they changed their minds but still the answer was "NO!" I was very disappointed and didn't know what to do. Every day I felt like I had received physical and mental abuse from my mother. I felt that I was not welcome at her house; I knew she didn't want me to be with her at that moment. I was sure when she woke up every morning, she hated seeing my face because I couldn't take her anywhere and I couldn't buy anything for her. I thought I had better go back to the capital city and try my luck there. So the next day I told my mother that I wantd to go back to Kuala Lumpur. She knew that I was in a very difficult situation financially but she never tried to stop me. She didn't worry about where I was going to stay or how I was going to survive.

I needed my mother to lend me some money for my ticket to the capital city so I asked her, "Mum, could you lend me a few hundred so I can purchase my flight ticket?"

Straight away she said, "NO! I don't have any money."

I knew she had a few thousand that I had given to her and in savings. She could help me if she wanted to. I held the pain in as much as I could because she is my mother.

I went to see Zambri with Nurul and asked him to lend me the money. I told him that I would pay him back as soon I as I was back in the capital city. But the answer that I received was "NO!" I felt so hopeless; I couldn't even stand on my own two feet. I felt like a homeless person begging them for some help. Why were they doing this to me? I did not deserve to be treated like this. My heart, my soul and my whole body hurt badly. I couldn't bear to stay with my mother any longer. I was so desperate to get out of that place. Without using my head, I asked my sister; she was the last person who I could ask for help. I knew I shouldn't ask her because she was still a young girl, but

I had no choice so I said, "Kak Cik, I can't stay here anymore, I want to go back to the capital city and live in my own place but I need your help. But if you can't hepl, don't worry about it."

She said, "Of course I can help you."

I said, "Sorry for asking you but I'm sure you understand, could you please help me borrow a few hundred from your friends so I can purchase a flight ticket to Kuala Lumpur? I promise I will pay you back as soon as possible."

Without any questions a girl of just fourteen years old rushed out for a few hours and returned with a few hundred in her hand, which she handed to me. I felt so useless and embarrassed, and I can never thank her enough for what she did. It really touched my heart; she saved my life and I will remember that for the rest of my life. The next day I was packing my clothes and ready to leave the place that had given me so much hurt. But this experience had taught me a lot about my family, and about life.

When my mother found out that Nurul had helped me out with the money she got really angry with my sister and said to her, "Where did you get the money from?" My sister didn't say anything. I said goodbye to my mother and looked into her eyes. I thought, you are unbelievable, you always hurt me and you will never love me.

I was now returning to the capital city, which I called my town. My life didn't get any better though as Kazmin's wife continued to harass me. I tried to find a way out, a way to return to London. Thanks to a lot of patience and the help of God, someone walked into my life with a huge heart and offered me some help. Out of the goodness of his heart, he put my wings together and let me fly back to where I belonged. That moment changed my life and I can never thank that person enough.

It took me quite some time to get back to my normal life. I struggled a lot of the time, but I never gave up. I knew I could do it and that whatever happened I would survive. With patience and a fighting spirit at last I had the power back over my life, and I no longer cowered in the darkness.

Soon after, I started thinking about my responsibility to look after my family, especially my mother. As soon as they received some money, they all started being nice to me again. Of course I felt hurt, but I needed a family so I put everything in one corner of my heart and continued helping my family even though I was struggling. As long as I could speak with my mother and the rest of the family whenever I wanted, I was happy.

CHAPTER 34

Pressure from My Mother

My brother Nas and I stayed with my mother for six days. Nas had only two weeks' holiday, so he was keen to go back to Kuala Lumpur as soon as possible. Every day he asked me, "Sis, when are we going back to the capital city? Because I don't have much time left."

I think he wanted to stay in the hotel away from all the people and noise and have some time on his own to rest. I knew what he was going through in his life at that time, so I said, "Don't worry we'll go soon."

When I saw the smile on his face it pushed me to make our stay at my mother's house shorter. As my brother was no longer a country boy it was quite difficult for him to settle himself, especially after seventeen years, which I completely understood. I am also a city girl, I love nightlife and I love to have a fun time. Because of that I can't stay in the countryside for a long time, especially with my mother's behaviour.

Nas started to have problems sleeping because my mother had told us a story about the ghost that lived in the house. My mother said that one night while she was watching TV, she saw someone walk pastf her and enter the bathroom, but they never came out. I asked her who the person was and she said, "It must have been a ghost, who else could have entered my house at eleven in the evening, when all my doors were locked?" Then she told us that once when she was siting downstairs, she could hear someone walking and running upstairs. She told us that she talked to that ghost, or whoever that person was. She told them. "You can do whatever you want to do but just don't disturb me." It was hilarious! We all burst out laughing and I laughed until I got my stomach pains. Then I said, "You talked to the ghost? Errr…! Mum! Weren't you scared?"

My mother was so proud. She said, "NO! Scared of what? Well! After I talked to them, they never came back."

After my mother told us about the ghost, every time she asked me to go upstairs to get something, I was terrified. As soon as I had got whatever I had gone up for, I ran down quickly like a rat because I felt like someone was following me. It was like a nightmare. I felt sorry for my brother because he was so scared about going to bed. Every time he went to sleep, he would open his bedroom door wide and leave the light on all night. But I slowly closed the door when he was soundly asleep, and switched off the light. Luckily I was sleeping with my mother, but I was still too scared to go to the bathroom as I thought that maybe the ghost would come with me. Scary! So I went to bed and waited until the morning to use the bathroom.

Every time I return to Malaysia, I stay in a hotel for a couple of days before I fly back to see my mother. There I have a good rest and do everything that I need to because I know that as soon as I am with her, she will give me such a stressful time, and she will put me under a lot of pressure. She won't allow me to go out with my friends, my time is only for her. Even when I want to go out with my sister or my brothers I have to have a good reason and sometimes I have to lie, and then she allows me to go but for no longer than one hour. She doesn't want me to have a good relationship with my brothers or my sister. When I have a nice conversation with my sister or my brothers, and am laughing and joking, she gets angry with me. and I can't understand why.

The day before my departure, I went out with my sister. We went for a good lunch, a beauty treatment and, before we knew it, we were already a couple of hours late. I had told my mother we would only be an hour. If I had told the truth, she wouldn't have allowed me to go out.

I called her and tried to give as good an excuse as possible, but she asked me in a high-pitched voice, "Where are you?

I said, "Back soon" and straight away hung up the phone.

On my way back home I was so worried. As soon as I walked in, she looked at me and I could tell by her face that she was angry. I tried to talk to her but she replied in an angry voice, and it went on for a couple of hours. At the age of forty-five she was still shouting at me like I was a little girl. I am her daughter but she has never shown me any respect. She only ever wants me to stay at home and do everything for her.

The day before me and my brother flew to the capital city she asked me to get her a dining table and, without saying a word, she received her request. When Nazeri found out about that he got mad and said to her, "You already have a dining table so why do you want another one, and where you going to put it?"

What my brother didn't know was that my mother wanted to replace the old table with a very expensive one. He didn't know that every year when I returned home, this is what I had to do. He was really confused and upset when he saw how scared and worried I was around my mother and how much I spoiled her. He was ery angry and raised his voice to me in front of my cousin and my cousin's friend. I was already so depressed about the situation with my family and now my brother had upset me too. All of sudden my mind went blank and without thinking I shouted some bad words at him, and then I ran upstairs to be on my own. I sat in my room and cried. I thought, why did have to shout at me in front of other people? Why doesn't he respect me? He hadn't seen the family for seventeen years and many things had happened that he didn't know about. I had explained to him how much pressure I was under but he hadn't taken much notice. Instead he had caused problems for me. Why didn't he try to understand the family situation?

Suddenly someone knocked on my door. As soon as I said come in, my cousin Kamal walked in. He had come upstairs to say goodbye because he wanted to go home. I couldn't control my emotions and, lost for words, I just cried like a baby. He spent a few minutes chatting to me but then he had to go because his friend was waiting for him.

Not long after, Nas came into my room and, in a high voice, he said, "We need to talk."

As soon as I heard that voice my blood pressure jumped right up. Angrily I replied, "I don't want to talk."

"Why?" he asked.

I replied, "I just don't want to talk."

He started shouting at me, "WHY?"

He made me really angry. I faced him and said, "Don't you shout at me, get out of my room, I don't want to talk you."

He still wouldn't back off. he just stood there and said loudly, "You are crazy!"

I thought, damn you! This time I could feel my chest blow up like a volcano. I looked at him and he looked evil, then I started screaming, "Yes! I am crazy, crazy because of all of you."

I completely lost my temper and my mind went blank, the only words I heard was when he said, "Give me back my passport."

For some reason he had asked me to keep his passport for the past few days. I said, "You can take back your passport and do whatever you want to do."

Then he said, "Do you remember the last seventeen years?"

Before he continued I cut him off. "Yes! So you should think about why I have done all of this for you."

I almost had a panic attack and was out of breath. My mother was now standing between us. She knows that when I get angry, I can get really mad, so she tried to stop my brother and asked him to go to his room. Whatever my mother said, he didn't give a damn, he just stood still in my room looking at me and talking non stop, just like a grumpy old man. It made the situation even worse. Bloody hell! I didn't know what language I should speak to make him move away from my face before I got any crazier. At last my mother had no choice but to push him out of my room and into his room. I could hear my mother having a talk with him.

Thank God he was out of my room. My heartbeat gradually slowed down. I sat on the bed thinking, after all I have done for him, this is how he repays me. I have given him my time, my energy, everything so he can be with the family and now he doesn't trust me with his passport. I couldn't believe he was doing this to me. No other sister would do what I had done for him. I was so sad that night. Each time I closed my eyes I saw my little brother Nazeri when he was a young boy. He was so sweet and gentle, whenever I was angry with him, he never fought back. I missed that little boy. Now he kept to himself, he didn't talk to me much and sometimes he could turn very moody, which made me stay away from him. My mother walked into my room and asked me, "Why were you two arguing?"

I said to her, "Why don't you ask him?"

At that moment I couldn't explain because I was too upset, but my mother said, "He's angry because you bought me the dining table? If that's the reason, you can send it back to the shop."

The way my mother said it made me feel so guilty because I knew she really wanted it, so I said, "Don't worry! You can keep it."

A soon as my mother left the room I closed the door and I stayed awake all night. My mind was left racing with the sad fragments of other people's lives.

I don't know what time I fell asleep but I could hear my mother's voice calling my name. My eyes were so swollen I couldn't even open them, and my head was spinning because I hadn't really slept all night so I couldn't get out of bed. But my mother wouldn't stop mumbling. I just wanted to shout at her, "Mum! SHUT UP!" But instead I kept quiet and just ignored her.

Suddenly she came in. I quickly closed my eyes and pretended to be asleep. She said something but I have no idea what she was talking about, then she left my room. I was sure she had got frustrated waiting for a response from me. But then I could hear her voice in my brother's room. I hopes she was giving him a good lecture.

A moment after, somone knocked on my door. Without waiting for an answer the door was pushed open and Nazeri came in. He hugged and kissed me and said, "I'm sorry, sis!"

I replied, "Don't worry! Forget about it, pretend nothing happened last night."

He said, "I love you and I am really worried about you because you have done too much for the family. Like the dining table; she already has one table and she wants more? Since we have been back Mum has never gathered all of us to eat at the table so what is the table used for? And she's got too much stuff inside the house, you spoil her too much."

He got the point and I totally agreed with him. I replied, "Yes! You are right. I know I do everything Mum and the rest of the family want and if you want to know the truth, this is the way it is every time I come back home, and it has been for the past twenty years. If I don't do it, she won't be nice to me and I don't want that. I am sure you are confused seeing the family like this after seventeen years, and I do understand tht you worry about me, but don't shout at me, it makes me very upset, especially as I am under a lot of pressure."

He said, "I don't mean it; I just get really angry with the situation in the house."

Before the conversation ended I said, "Never again ask for your passport back, you have to trust me. I am not your brothers; I would never do stupid things to you. I brought you back to see the family and I have looked after you more than myself. I am very disappointed and very upset with you."

I kept my sadness to myself and carried on for the rest of my time with Nazeri and tried to make him and everyone happy.

Our last day in the countryside was approaching. On my last day I wanted to go out with my sister and do girlie things. We hadn't done anything like that in such a long time, especially since she got married and had children.

But one big problem was my mother. She won't allow me to go out unless I have something to do, and then she will ask me so many questions before she opens the cage and lets the bird fly freely. I really don't understand why she has to do that. I live by myself for most of the time and she doesn't know what is happening to me, and I'm a big girl so she has no reason to worry.

I have no freedom and a lot of pressure from my mother, because she only wants me to do things for her. Anyway, I used my clever brain to come up with a good reason to go out. As I had bought my mother her house, I told her that I had to go to the lawyer's office because they needed me to sign the paperwork, and then I needed to go to the bank. I told her I would be home late because I had a lot of things to do. After this explanation my mother allowed me to go out.

Hooray! I had done it! I drove happily away from the house and straight to the bank to cash some money, but unluckily the bank was still closed because of the Eid celebration. Hooray again! That meant I had plenty of time with my sister. While I was driving I was on the phone to my sister, and I asked her to give me directions to her house.

I arrived at last and she happily welcomed me into her house and showed me around. She lives in a two-bedroom flat. It is very nice and comfortable and big enough for the four of them. I was very happy for her. Four years she had been married and this was the first time she had invited me! As I had promised my mother I wouldn't go home late, I told my sister that we had to go because I wanted to spend some time with her doing things outside the house. So we made a move and did what we had planned. We only had a couple of hours together but the time that we had felt so precious to me and we both enjoyed it so much. She asked me a lot of questions and joked and teased me, making me laugh all the time. My sister has a wicked sense of humour, which I remembered from before, and this made me love her more than words can say.

On the way back I called my mother to ask her if she wanted anything. She shouted at me angrily, "Where are you? Why are you late?"

Without answering her I hung up the phone and then discussed with my sister what reason I should give our mother for our late return home. The nearer we got, the more scared I was about how my mother would react. I really didn't want her to create any problems because tonight was my last night and I wanted my sister to sleep at my mother's place so I could have more time to chat with her. We arrived home safely but my heart was running at one hundred miles per hour as I waited to see what was going to happen. My sister just worried for me; if my mother got angry with her, she could just go back to her house, where her husband would be waiting for her. What about me? I had nowhere to go and no husband waiting for me. It was really sad. We walked into the house and there we found my mother sitting on the sofa waiting for us with an angry face, like a hungry lion waiting for its prey. I said hello to her but she didn't reply or even look at my face. I went to the kitchen and put the food I had bought her on a plate, then took it to her and asked her to eat it, but she said, "That food doesn't look nice."

But I said, "Why don't you try it first?"

Then she said, "Just leave it there."

I sat in the living room waiting for her to come around but she just ignored me, which I was really sad about, especially as it was in front of my brother Nazeri, who didn't really understand about my mother's character yet after seventeen years of not seeing her.

To start the conversation I told my sister, "Kak Cik, I am going upstairs now to wash my face, after half an hour could you come to my room because I have a few things to chat to you about?"

My sister answered, "OK!"

But as soon as my mother heard, she got really angry and raised her voice. "Why? So tonight your sister is going to sleep with you? Fine, I can sleep down here."

I lost my patience too and said, "Mum! I didn't say you can't sleep in the room; you can go into the room anytime. I asked Kak Cik to go upstairs because I want to chat with her, that's all, Mum! You always think badly of me, that's very silly."

Then she said something to my sister in the kitchen, I have no idea what but suddenly my sister took both of her children and got ready to go back to her home with sadness on her face. I got really mad with my mother and said to my sister, "Come on! Please don't go home, you know that I am going tomorrow so please stay tonight. I'll be really hurt if you go so please stay for me."

Without a word she walked back into the house. I said, "I am going upstairs now so come to my room in fifteen minutes." My mother didn't understand any of what I said because I spoke in English.

I was in my room waiting for my sister to come in but instead my mother walked in. As soon as she sat on the bed I started to lecture her angrily. She didn't answer, I think she was just waiting for me to shut up. As soon as I shut my mouth, she quickly ran downstairs. Good for her.

While waiting for my sister, my phone beeped; I had a message. It was my sister saying sorry but she couldn't come to my room because of my mother. I was really frustrated with my mother's behaviour towards us. I lay in bed thinking, why does my mother treat me worse than the others? This is ridiculous, for a long time she has hated me. I would like to know why. Suddenly she walked in and sat beside me on the bed. This was the last night I would be with her so I asked her for the second time, "Did you want me to read my book to you?"

She replied, "Next time, I am sleepy now."

The way she answered hurt me deeply. My first book, *Life Behind the Silence*, was like a heaven to me. All through the process, she gave me so much encouragement and moral support, until the book was completely done. When the book was published, I was on top of the world and wanted to be with her and hand her the book. I told her the day my book was published and she was very happy, and I told her that this was going to be the best present that I would ever give her. One month later I flew back home and as soon as I arrived I happily showed her the book. But her face changed; she wasn't happy at all and I wondered why. She held the book for only a few seconds then handed it back to me. I felt so hurt at the time. I had flown a thousand mile to show ehr the book I had worked so hard on, and that meant so much to me, and she wasn't the excited to receive it and she didn't appreciate it at all. The question kept buzzing around my head, why is she doing this to me? I couldn't understand it.

I closed my eyes slowly, pretending to sleep, then I saw my mother get up and go downstairs. Ummm…! When I wanted to read the book to her, she said she was tired and sleepy, but now she was awake. Well! Whatever! I was so tired so I put the question to one corner of my mind and I slept soundly until the morning!

CHAPTER 35

Last Day

It was the last day my brother and I were going to be with the family, but I could see that Nazeri was anxious to go back to Kuala Lumpur. I was happy to see the smile on his face; it reminded me of when I took him from my mother's house to the capital city to stay with me when he was a kid. I stood in one corner and looked at him; to me he was still a little boy. He was still such a good boy, he helped my mother with the cooking and cleaning round the kitchen. I left them alone and went to my room to pack my stuff. Redzwan walked into my room to have a chat with me while I was packing. A few minutes later my mother walked in and sat between us, interrupting my conversation with my brother.

That is my mother, she has always done that to me, she has never allowed me and my brother to have any private time. She started bringing up all of her probems. I was really tired but what could I do?

My mother and my brother sat on the bed watching as I packed. I opened my handbag to check I had my the passport and to make sure I had left nothing behind and in there I found all my documents about my IVF treatment. I had a big smile on my face as I happily brought them out to show my mother and my brother. As my mother already knew about this, I only had to explain to my brother why I had made the decision to do it this way, and I handed him the pictures of the scan. Without question, he was very happy for me and wished me all the best, which was so generous of him. But then my mother said, "Ummm...! You are already old, that's all you can do."

I was really shocked and I looked into my mother's eyes with a broken heart. I then began to get angry but I said, "Mum! Before you gave me so much support and agreed with everything I was doing but now you you're talking like this, you've really upset me, Mum! How could you? To have the treatment and have my embryo frozen cost me a lot of money and I went through hell. I want everyone in our family to know that I did it this way."

My brother agreed with me one hundred percent and told my mother off. She didn't say anything but there was a smile on her face and that smile was full of meaning. I excused myself to go to the bathroom to have shower. In there I sat on the toilet and was very tearful. I thought, how could say something like that to me, especially in front of my brother? It was so embarrassing and she had no idea how hurt I was. When we are far apart, she is like my best friend, we can talk for hours and she gives me the advice that I need, but when we are close to each other, she is like my enemy.

I had done my packing and now needed to go out and do some shopping, just to clear my mind after what my mother had said. I took my sister along with me, we were going to the supermarket, to have lunch and to do some other stuff. We had a little time together before I left her, which I was very pleased about.

I drove back home. In two hours' time we had to leave for the airport so I was surprised to learn that they had not even had lunch yet and my brother had not even packed his stuff. I kept looking at the clock and at my brother. He took his time enjoying his lunch, laughing and not worrying about anything. I was sure we were going to miss the flight, particularly as he eats very slowly – he does everything slowly. I already had ready everything so as not to be late. I tried to make him go a little faster but he still took his time. I thought, eeerrrr…! Come on! I quickly went to my room to check if I had left anything behind then a few minutes later my mother came into the room to get something. I looked at her; my heart really didn't want to do it but my soul whispered, "Why don't you try one more time"" So I held my book out to her and for the last time asked, "Mum! Do you want to keep my book?"

She looked at me and said, "What am I going to do with that? I can't read it."

I told her, "But you can keep it, as I told you before, this book is the best present I could ever give you."

She looked at me like I was an idiot and said, "NO! Take it back with you."

As soon as I heard that my heart broke into pieces. I was lost for words, I couldn't explain how disappointed and frustrated I was. I walked slowly out of my room with an empty mind, and with so much hurt in my soul, but I still loved her.

At last everyone was in the car but on the way Nas wanted to stop at Zambri's workshop. Well! Without question we were definitely going to miss the flight. We spent about thirty minutes with Zambri, taking photographs of his antique car collection. Zambri usually hates having his picture taken but surprisingly he was now posing with everyone. I tried to cut the conversation short and told Nas that we had to go. My brothers shook hands and everyone hugged each other, and I kissed Zambri on the lips. It was very funny, he kept wiping his lips because they had lipstick all over them. I was very naughty, the more he wiped, and the more I kissed him. Everyone was laughing.

Nas drove to the airport and I sat in the front with him thinking, I wish I could drive, maybe then we would catch the plane. My mother, my sister and her two children sat behind us. I kept looking at the time almost every minute then I said to my brother, "I don't think we will be there on time. No, we've definitely missed the flight so slow down."

He sped up to try to get there on time but it was too late. I sat quietly, just waiting to see what would happen when we arrived at the airport. We got to the airport at the exact time the plane was taking off. Well done, Nas! I really hoped that I wouldn't need to pay for another ticket. We got our luggage out of the car and went straight to the counter and tried to explain why we were late. We made an excuse about the traffic – that's the best thing to do in these situations. Because I had bought business class tickets we only had to pay the fine, which was just 100 ringgit each.

Luckily a few flights a day go from there to the capital city so we booked on the next flight, we just had to wait for two hours, so that wasn't too bad. While waiting I took everyone for dinner and took advantage of the extra time to chat to them before we left. As usual my mother's problems were still neverending; she was asking me to do this and that even in the last minutes. I was so knackered, I just couldn't wait to be at the hotel resting my whole body and my mind in peace.

It was time to say goodbye. We hugged and kissed each other before walking to the gate. My sister had tears in her eyes; she was sad to see Nas go because they had been very attached to each other since she was a little girl. And at the same time she was upset with my mother for some reason. For that reason I got very worried because she was going to drive her back home. I told her with a tender voice, "I know you're upset with mum, but I am sure you know her character so forget about everything, and don't answer back, whatever she says. Remember, she is an old woman and the kids will be in the car, so drive carefully back home. I love you and I always will."

Then I told my mother in secret, "Please don't say something to upset her while she's driving. You know how she drives when she gets angry, so keep your mouth shut. Whatever you want to tell her, just wait until you get home." My mother agreed, and I hoped she would keep her word.

My sister looked at me with floods of tears in her eyes, and agreed without words.

She is a clever girl, I was sure she understood everything that I had said, but before I said goodbye again I reminded her, "Drive home safely. I'll call you as soon I get to the hotel." I left them behind with tears in my eyes but relief in my heart.

CHAPTER 36

Time Together

We arrived at Traders Hotel, the same hotel that I always stay at. I treated my brother the best I could to make him happy; he had been through a lot of hard times in the past seventeen years without me in his life. I hoped he would like his room and appreciate what I had done for him, otherwise I would be frustrated. I had tried my very best to make everyone in the family happy, including him, but sadly no one had made me happy. We walked along the corridor to the room and he said, "This is a very nice hotel."

I was pleased to hear that and agreed with him. I had a big smile on my face, I just couldn't wait for him to see the room. We arrived at his room, 3011, which was connected with my room, 3010. As soon as we walked in, I took him straight to look at the Petronas Twin Towers, standing beautifully and full of light in the night sky. We both stood for five minutes and gazed at the stunning towers. The first words that he said were, "WOW! Sis! This is awesome! I am lost for words, I really don't know what to say."

I stood in front of him full of smiles and with happiness in my heart, feeling like a mother trying to do the best for her son. Then I asked him, "Do you like it?"

He came towards me and gave me a big hug and a kiss annd said, "Thank you, Sis."

I said, "That's all I want." To know that I had made him happy gave me so much happiness.

He said again, "Sis! You didn't have to bring me to an expensive hotel, I would have appreciated even a cheap hotel but the main thing is I get to see you."

I replied, "Don't worry about that, I just want to treat you. I treat all the family the same way I treat you or maybe even better. I don't want anything in return just look after my heart, that's all I need."

He replied, "Come on, sis! You know that I love you."

I said, "I love you too."

Then he said, "But, sis, you're spoiling me now."

I smiled and said, "You deserve it after all this time."

The night was still early and our stomachs were hungry so we decided to go out for dinner. It was almost eleven at night. I could remember only one hotel that served food twenty-four hours a day, the Concord Hotel, which was not very far from where we were staying. I went to my room to drop my luggage off and then we were ready to go out. We got a cab, which only took ten minutes.

We walked into the coffee house, which I could see was full of Malay people sitting in groups, chatting and smoking while enjoying traditional Malay food. We could either choose from the menu or the buffet; usually people go for buffet, me included. There is so much food and it's all delicious, when I look at it, I feel like I want to eat it all!

Dinner is from seven until ten thirty and then supper follows from eleven until one in the morning, and then they serve breakfast from two until ten thirty in the morning, it's fantastic. My brother and I stuffed ourselves with food until I felt sick, it was very bad! After dinner I took him to the Hard Rock Café to have a few drinks. Luckily they had live band and the group were playing awesome songs. As I love to watch live bands I decided to stay until the end. It looked like my brother was enjoying himself as he danced with a pint of beer in his hand. Man! He was drinking like a fish!

Back at the hotel we wished each other a good night and I left him on his own to enjoy his sleep in the hotel. As soon as I walked into my room I could see the huge bed waiting for me to jump on. My body was feeling so knackered, but I couldn't do that yet. I had to unpack my luggage, tidy up and hang up all my clothes. Seeing all my clothes hanging up makes me so relieved. I can't ever do that at my mother's house. If I was to choose between my mother's house and a hotel, I would choose the hotel. I feel like the hotel is more like a home, it gives me so much freedom, I can do whatever I want without worrying about anything.

I looked at the time; WOW! It was four in the morning. I should jump into bed now. I left everything as it was, I would continue tidying up the next day. I jumped into bed and slowly dropped my body down, feeling so much relief. I closed my eyes and within a second my soul was flying to a different, more peaceful, world.

My alarm was ringing but my eyes were stuck together so I couldn't open them. I tried to look at the time; it was six in the morning. My body felt so heavy, I couldn't even make a single move. With my eyes still closed I thought, should I go to the gym or not? My mind said yes but my body said NO! And I said, come on, Gina, get up! Straight away I jumped out of bed and got into my gym gear. I quietly left the room, slowly closing the door so as not to wake my brother up because it was still early. I was walking like a zombie with both of my eyes half closed. I thought, I am killing myself but I know I will be fine soon as the exercise is over. There was only had a few people in the gym. I started my warm-up on the bike and as I had had only two hours sleep it was quite hard at the beginning. But I pushed myself for forty-five minutes on the bike and then my brain started to wake up and my energy started to jump, and I ended up spending two hours in the gym. Now I was fresh and ready to start the rest of day.

Back at my room I couldn't hear anything from my brother's room. I was sure he was still soundly asleep. I wouldn't disturb him until he woke up by himself. I wanted him to have a good rest and let him enjoy his time in bed. I decided that before he woke up I had better get ready because I take longer to get ready than him. I am not a make-up person but it takes time for me to choose what clothes I'm going to wear. I usually jump in the shower and spend about an hour in the bathroom but the best part of getting ready for me is trying my clothes on. I love fashion. I would love to be fashion designer but I hate sewing. I would love to be a model but I am not tall enough. Actually I did do part-time modelling for the company where I used to work as an aerobics instructor for a short while; that was fun and I loved the catwalk.

I tried a red top, then a white one, then decided to wear a jacket but it was too humid out there. And perhaps shorts, instead of a summer dress or skirt… I kept changing over and over again until I heard someone knocking on my door. Of course it was my brother so I said, "Come in!"

He pushed the door and walked into my room. He was all dressed up. He asked me, "Are you ready to have breakfast?"

I was shocked and said, "What?" Then I asked him, "When did you get up?"

He said, "Half an hour ago. What time you wake up?"

Instead of answering his question I asked him, "Did you have a shower already?"

He replied, "Of course, look at me."

I said, "Right! I won't be too long, just give me fifteen minutes."

He turned around and went back into his room. I thought, man! In half an hour he can get completely ready. Why is he so quick? And now, as he was already ready, I had to get ready as fast as I could. Luckily I had already decided what I going to wear, I just needed to drop something in my bag and I would be ready to go.

We ate breakfast at the coffee house. The waitress took us to a table for two right in the middle of the room. I could see the breakfast buffet, there was so much food. I felt so hungry after my workout. As soon as we arrived at the table, instead of sitting down I just hung my bag on the chair then went straight to get some food. WOW! Yummy, yummy! I was so greedy, I wanted to eat everything. My favourite breakfast is wild Alaskan salmon. Well! Surprisingly there was salmon, not wild salmon but that was still fine. I put everything that I wanted on my plate then returned to my table and enjoyed my food. As soon as I had finished I went to get more food. I really stuffed myself, it was like I had never seen food before in my life. My brother was so cool, he took his time getting his food and ate very slowly, he even took a long time to chew and swallow his food. Man! I couldn't stand that, but he can really eat, I was just wondering where he was putting all that food.

It was Nas' first day in the city so we decided to go shopping at the Petronas Twin Towers. It took us only five to ten minutes to walk there from the hotel. As I don't like the sun and worry about my skin getting tanned, I rubbed my body with SPF 90 to protect my skin. Still, I was very conscious of avoiding the sun and walked under the shade, leaving my brother behind. But my brother was so relaxed walking in the sun with his chubby belly, like it was nothing to him. Well! I guess that's because in Australia in the summertime it can reach forty degrees. There's no way I would go there during the summer.

Shopping with him really pissed me off, getting one thing took hours. I hate waiting and am usually really impatient but because I hadn't seen him for seventeen years, I had to be patient otherwise I would have left him on his own for a long. I am shopaholic but the way I shop is really easy, I go into a shop and grab what I like. I won't try it on in the shop, it just causes a lot of hassle, queuing and having to remove my clothes. I prefer to try clothes on at home and take my time.

Anyway, back at the hotel we decided to go to the Sky Bar for a few drinks then, after we got back to the room, we rested for a few hours before we went out for dinner.

It was the second day in the hotel with my brother and my schedule was the same, as it was every morning. I woud go to the gym while my brother was still snoring and sometimes I had to wake him up. On this day he had planned to rent a car. It was a shame my licence had expired otherwise I could have driven; it was really frustrating because I love to drive. I got my first car when I was nineteen and from that time on I would change cars every six months. I drive fast and crazy. Sometimes I go for long drives on the motorway, and sometimes I have a race with someone at the weekend after I've been clubbing. I am so in love with driving, and I become so crazy. I remember taking driving lessons for the first time when I was eighteen years old. I knew I had completed my test without any mistakes, but then suddenly the instructor shouted at me, "Get out!"

I really thought that was it, I had failed my driving test. I got out of the car and walked away, I was so upset Suddenly he shouted at me again, "Where you going?"

I said, "Home."

He said, "No! Come here! You have passed your driving test."

I hadn't understood what he meant when he said "Get out", I thought I had failed, but what he meant was "Get out of the car, you have passed."

I couldn't believe it when the instructor told me that I had passed the test! I was so happy, it felt like a dream. As soon as I got home I packed my stuff and the same day I drove back to my mother's city of Kulim. The journey took about seven hours back then but now they have built a motorway so it only takes about five hours. I only knew how to fill up a tank of petrol. Changing a tyre, putting water into the car – I didn't have a clue. It was the first time I had driven back to my mother's city so I didn't even know how to get there, I just followed the signs. I left at night-time so there would be less traffic and it wouldn't be as hot.

I arrived at my mothers home about six in the morning. She was really shocked to see me arrive in a car on my own. But I just smiled and was proud to show her my new car and that I could drive. I was just so happy to be driving at that time but when I think back now I think thank God nothing happened to me! What would have happened if one of my tyres got a puncture? Or something else! What would I hve done? I feel scared when I think about it.

I love sport cars and I even had one once, a Mazda RX7. I drove back in that car to see my mother in one day. I took her for a drive and to do some shopping. She just complained that my car was too small and didn't have any boot space to put her stuff in. She asked me to change it for a bigger car. I looked at her and smiled but didn't bother to explain anything to her because she would have never understood why I liked that car. Instead I burst out laughing when I looked at her sitting in this sports car, I couldn't even see her head, it was hilarious!

Anyway, after breakfast we tried to find information on where to rent a car. It was really hard for us because we had no idea where to find a rental place as neither of us had lived there for a very long time. Then my brother had a brilliant idea, he stopped a taxi and asked the taxi driver to take us to a car rental place, and in twenty minutes we were there. Nas chose the car and once we had paid for everything we were ready to make a move. That evening we would have to go to the airport because Giovanni was arriving from London but in the meantime we decided to go for lunch in the area of the city called Bangsa. My brother drove of course, while I was busy giving him directions. Suddenly my phone rang; I thought, who the hell is calling me now? Kazmin's number showed up on my phone. I thought, should I answer or not? Then I decided to answer because I had told him that I had found my brother and he knew that I was coming back to Malaysia with him. I wanted Kazmin to see my brother because he had known him since my brother was a little boy, and my brother had stayed with us. He loved Nas dearly. Ever since my brother had gone missing, he was the only person who had always asked me if I had found him yet. It really hurt me because none of my other brothers had ever asked me about Nas. As soon I told Kazmin that I had found my brother, he was so happy and wanted to see him so much. I had promised him that if I went back to Malaysia, I would take Nas to see him so now I had to keep my promise.

I quickly answered the phone. "Hi!"

Straight away he asked me, "Where are you?"

I said, "In Bangsa with Nas."

He was so excited about seeing Nas, he begged me to wait for him. I knew he had missed my brother so I agreed to wait for him without discussing anything with my brother, but I knew he would be OK with it. As soon as I hung up the phone, I looked at my brother and said, "Nas, Kazmin is coming to join us for lunch, he has missed you and wants to see you so much."

Life Behind the Silence

My brother said, "Well, for me it's no problem, but I'm just worried about you."

I asked, "What are you worried about?"

He said, "How do you feel tabout seeing him again?"

I laughed and said, "Don't worry, I have no more feelings for him. I am doing this because I promised him that I would take you to see him, that's all."

My brother said, "OK!"

Kazmin suggested that we wait for him at the Chile restaurant. I had heard about the Chile restaurant, they served a kind of Mexican food, but I hadn't been there yet. Well, I thought, it is nice to try something new. We have arrived early, before Kazmin. My brother decided to sit at the bar. I wasn't surprised that he was happy at the bar, he had been missing his Fosters beer since he had been at my mother's. I was bloody right. Straight away he asked for a drink and I ordered a margarita. We chilled out at the bar while waiting for Kazmin to arrive. After a second round of drinks, I saw Kazmin walk in but I pretended not to see him. He saw us though and he walked straight towards us and hugged me and shook Nas' hand. He was shocked to see the fourteen year old boy who used to stay with him now sitting in front of him as a thirty-five year old man. At the same time he was so happy to see my brother. For the first time I saw them communicate as adults. I was very pleased for both of them.

The three of us moved to the table for lunch. My brother ordered steak and Kazmin and I ordered fish. As I had not really been looking forward to seeing him again, I had nothing exciting to talk to him about and so just enjoyed my meal and let them chat. They chatted a lot, thank God. They kept asking each other about their lives and work, and then Kazmin started to talk non-stop about his business.

He looked so miserable with his long, untidy hair. He rubbed his face every single second and he couldn't stay still. He looked like he needed something, like someone addicted to drugs, it was very strange. When my brother excused himself to go to the toilet, I took the opportunity to ask Kazmin about his life. My first question about was, "How's your wife?"

He said, "We're not together anymore, now I live on my own."

I said, "OK."

Of course I felt sorry for him but I thought, for everything that he has done to me, he deserves it. He didn't look at my face when he talked and he looked very nervous, I was sure he was taking some kind of drugs. Then I asked him, "How is your business?"

He said, "I'm having real financial trouble and my business is in a bad way, I need your help please!"

I thought, here we go again, money, money never ends.

I was very curious to know the amount that he needed so I asked, "How much do you need?"

With excitement he replied, "A hundred thousand!"

I was shocked. Fucking hell! What was he thinking? He must be joking! I couldn't believe what I was hearing. Then he started to explain how his business was going to be fantastic if I gave him a hundred thousand. I thought, Kazmin, I have known you long enough to understand who you are, so stop giving me all this bullshit. I wasn't even focusing on whatever he was talking about, it didn't even enter my brain, I just looked at him and smiled. What kind of life do you have, Kazmin? I thought. How much longer do you want to go on like this? I know he used to help me and give me money, but that was when we were together, now it was over. I had helped him a lot too, so I owed him nothing.

My brother returned to the table and I told him that we needed to leave to go to the airport, especially as we didn't really know the way.

Kazmin asked me, "Why are you going to the airport?"

I said, "My boyfriend is coming from London to stay with us in Kuala Lumpur for a week or so."

He looked at me and said, "Oh! OK!"

As we didn't know the way to the airport he offered to take us there but I said, "No thanks! We will find the way but thank you anyway, that is very kind of you."

The three of us walked outside to get our cars. His car was parked right in front of the shopping complex and our rental car was in the car park. He took us to show us his car. Umm…! It was a new model Porsche; beautiful. But he had said that he had financial problems. It was bonkers! Before we left him he asked me, "How about the money? Can you help me or not?"

So as not to upset him I said, "At the moment I can't promise anything, but I will think about it."

He said, "Please! I need it as soon as possible."

I smiled but didn't say anything. I thought, there is no way he is going to get that amount of money from me. Even though I have it, why should I help

Life Behind the Silence 255

him after he has damaged my entire life? I would rather give my money to poor people who genuinely need it than give it to him.

Anyway, he asked us to follow his car, which was very kind of him. He took us to the motorway that goes to the airport, and then he left us. From there we followed the signs without any problems until we reached the airport. We had plenty of time so we walked around while waiting for the flight from London to arrive. Half an hour later we looked at the screen; the flight from London had landed so we went to Arrivals to wait to welcome Giovanni. As usual, I was impatient and talking mambo jambo to my brother. I kept asking him, "Where is he? Why is he so late coming out?"

I'm sure I was giving my brother a headache with all of these questions. Nas said, "Relax, sis! Don't worry, he will come out soon."

I said, "OK! I better shut my mouth."

From afar I could see him, with his curly hair and big forehead. As soon he saw us, he walked straight towards us with a trolley full of my brother's stuff. I can never thank him enough for coming all the way from London just to help me bring all my brother's things. He is such a kind person and that makes me adore him. As it was the first time my brother and Giovanni had met, I introduced them to each other. As he is Italian, Giovanni is a very loud person. He talked to my brother like he had known him for a long time and jokingly said, "Look at this, take all your stuff."

My brother laughed while he took the trolley from Giovanni's hand but they pushed it to the car together. All the way to the hotel they talked and laughed. I sat behind watching them both, so pleased that after just thirty minutes they were getting on so well together.

At the hotel, Giovanni was so happy with the room and the view of the Twin Towers, and I was so happy with that. I asked my brother to open his luggage and look at everything that we had got for him. I was even more excited than him, I was over the moon seeing him happily trying his clothes on like a little boy. My heart whispered, I love you, my little brother.

Then we went out for dinner. Giovanni's stomach is like a rubbish bin, he is always hungry and is always thinking about food. Well, he is Italian! He loves food and always looks after himself, which is what I love about him. Well, he was in very good company because my brother loves eating too; they could have competitions and I could crown the winner. After dinner we went out and didn't get back to the hotel until almost two in the morning. Giovanni stayed in my brother's room with him and I said goodnight to them.

CHAPTER 37

Sad in My Heart

My brother was due to leave us the following day, but Giovanni begged him to stay another day so we could have more time with him. At Giovanni's suggestion we jumped in a taxi to the station, which took about twenty minutes from the hotel. In the taxi my brother didn't talk much but Giovanni kept teasing him. I knew he had had so much fun and wanted to spend more time with us, but he was really worried about the restaurant and even more worried about his partner. I suggested that he call his partner to tell her that he was going to stay one more day. Come on! One day wasn't going to make a difference, surely she would understand that my brother hadn't seen his family for a very long time.

We arrived at the station and he took his time wandering around. He looked so worried, I felt so sorry for him. But I had to change his ticket now before it was too late. This was crazy, so I came to a solution. I handed him my phone to call his partner and told him to explain that Giovanni had arrived from London yesterday and he would like Nas to stay another day to get to know each him. Nas agreed with my brilliant idea and he walked away from me and hid himself in a corner to speak to his partner. Well, I thought, he might want to have a personal conversation with her, so I left him alone.

Fucking hell! He had been on the phone for almost forty-five minutes. What kind of explanation was he going to give us? For God's sake! I hoped he wasn't having any trouble. Me and Giovanni patiently waited for him. If it hadn't been my brother I would have been gone after five minutes. Finally he came back over to us with a smile on his face. Thank God, he had finished. I askedhim straight away, "So what happened? Can you stay another day?"

Life Behind the Silence 257

With a smile, he said, "Yes! But just one day, OK, I'm only doing it for you, sis."

I was so happy to hear that and said, "Thank you, darling, I appreciate that."

That was very sweet of him, as I knew his partner was not happy for him to stay another day. And I knew something was not right because before that he had warned me not to tell his partner that I had treated him to a room at the hotel for a few days. He said the reason for that was because he didn't want his partner to get upset because he was having a good holiday while she was at home waiting for him. I wanted to ask what was wrong with that but I thought, not at this stage, for the moment any time that I have with my brother is priceless.

Anyway, I quickly ran to the ticketing office to change his ticket before it was too late. I can't explain how happy I was that he was staying another day. That one extra day meant a lot to me, and I just wished he could spend more time with me. The ticket was changed without any problems then we all went back to the hotel with smiles on our faces, especially Giovanni, who was talking non-stop. Well! He is Italian so it didn't surprise me, I was used to it. I hoped my brother wasn't getting pissed off with him though, but I was sure he understood. If he didn't, he would have to keep it to himself as that is Giovanni's character.

For the past two days I had found my brother a bit strange. He hadn't talked to me much and he always kept to himself. He only came into my room when he needed my help to do his hair then he would be gone without a word. I tried to talk to him but he wouldn't respond much, and he looked like he wasn't interested in having a conversation with me at all. That made me really disappointed with him. What I expected from him was totally different to this. Every time we had breakfast we sat facing each other and sometimes he wouldn't say a word. I always had to find a subject to start a conversation with him about, otherwise we looked like strangers. Even when we went shopping, he only spoke a few words if he needed to. His face was always moody and I had to make jokes to make him smile, but I couldn't make jokes all the time. This was really upsetting me. I had tried to do everything I could to make him and everyone else happy. What had I done wrong, what else wasn't right? I was the only person who thought about them so why didn't they start thinking about me and my feelings? I was really hurt and pissed off but I tried to hold my sadness in as much as I could.

The extra day my brother had decided to stay with me was my birthday, 23rd September. His birthday is on 15th September but we were in the countryside at that time so we didn't no celebrate. I had told him that I wanted to celebrate his birthday but he said no, he wanted to celebrate his birthday on my birthday in the capital city. That was very sweet of him. I can't explain how happy I was that he was staying for my birthday because this was the first time that we would celebrate our birthdays together.

I was so excited to celebrate with him and I had organised something in secret. I had booked a restaurant in the KL Tower, which is one of the tallest towers in the world. I had requested a birthday cake with 'Happy Birthday to Gina and Nas' written on it. I did it all in secret. I tried to do the best I could to make him happy and make him have a good time with me. I love celebrating my birthday because that is the day I was born. Each year I would make it very special, I would have special treats from loved ones and go out partying with friends all night long. The last one I had celebrated was my fortieth birthday. Since then I hadn't celebrated, my life wasn't fun anymore. I no longer had friends to go out with and wouldn't get a single call from anyone for some reason, which was really sad. For five years I had been living in the dark. How could I have let this happen to my life? I needed to wake up and smell the coffee and face the world again.

It was the night of my birthday and we were all dressed up ready to go for dinner. I had been in this revolving restaurant a few times. The first time I had dinner at this restaurant, I secretly made a wish that one day my loved one would surprise me by going down on his knee and proposing to me. WOW! That would be so romantic, but that has still not happened, I am very disappointed.

This was the second time Giovanni had been to this restaurant but for my brother it was the first time. I was so excited, I just couldn't wait for him to see it, I was sure he would enjoy it. I really hoped so because I was becoming exhausted with everyone's behaviour. Dinner was booked for seven thirty but we were half an hour late because of the traffic. We had to get the lift to go up to the restaurant, which is named Seri Angkasa. It revolves at a height of 282m (948ft), 20ft above the observation deck. You dine at the top of the 421-metre high KL Tower, where you can get a 360-degree view of the city while enjoying your food. As soon as we walked into the restaurant we could see the beautiful view of Kuala Lumpur lit up at night.

I was so proud of myself and took charge of my brother by telling him about the restaurant but still he didn't look as happy as he should have been. The food was an international buffet including a wide variety of desserts. We all enjoyed the food very much and ate like pigs, especially Giovanni. Because it is a revolving restaurant, each time I looked out a different building would appear at my window. When I'm there, I always think I'm dining among the clouds. But I don't think that I was doing a good job of making my brother happy because he still carried on behaving the way he had been, it was really frustrating. I tried to enjoy my time; the food was fantastic and that's all my brain was trying to focus on at that moment. Before we left, an announcement was made wishing a happy birthday to Gina and Nas. I looked at my brother to tell him that it was a surprise for him. There was a smile on his face but I knew that smile was not genuine at all. The waitress came with the cake and put it on our table so we could both blow the candles out. I was waiting for Nas but he just sat there until Giovanni asked me to blow the candles out and asked Nas to stand beside me so he could snap our picture. I thought, why doesn't he bring his ass to me rather than wait for Giovanni to tell him to? I really didn't understand why he was behaving like this. I was getting a headache and feeling sick to my stomach from thinking too much.

He made me feel really stupid and hurt me a lot that night, especially as it was my forty-fifth birthday. At that time celebrating my birthday didn't mean anything to me, I was just doing it because of my brother. I didn't even want to think about my age, it just made me feel so sad. Because at the age of forty-five I didn't even have a family yet, and it was children of my own that I had wished for all this time. I was really frustrated about my life and heartbroken, but no one cared, not even my own family – not even my mother, the one person who knew everything about my life. Thinking of that made me so emotional, it was hard to control, then I became moody. Many questions were running around in my head and eventually it made me burst into silent tears. After dinner we went back to the hotel because my brother wanted to change his top and get his jacket. I was so pleased about that because my mood had changed and I had become unhappy all of sudden. I wanted to pick an argument with Giovanni to relieve my anger and the tension in my head that I had carried around for quite some time.

But at the same time I didn't want my brother to get upset because he didn't know much about my personal life. The longer I held my feelings in, the more stressed I felt. As soon as we arrived at the hotel, I walked straight to my room feeling very sad. I tried not to think about it because it was too much for me, but I couldn't help it. I am just like any other human being, I have a heart, and at that moment my heart was feeling so hurt. I cried and cried and cried. Suddenly I could hear knocking on my door. I knew it was either my brother or Giovanni so I quickly wiped my eyes and pretended to be doing something. It was my brother; he wanted to go to the clubs. I didn't feel like going out as my mood had completely dropped, but I pushed myself and hid all my sadness just for him. I didn't want to spoil his time, and I didn't want him to get upset. At five to midnight I was still waiting for both of them to wish me happy birthday but sadly these two bloody men didn't even bother, I hadn't even received a birthday card, how fantastic is that?

I felt I wanted to kick them both, I wanted them to get out of my face. The question is, why hadn't they bothered to take my heart into considersation a little bit, and just make me happy that one night? Giovanni did give me a couple of presents and I did appreciate that he had thought about my birthday. The presents were Prada and Gucci and they were beautiful. I love designer stuff, my favourite is Valentino. As much as I loved the presents they didn't excite me at all, and they didn't make me happy, because I was too hurt. Giovanni looks after me well and will give me anything that I want but he couldn't give me what I asked for. I was hurt, disappointed, really frustrated and my heart was breaking. Why was he doing this to me? I didn't deserve it.

Anyway, my brother was still waiting for me, so I was left with no choice but to agree to go with him and Giovanni to the Hard Rock Café. We were there for a couple of hours but I sat on my own and didn't talk to either of them. That is me; if I am upset it can go on for the whole night. I was just enjoying myself, watching the live band and enjoying the songs that they were singing, and my brother was enjoying himself drinking his pint and smoking, and Giovanni was doing the same except he doesn't smoke. The three of us looked like strangers.

Eventually I felt sorry for them so I broke the silence. I started to talk and made a joke. I was keeping my own sadness in one corner of my heart and trying to make the best I could of the night before my brother left me the next day.

I took them to a club where there was a group from Columbia singing Spanish songs and doing salsa dancing. I used to learn salsa and taught a bit to my students, but I haven't danced for ages. Well! I can still move very well. I love Latin music very much. I find salsa beautiful and very sexy, especially if you dance with the right partner. That night I had two guys with me, but

I could use neither of them on the dance floor. As usual my brother was sitting on his lazy bum and looking around with a glass of whisky in one hand and a cigarette in the other; he smoked non-stop. Suddenly they played my favourite song, I couldn't hold my feet still any longer, so I grasped Giovanni, dragged him to the dance floor and started my sexy salsa dance moves. But when I looked at Giovanni, oh dear, he was really making a mess, he was moving everywhere. I pulled him close to me and taught him a few moves. Well! At least he tried. After a few songs we stopped and joined my brother. I continued to dance on my own in the bar area where we were standing and sometimes Giovanni joined me. My brother couldn't care less, he just sat and enjoyed his drink, but in the end we had good time.

For our last stop of the night I took them to a club called Beach Club, which is famous because it is full of prostitutes and foreigners. I took my brother and Giovanni there just for fun. As soon as we entered the club a few girls looked at my brother and Giovanni and watched which direction we were going, and some of them slowly followed behind us. We stopped at a table and the girls kept passing in front of us, looking at my brother and Giovanni and then at me last. I knew all of the girls wanted to offer my brother and Giovanni their company but they weren't sure what kind of relationship I had with these two men because, on purpose, I was standing right in the middle of them. Every time they looked at me, I made my face very serious. They were obviously scared to approach these two guys while I was with them. All the girls were young, pretty and sexy of course. I teased them both every single time a girl walked past us. Giovanni's eyes popped out like a frog, and my brother smiled in kind of a shy and he started moving around. Poor him! I thought I had better give him some space so I asked Giovanni for dance.

We danced non-stop until the crowd started pushing us. I stopped dancing and went to find my brother. There he was, wandering around, his eyes open wide looking at all those girls. He gave me a smile and raised his eyebrows. Umm…! I was sure that meant something. Well! At least he was happy; that made me happy. But I kept my eyes on him. I knew he was big enough to look after himself, but he was still my responsibility. As long as he as with me I would look after him. I didn't want him to go too far and I didn't want him to spend money on something stupid. He could have fun chatting and flirting, I had no problem with that. I could see that he had started to chat to some girls. Then I got a bit worried when I saw that one girl was standing very close to him. I didn't want to interrupt him so I just sat in a corner with Giovanni and looked over him. He took that girl to the bar and got her pint of beer and a pint for himself. I really hoped he would just buy her a drink then say goodbye. Now I felt guilty for bringing my brother to this club.

I looked at the time; it was already three in the morning. Time to go. I decided I had given him long enough so Giovanni and I walked towards him and I said, "Nas! Come on, we have to go."

My brother looked at me and smiled, then he looked at the girl and smiled but he didn't move his feet or say even one word. I stood right in front of them and looked straight at the girl. She moved slowly, pretending take a drink, but actually she was hiding behind my brother's back. I was sure she was scared of me. My brother was still looking around, there was definitely something on his mind but he didn't know what to do. Suddenly he introduced me to the girl. She said hello to me in a timid voice and I replied in a powerful voice but she didn't even look at me. She was a very small, innocent-looking girl. She looked Philippino or maybe Thai. At that moment I wasn't really sure how much longer I would have to wait there. As I could see that my brother still didn't want to let her go I thought I should leave them to discuss things. So I said to my brother that I would be back in ten minutes then me and Giovanni walked away and left them on their own.

Exactly ten minutes later I went back to my brother. In the back of my mind I already knew what my answer would be, whatever my brother asked. When we got there, surprisingly my brother was on his own, so I said, "Where is she?"

My brother said, "She's gone, so let's go back, you ready?"

I said, "Of course." He didn't look happy. I hoped it wasn't because of me.

We got a taxi straight to the hotel. In the taxi my brother said, "You know what that girl said about you?"

I said, "I don't know, what did she say?"

He gave a little laugh and said, "She said you look so vicious and she was so scared of you but I told her not to worry."

I smiled and said, "Good!"

As soon we arrived in the room, I looked at my brother's stuff, which was still everywhere. He hadn't done any packing yet, but he had already jumped into bed. I turned to him and said, "You only have three hours before we leave for the airport, so you better pack your stuff now." Giovanni agreed with me.

Life Behind the Silence 263

With his eyes closed, he said, "Umm…" then Zzzzz…!

Within a minute he was soundly asleep, leaving me and Giovanni standing in front of him looking stupid. I thought, he's such an idiot, I have been talking to him and he's asleep. I left him and Giovanni and walked into my room and jumped straight into bed. I closed my eyes and without thinking about anything I slept for three hours before waking up to take my brother to the airport.

I didn't talk much on the way to the airport. I tried to keep it cool as much as I could but it was sad to see Nas go after we had had such a good time together, even though he had hurt me with his behaviour, but I was sure he hadn't noticed that. When we arrived at the airport he checked in his luggage straight away and then there was just enough time for him to go through customs and to the gate. I waited to one side because Giovanni was having a talk with him. I had no idea what they were talking about. Then my brother came up to me, gave me a big hug and said, "Love you, sis!"

I replied, "Love you too, darling!"

We said goodbye. I was in tears for a few reasons; I was sad to see him go and also a bit disappointed about his character. I remembered the first time I had spoken to him on the phone, when he had told me that he had changed. Yes, he had. But I should understand, seventeen years is such a long time, anybody can change and become a different person, so I couldn't expect him to be the person I used to know. But I missed my little brother's character. He was so arrogant and snobbish now, and I hate that kind of person. But he was also very caring, and I will always love him because he is my dear brother.

I looked at him until he had disappeared from out of view. I wished him all the best for everything he did in his life and of course I said I would get in contact with him as soon as I got back to London.

Back at the hotel, I was relieved that I had done my job as a daughter and brought back my missing brother to my mother, like I had promised the rest of the family I would. I had rid myself of my guilt and I was proud of myself.

I respect my brother's adventures and his independent life and I am very proud of him. I wish him all the best for his future and hope his dreams come true.

I am also happy for my brother Redzwan at last. He has married his dream girl and has two good-looking boys. His work is very basic and he lives a very simple life but he works hard for his family. I am still concerned about his married life, because he doesn't seem happy and always talks about divorce. My mother has told me that he is under a lot of pressure from his wife. I don't want to get involved. I am sure he knows what to do and I wish him and his two boys all the best.

After seven years, my brother Zamberi is also married at last. He has one beautiful daughter and one handsome boy, just like his father, and he has become a fantastic father to his children. He too works hard and is doing very well with his business. I am very proud of him.

I am very disappointed with my sister Nurul, because I wanted so much to bring her to London to study. She was very young and very clever but then she made the decision to get married to the man of her dreams, and they now have one boy, one girl and one on the way. Her two children are very sweet and clever, just like her. She lives a very simple life but they are very happy together, and I am very happy for her. I wish her all the best in this world for her future with her husband and her children.

As for me, I am still on my own, without a husband and without children, but I am happy to see all my family in a good place. I want to watch all my neices and nephews grow up into beautiful people. I am sure they will.

After my brother left I decided to take Giovanni to Penang Island. As Giovanni had never been there before, he was so excited and asked me so many questions. Even though I am from Malaysia, there were many places that I had never visited on Penang Island, so it would be intersting for me too.

After three days on Penang Island we started to go on tours with the guide from Nature Adventure, and it was very interesting. To do that we had to go by boat. It took me a long time to decide whether or not to go because I was worried about my seasickness. But luckily the boat went very slowly. The guide showed us a few animals in the water and explained to us about many kinds of birds. Seeing the oean was amazing. It was so blue and beautiful; even though I am scared of water I could still relax my mind and soul. For the first time I really appreciated the beauty of nature. I really enjoyed my time on the boat. I wished I had done it a long time ago but I am still scared to go on a boat now.

After forty-five minutes the boat dropped us on a beach and the guide took us on a walk. I don't like the beach because I have to walk in the sun but luckily I had already put SPF 60 all over on my body and I was wearing a big hat that covered my face. The guide took us to the area that had been hit by the tsunami that had also hit Indonesia. I stood in exactly the same spot that the tsunami had hit and he explained that the big rock that was there now didn't used to be there before the tsunami had hit. Oh shit! I felt so scared. I looked at the sea and I could see a wave moving towards us; I hoped it wasn't a tsunami. I started to worry and looked at the ground, I could feel my legs moving. Oh God! Please! Not now! Damn! My imagination was getting worse, I couldn't stay any longer but he was really taking his fucking time walking around the area. I thought, what happens if a tsunami comes, where am I going to run? My eyes kept looking at the sea and my mind was full of stupid things. After one hour he decided to leave that area. Thank God, my life was safe now. Then he took us for a walk through the jungle back to the hotel. It took us about three hours, which I loved very much because this was exercise for me.

On the last day we were on Penang Island Giovanni decided to climb Penang Hill. The guide was going to pick us up from the hotel at seven in the morning. I know Penang Hill but I had never climbed it, it would be a first for me too. The guide had told Giovanni the kind of shoes we had to wear and how much water we had to bring and a few more things, and I thought that was a lot of hastle. Giovanni got everything ready in advance and made a big deal about climbing the hill. I thought, just relax; when the time comes, just go and climb the hill. We went to the lobby to look for the guide; there he was waiting for us, a Chinese man with long hair like a ninja. As soon as he looked at us he said, "Are you ready?"

Giovanni was so excited. "Yes, we are," he said.

I just smiled and agreed, but the guide looked worried about me. He was so confident with Giovanni but not me. Well, he might be wrong. He drove us to the hill; it was raining when we got there but not too bad. Without wasting any time we started to climb Penang Hill. It was eight o'clock on 3rd October 2010, and a very wet morning. The guide was in front of us, I was in the middle of course because I was the only women and Giovanni was right behind me. I looked at Giovanni; he was just like a monkey, so excited to be climbing and talking non-stop. But then after thirty minutes he went silent. I turned around look at him, Man! He was drained! He looked so exhausted and could hardly walk, bless him! To keep him moving I started talking and asked him, "Are OK, darling?"

He answered in a loud voice to show off that he was still strong, "Yes, I am fine and you?"

I replied, "I am very good."

Then he went silent again. It was amazing walking in the forest, it reminded me of when I was a child. I always used to walk in the jungle but I never climbed the hill, this was my first time and I was enjoying it very much. I didn't feel tired, especially as I could hear many different kinds of birds singing with many different kinds of melodies to welcome us to the jungle, it was so cheerful. The jungle was also full of the noise of insects which I had never heard before. They made my ears drum and I don't think they were happy that we had entered their world. My energy pushed me and kept me moving, and I was keen to find out more about the forest. Our guide explained to us about every single thing that I had been missing in this beautiful world, it was very intersting.

After one hour of climbing we stopped at the first station for just ten minutes for a quick drink and I stood for a few seconds looking at the sea; it was so beautiful from the top. I closed my eyes and breathed in slowly and then let go. I felt all the pressure, depression and sadness that I had been carrying all my life fall away at that moment. I then turned around look at Giovanni. I burst out laughing; he was soaking wet from head to toe, like he had had a shower. Anyway, we continued our journey and this time it started to feel a bit tough but I loved the challenge.

When we first entered the forest I had started to pray non-stop in silence that nothing dangerous would happen to us because there was only three of us there. I was most worried about the guide because if something happened to him, Giovanni and I would be lost and wouldn't know what to do, we might even end up staying in the forest. I kept up with the guide all the way and left Giovanni quite far behind. I tried to push Giovanni to walk a bit faster but I was worried he would slip down because the pathway was very slippery and narrow, and he had never walked through a jungle before. Even for me it was really difficult and I had to be very careful. I was enjoying my time climbing but my mind was worrying about both of them and my eyes kept looking around in case something jumped out at us, and I really hoped the climb would end soon!

When we stopped at the second station, I dropped my ass on the ground like a bomb. I could feel sweat running like a river inside my shirt. I had never sweated like this before. It was fantastic because I knew for sure that I had lost some pounds, and I couldn't wait to carry on climbing so I could lose more. Giovanni look terrible but he was still managing to keep up. As we only had ten minutes to rest, I quietly drank some water and then walked up to the end of the hill to look at the view. It was like a different world. I can't explain the feeling that I had in my heart.

We continued climbing and this time I brought out my walking stick. For some reason I had bought this walking stick in Kuala Lumpur before we went on holiday to Penang Island. I hadn't even known that we were going to do the climbing, it was just lucky really, and it really helped me a lot. The climb was getting harder, but the harder it became, the stronger it made me. But I wondering how much further we would have to climb. When I looked down I could see that there was no way I could turn back, so I was left with no choice but to climb until the end.

Giovanni was the youngest in the group but he was also the slowest. He looked so knackered, I was really worried about him. I kept talking to him to make sure that he was OK. Surprisingly he still kept up even though he was having problems with his legs. I ignored him; I didn't want to say anything in case he gave up. By the time we stopped at the third station, I was soaking wet but Giovanni looked like he had drowned and his face was as flat as a pancake. I could see that his feet were shivering a bit but I pretended not to see anything. I don't like telling Giovanni off so I knew I had better leave it and give him some support so he could continue without any problems. I left him and the guide tochat while I went to look at the view. Woops! I could feel my heart thumping and my body flying away. It was really high and I am scared of heights but the view was divine.

We continued to climb and now I kept asking the guide how much longer until we would arrive since it seemed the climb would never end. I was surprised at myself because I just kept going and never felt like giving up. I didn't even know where I got the energy. It was no doubt thanks to the exercise that I do every day, it has really kept me fit and I also really watch what I eat. Now I was able test my fitness.

I could see Giovanni starting to walk quite clumsily, he could hardly carry his feet. Then he told us that one of his sandals had broken. I wanted to laugh but I had to hold it in case I upset him. I asked, "Can you walk with the broken sandal?"

He answered, "Yes, I can."

Well! I didn't think so but he is very proud so his answer didn't surprise me. I asked him again, "Are you OK, darling?"

He replied, his voice full of his ego, "Yes! I am completely fine."

I knew he was half dead but he still wouldn't put himself down, which made me really pissed off at him.

Yippy! At last we arrived at the end of our journey: the last station, at the top of Penang Hill. It had taken us five hours to climb right to the top. I dropped my bag and my whole body on the ground. I was so relieved to have finished this challenging journey. I told our guide, "I am a fitness instructor but this is the hardest exercise that I ever done and as a forty-five year old I am very proud of myself." I was the oldest in the group. When I told him that I was a fitness instructor he was very surprised. Then he told us that, when we had decided to climb Penang Hill, he had been most worried about me. He said that he didn't think that I would make it right to the top. Well! There I was! I walked to the edge to see the view. WOW! It took my breath away, the view was stunning, I could see the city of Penang and I could even see Penang Bridge, it was magnificent. I couldn't take my eyes away from that view, it was magical. I still couldn't believe that I had done it. Well done, I thought, you did it, Gina!

But it wasn't over yet, because we still had to walk back down the hill. I was so relieved when our guide told us that we would follow the tar road, it really put a smile on my face. The road going down was harder than the uphill climb but for me it was very easy. I jumped like a grasshopper and left them very far behind. When I looked back I could never see even their shadows. I thought, where the hell are they? Fuck them! I had no time to wait so I left them and continued walking on my own. It was so easy to walk down, what was wrong with them? I had walked almost halfway when I decided to wait for them. Ten minutes later, there they were, walking down like turtles. As soon as I saw them I started walking again but then Giovanni shouted at me, "Gina! Could you stop right there please!"

I thought, what now? But then he said, "We are going to stop at the café just in front of you."

I looked at the corner up ahead. Oh yeah, there was a café. Our guide must have told him, but what did they want to stop at a café for? I was bit worried about the time because we had to check out of our room and go to the airport because that night we were flying back to London. I hoped they wouldn't take long. But first at all I went looking for the toilet, I was dying for a wee after drinking so much water. Luckily they had a toilet. I couldn't wait to relieve myself. We sat in the café, both of them drinking coffee and me just drinking water and sucking my lollypop.

After half an hour of rest we were ready to make a move. At first I walked with them, then I got pissed off because they were very slow and took their time chatting and laughing, they were worse than women. I really didn't have time for that so I left them to enjoy their own company. The road had a lot of corners and was very narrow so it was really hard for some people but I found it easy and I enjoyed it so much that I wished it would never end. But I was also really scared on my own because everywhere was the jungle and wild animals could catch me anytime. Luckily I bumped into a few Chinese people walking up the hill for exercise. I would walk down very slowly if I didn't see anyone but then as soon as I saw someone I would speed up. I kept doing that until I saw a lot of people and a few cars. Yippy! I was so relieved to know that I had completed the adventure; the journey down was 11300m. I rested under the trees while I waited for Giovanni and the guide to arrive.

Now I can tell you a little bit about Penang Hill. Also known as Bukit Bendera, Penang Hill is the highest peak on Pulau Pinang, at 830m above sea level. It is one of the best places to catch a bird's eye view of the island.

Dear Lord! At last I saw them walking down, after fifteen minutes of waiting. They both looked like old men. I asked, "Why did you take so long?"

Giovanni said, "It's really hard going down."

I just smiled then turned around to look at the hill and whispered, "Penang Hill has left a good memory with me for the rest of my life." Saying that, if I were ever asked to do it again, the answer would be never because it was bloody tough.

Anyway, we had to go back to the hotel as soon as possible to pack our stuff because our check out time was at five and it was already three. Our guide took us back to the hotel. Luckily everything was done on time and we were at the airport at the time we had planned to be. From Penang Island we flew to Kuala Lumpur airport and there we checked in our luggage. At eleven forty-five the flight took off to London. Goodbye Malaysia. The journey would take thirteen hours. As soon as we settled down in our seats we both passed out straight away because we were so exhausted from climbing Penang Hill. I was sure that by the time we arrived in London I would be dead. I was thankful to Giovanni for that holiday as I had never felt like that before. I slept all the way to London.

CHAPTER 38

Muslim

The name of the Muslim religion is Islam, which comes from an Arabic word meaning Peace and Submission. Islam teaches that one will only find peace in one's life by submitting to Almighty God, Allah, in heart, soul and deed. The same Arabic word gives us Assalaamualaikum, which means peace is with you and which is the universal Muslim greeting. A person who believes in and consciously follows Islam is called a Muslim, which also comes from the same root word.

It was a late Saturday afternoon on another freezing day and my plan was just to stay indoors and keep myself warm. I hadn't had a single chat with my mother for two days, so I was wondering how she was. I looked at the time; it was two in the afternoon in London so it would be nine at night in Malaysia. I knew she would be awake. My mother never goes to bed early, the earliest she goes to bed is one in the morning but she might fall asleep at eleven if she is very tired. After two days without speaking to her, I was sure there would be many stories that she would want to talk about and that should would have a lot of gossip to tell me. I picked up the phone and dialled her number Within a second she answered the phone. "Assalaamualaikum!"

That is the way she always answers the phone with her soft and sweet voice, she sounds like a young woman, in fact she sounds younger than me. I can't answer the way she did.

I said, "Mualaikumsalam, Mum! How are you?"

After a general conversation she told me, "I have many stories to tell you."

I told her that was exactly what was on my mind before I called her, then I could hear her give me a small laugh. First of all she obviously told me about her two eldest sons, who I will have to hear about for the rest of my life. Then she told me that her friend had been round to see her to tell her that the book that I had sent him, *Behind the Eyes,* had arrived. Her friend is in charge of everything in the mosque and every time I go back to see my mother, I go and see him to tell him that I want to make an offering. His name is Wahab, the same as my father, but he is a lovely person with a beautiful character, totally different to my father, only their name is the same. I will tell him which day I want to make an offering and then he will go and tell everyone to come to the mosque on that day. He will tell me the amount of money that he needs to buy all the ingredients for him to cook. I then have to go with my mother and find the goats for my offering. Luckily my mother knows someone who is a farmer and he has many goats for sale. After I have paid for the goats, he will do the process, and then he will bring them to the mosque on the day of my offering.

As Wahab knew about the book, every time I made an offering he asked me about my book. I returned to Malaysia at the end of August for a holiday and one morning, on 10th September 2010, I went to Wahab's house to tell him that I wanted to make an offering and this time I brought him news about my book. He was so happy for me and asked me to send him a copy. And he told me that he wanted to tell everyone in the mosque that my book was published. I just smiled and appreciated his generosity. As I had promised to him, I sent him a copy, and he was very happy to tell my mother that he had received the book. Anyway, he told my mother that the book's content was very sad.

My mother and I were so pleased to learn that someone had read the book and then commented on it, no words can describe how happy and emotional I was. But I was very sad about my mother and told her, "You know, Mum, as soon as I told him the book was published, he asked me for one straight away. Can you see, Mum, how thankful people are for what I have done? But not you! I told you from the beginning that my book is my best ever present to you because that book means a lot to me and I am sure it will to you too. I am sure you remember that as soon as I arrived back home, the first thing that I did was hand the book to you, but you gave it back to me, and that hurt me. And again I handed it to you before I left for London, but you asked me to take it back with me to London. Can you imagine how upset I was?"

My mother was silent for a few minutes then she said, "Next time when you come home bring it back for me."

I said, "Whatever!"

After a two-hour conversation with her, we said goodbye.

As I was born a Muslim, I am proud of and respect my religion but I also respect other religions and I am very open-minded. Before I met Kazmin, my ex-boyfriend, I had a few boyfriends and they were crazy about me. That's because I was very attractive and quite a flirty girl at the time. So I took advantage of that and played around with the boys' minds. My plan was to get pay back for what my father, grandfather and my uncle had done to me. When I reached my teens, for many reasons I didn't like Muslim boys. Don't get me wrong, they are very nice, caring and very polite but something that I had seen had made me aware. I had a few non-Muslim boys who wanted to marry me and who converted to Islam but without telling me. I thought, how stupid is that? Who asked them to convert to Islam? Of course, what they did was wonderful, but it didn't impress me at all. I was very young at that time and the word *married* didn't even cross my mind. For them to do that was ridiculous. I am sure they wanted to surprise me, and to show me how much they loved me, be to be honest they could go to hell! It didn't mean anything to me, in fact they would get big surprise from me, a nasty surprise.

Kazmin was the first Muslim man that I fell in love with. His family was very religious but he was very open-minded, which was what I loved about him. The first time I arrived in London my mind went wild for an English man but I am the kind of person who is very honest with the person who I am in love, and he eventually broke my heart.

After Kazmin I never fell in love with a Muslim man again. He was the first and the last Muslim man I have been with. I did go out with an Indian man and I went to the temple with him just to learn about his religion and his culture. It didn't mean I was going to join his religion, just that I respected it. We are all the same in this world, we are only divided into groups by different religions. Our hearts, souls, minds and feelings are the same as we ar all human. All my friends, including a few of my boyfriends, in London are Christian and I do go with them sometimes to church. They only offer that i join them, they never force me. I wanted to go and look inside a church, and to learn something about them. I sat with them and watched how they prayed. Well! I did sing with them, there's nothing wrong with that, but I didn't do anyting that I wasn't supposed to. I went to church a few times, and for Midnight Mass on Christmas Eve, just to see and learn more things, as every day we learn new things in our lives. Everyone has their own opinions in life.

I love people; I love children and I love young and old people. It's the same with religion, I love to know about all the religions in the world even though I am a Muslim, no one can stop me.

I don't think I will marry a Muslim man but I would never say never. I think I have made my decision but nobody knows what is going to happen in the future. I could end up married to a Muslim, who knows? Muslim men are not bad people. Like in any religion, men have good and bad points. But the majority of Muslim men like to have several wives, which make me hate them.

Before they are married they are fantastic lovers and very caring. A few months after being married the relationship is still fine, but then as soon as the wife gives birth things start to change. When they have a second or third child they start having affairs with younger girls. They go out almost every night to the clubs or somewhere else, having fun with all the girls in the clubs while their wives are at home looking after the children. They get back home in the early hours and give a lot of excuses and of course their poor wives believe whatever explanation the idiot husbands give. And most of them end up marrying a second wife and having a child with them without the first wife knowing. Then when they get bored of the second wife, they will find a fresh new young girl, who could end up as a third wife. So they spend less time with the first wife and second wife, and most of the time with the young one.

When they divorce the first wife or second wife, they leave both of the wives without feeling any responsibility. Then the women have to go to work to feed themselves and to look after the children. That happened to my mother when my father divorced her and left us without any money, and exactly the same things happened to all of my friends whose husbands married new women, they left them without anything. It also happened to me with my boyfriend Kazmin; he had an affair with a few girls when he was in love with me, and when he was married he still wanted to marry me so I could be his second wife. I was stupid enough to agree at the time because I was still in love with him but, thank God, things never happened the way he planned. At the same time that he was saying he wanted to marry me, he had affair with a young girl. One day he introduced her to me on the phone. Obviously I was not angry or jealous because I was no longer in love with him, but he didn't know that because I was playing my own game to see how clever he was. Then one day he told me that he wanted me to be his second wife and his young girlfriend to be his third wife. His suggestion was that we live together in one house and that the three of us have a sexual relationship. Absolutely disgusting!

It came to the point where I had had enough of his immature personality. So I told him, "I am very disappointed with you, how could you ask the first woman in your life something like that? You have never respected me and you never will. You have hurt me a lot in the past and you are still hurting me now. I am holding in the pain in my weeping heart until you walk out of my life, but you couldn't care less. Is this what you call love?"

I expressed feelings to him that I never had before. My warm tears started to run down my cheek. He was silent then I said, "You should think about what you have done to me." Then straight away I hung up the phone and after that day I didn't communicate with him for almost a year.

The worst thing that he wanted me to do is bleach my skin so I would become white. Malaysian men love women with white skin, for them women with white skin are beautiful. That's why he wanted me to bleach my skin, so I would be pretty for him. I did not understand that; if he didn't find me pretty, why didn't he leave me alone rather than chasing me around? He was such an idiot and very selfish!

Since the day I stepped onto the ground of the city of London I have been learning a lot about life and culture, especially about myself. I am thankful to God, who took me away from the other side of the world, where the sun sets, and brought me to where the sun rises.

I learnt about my religion at school, but neither of my parents taught me how to pray or how to read the Al Quran so I didn't know any Arabic words. I am not a very religious person but I do pray sometimes, and I wanted to know more about Islam. As I come from a Muslim family, I do respect my religion. So I learned by myself how to pray from the Malay version of the Quran. I don't know whether it is right or not, but at least I tried to learn and to to pray.

Islam in Malaysia is totally different to Islam in other parts of the world. We don't kill each other or kill innocent people like some Muslims do. I have never have found where it says in the Al Quran that we have to kill people or that if we kill Christians, we can go to heaven. I never heard such silly things. Our country has Christian, Hindu and Buddhist people and we don't hate them, we live next to each other and become good neighbours and have good friendships. Women in Malaysia can cover their hair if they want to or they can enjoy Malaysia's nightlife like in any European country, it's their own choice. But for me the most important things that I have learned and that I have always programmed in my brain are: Muslims can't eat pork, can't touch dogs and can't drink alcohol. Well! Actually, we can touch dogs but only if the dog is dry, we can't touch them when they're wet. I honestly don't know for what reason. I don't eat pork but I do drink alcohol sometimes and I have my little Chihuahua, and I pray. How did that happen? I don't even know myself. Well! This is between me and God. I do things because I want to, and I pray because I believe in God and will always love God.

That's one thing that I will never understand about Muslims in other countries. They shouldn't be called Muslims when they kill each other. They shouldn't be called Muslims because they are different from us. I had a friend from Iran and I saw the way they prayed, it was absolutely wrong. The way they pray is not in the Al Quran. That didn't bother me at all because I am not a perfect Muslim myself, but what did bother me was a little mistake they made; they have to mention Muslim and Allah. That is just an excuse, it has nothing to do with the religion, in fact they are not perfect Muslims so what are they going on about? Shame on them.

They hate Christians so why do they come to Britain in the first place? And why do they receive benefits from the government every week for their daily needs? Why do they come to this country and tell people what to do? Why do they come to this country and bomb people? It's not only Christian people they kill, of course they kill Muslims too. If they want to do that, they should just go back to their own country and play combat and kill each other, they shouldn't include other religions. I am not talking about all of them but the majority are like that. I really cannot understand what kind of Muslims they are. I don't hate Muslims because I am a Muslim myself, but I feel so embarrassed because of their behaviour. They cause a lot of problems in this world and because of them, other religions think all Muslims are the same. One day I went to Camden Market with my boyfriend to find some stones for my collection and happened upon an Indian shop where they sold many kinds of stones. While I tried to choose the stone that I wanted, all of sudden the owner of the shop asked me, "Where are you from?" That happened to me all the time.

I smiled and looked at him. Instead of waiting for my answer, he jumped to another question: "What religion are you?"

Since the Middle Eastern Muslims have caused a lot of trouble, I never tell anyone that I am a Muslim unless they ask me. Anyway, I felt a bit weird when he asked me that but I didn't think much of it. He was an old man and looked very kind so I told him, "I am a Muslim."

Suddenly he said, "Ya! Muslims kill people."

I was shocked at such an unexpected response. Those words really put fire in my chest and I was burning inside when I looked at his face. I looked around; luckily no one had heard what he had said. I tried to control my aner and calm down, then I said, "Yes! I am a Muslim, but I am not an Arab, I am from Malaysia and we don't kill people. You have to be careful saying something like that."

He noticed that I was upset so he quickly changed the story to try and cover it up. I felt like throwing the stone at his bald head, but luckily he was an old man so I was still kind towards him and I bought his stone. So that's what I mean, these people damage things for other Muslims like me. I am very proud of my country and all the Muslims in Malaysia; we don't kill people and we don't hate other people's religionss. Muslim, Christian, Buddhist, Hindu and any other religion in this world, we are all humans. Black, white, brown, they are just coloura. We only have one life so we should enjoy whatever we have in this beautiful world as long as we are alive, and we should make the most of it.

Malaysian women are very softly spoken and very polite, that is our culture. But behind the politeness, they like to gossip and bitch, and to make up stories that aren't even true. They have so much jealously in their heads and that jealously sometimes turns to evil in their hearts, which makes them find witchcraft. Even some men like to use the witchcraft as well. These people can get really jealous of other people's success in their careers, and that is something I really hate. That is because this happened to me. I had lots of good friends, but none of them had genuine hearts. When I told them about my success in my career, their behaviour changed and they became complete strangers. I wanted to share my happiness about my achievement with them but sadly none of them seemed interested, and instead they made fun of me. I even lost some friendships because of my success, it was unbelievable. I couldn't stop thinking how generous I had been towards them and that this was how they were paying back my generosity. I was hurt because I needed friends to share my happiness, but I was proud of myself because I had done something amazing that they haven't achieved. Well! I should smile and be happy.

I met a lady from Malaysia who was living in London, and she had her own business. I knew her from her workplace as I regularly went to her and gave her some business. We became friends and sometimes we went out for dinner. She was a very nice lady, and she cared about me a lot, which I was very happy about. I adored her kindness but sometimes the things that she said to me could be very nasty and that upset me very much. I tried to hold in my sadness and started to avoid her as much as I could. But because she was doing excellent work in her job, she left me no choice but to continue seeing her. I tried to block out my sadness and put on a brave face and look happy. But then the day I received my books, I was so excited so I decided to take a copy with me to show her so she could share my happiness with me. When I arrived at her place, I did the things that I had to do with her first. Then before I left her, with a big smile on my face, I showed her my book. I thought she would be surprised and hug me or congratulate me, but nothing that I expected happened. Amazingly she didn't even look at the book, instead she said, "Good for you, but I am not going to buy your book, you have to give me one for free." WOW! What a lovely friend I had.

I stood in front of her feeling so hurt, thinking, did I hear her right? Was she being serious or just teasing me? Maybe I was a bit naïve because I was still waiting for her to say something nice, but then she started talking about her charity work. She showed me the list of how many people had given money and how much they had given, then she said, "You have to give something because this it's for charity."

I have no problem whatsoever giving money to charity, but she shouldn't have said that to me, and she shouldn't have treated me the way she did. As she didn't ask anything about the book, I slowly put it back in my bag and left. It's not very far from her place to my flat, it took me fifteen minutes on foot. While I was walking back home, I was in tears and was thinking, I haven't done anything wrong so why was she so nasty to me? Dear Lord! I did not expect her to buy the book, I just wanted to share my happiness with her, that's all.

Since that time I tried not to see her again. I thought that was for the best as I can't face somebody who has hurt me. She did call me and leave me a few messages but I just ignored them, because the messages she left were nasty. I hadn't done anything to upset her, so I did what I thought was right for me. For me, that was it; my friendship with her was over. I thought, what is wrong with Malaysian people? Why don't they have clean hearta? And why are they so jealous? I will never understand.

But it was totally different with my friends from London. As soon as I told them about my book, they were so happy and everyone bought my book and commented on it; how fantastic. I am so pleased to have them as my friends. A few people really touched my heart, especially Giovanni's mum. She burst into tears as soon as Giovanni told her that my book had been published, and Giovanni's brothers was also in tears. She is such a genuine person with such a good sense of humour. I just wish Giovanni's father was still in this world because I know he would have been over the moon. I loved him dearly and I can imagine how happy he would have been about my book.

My lovely sister, Nurul, bought my book and read it twice, and she said beautiful things about it, which made me so happy. And she told me she will keep my book for her children, for when they grow up, and she will let them know that it is their auntie's book. That was so wonderful, it was the most beautiful thing that I had ever heard from her, bless her!

Malaysia is a beautiful country but my mind was never at peace there, that is why I love the city of London. It has brought me so many things in life. The people don't care what you do, they don't bother about your life and I don't worry about anything. That is what I have learned in this rich country full of adventures. It is an expensive life, but I live with peace of mind and I won't let the world ruin my life.

CHAPTER 39

Last in Love

My heart was breaking because my life, my dream and my wish had been destroyed by someone who had been promising they would give me what I wanted all this time. I kept away from everyone because I had totally lost my confidence, and sometimes I was just not my self. Sometimes I really needed someone to talk to and at those times I did meet up with my closest friends. I tried to be as confident as I could and to keep my smile as big as possible, and to pretend that I was happy and enjoying my life, and I did the same with my family, especially my mother. When they asked about my life, I laughed and said that it was fantastic, that Giovanni gave me everything I wanted, that I couldn't ask for more and that I was happy.

But that was not true. What they didn't know was, I had been lying all that time. I am so sorry but I lied for some reason. I didn't want my friends and family to know that I had an unhappy life. I guess that when I was a little girl my father left a mark on my life, and that mark has made me scared to face the truth in life, and so my life has become very personal to me. And that makes me cry when I am alone, and no one knew that until today. It was very depressing because I didn't share what I was going through in life with anyone. Because of that, some of my friends didn't understand me and I lost communication with them, which made me really sad. I am crying like a little girl. What they didn't know was, all I did was to protect myself, I didn't want them to look down on me. But I was wrong, it didn't happen the way I thought it would. Sadly, I lost some of my closest friends. I hope one day they will understand who I am, and why I did not tell them the truth. I will never change myself for anyone, I will always be the way I am, that is me: Gina.

The morning sun was bursting through my window, but we were still in the wintertime and it was a very cold day. I was at home trying to put myself together but my brain was kicking me badly and that made it really hard to concentrate on whatever I tried to do. I was sitting at my computer checking my emails, just hoping someone had sent me some good news to cheer me up. Well! Surprise! Surprise! Kazmin had sen me an email. It had been a long time since I had heard from him; I hoped he wasn't going to give me any hassle. I clicked on it and saw that it was a long message. I thought, what the fuck is that? It was like a chapter out of my book. Man! This scared me and made me think twice about reading it. I only read the first sentence and that was enough to raise my blood pressure. Without reading anymore, I got straight off my computer and picked up the phone to dial his number. It rang and, thank God, he answered. As soon as he answered the phone, without asking him anything, I started my lecture, "Everybody in Malaysia just thinks about their life and always about money, money, money including you, and my family, that's all you guys know. All my life I have tried to help my family and give them a better life, but no one cared and no one asked about my life. When they need money, they know how to find me. Do they think money grows on trees? As soon as they get what they want, they're gone, they disappear and only get back to me when they need help again. I have been helping my friends and family but who's been helping me? I should have learned to think about myself by now."

He didn't interrupt at all, he was silent and listening to every single word that I said. As soon as he was sure that I had calmed down, he asked me, "How are you?"

I said, "Frankly, at the moment my life is like shit and don't even ask me why because I really don't know where to begin, it's a mess and I'm pissed off with everything. If I can, I want to go far away from everybody and be on my own, that's how I feel right now."

He replied, "Well, it's life, that's normal."

Straight away I said, "Yes! You are right, life is normal but people are shitting on me and that life is not normal, it's really fucked up. I hate myself for wasting my time on somebody who doesn't appreciate my genuine heart, and I'll regret that for the rest of my life. Anyway, I heard that your stepdaughter got married. Well! My sister told me she saw your wife and her ex-husband in a magazine but you were not in there. Why?"

He said, "I didn't go for a reason."

Then I said, "OK!"

I thought, it's better if I don't ask him much about his personal problems, especially as I have enough problems of my own. He changed the subject and made a joke about something else, which made me laugh, and then we ended up asking each other about our lives. At the end of conversation he said he needed my help; of course he needed money. He needed it for a very important issue that he had to settle and because of that I helped him, but only with Giovanni's permission. Even though I hate Kazmin for what he has done to me, somehow, deep in my heart, he is still a part of my life and he is my best friend because he never hides anything from me, and he always listens to my advice. That is something that I will always love about him.

Soon I ended the conversation with him and went back to my computer to finish reading the rest of his email. I was very excited to find out what he had written. It was midday on Tuesday 8th March 2011. Nothing that he had written about me made any sense at all to me, but it put a smile on my face, especially the words, 'The Gina that I knew before is totally a different person now.' Well! Of course he thinks that, I am no longer the stupid girl that he used to know before, waiting and wasting my life for him.

Then he wrote, 'I believed you would die and do everything for our love.'

I thought, he must be blind. I have done what he asked, I did everything to satisfy him, he was the one who cheated on me and married someone else. Because of my love for him, I trusted him and waited for him to marry me, but he just wasted more of my life. Love really hurts and it has left me scarred; I will never recover.

The next sentence read, 'I congratulate you on your story book. Now you are happy because you have got what you wanted and you have satisfied yourself by talking about me, like you always dreamed.'

Well! I'm sorry but I didn't intend to hurt him. I just told the truth about my life and my feelings about my love life. It was easy for him to say these things, he had no idea how much he had hurt me. He had shared his life with me and with another woman too and I still managed to keep the relationship going for ten years before he got married. He has never cared about my heart. I was screaming and searching for help and love, but he didn't care. He got so much enjoyment from the other women that he was with that he forget that I was all alone waiting for him. Our relationship left wounds but I was strong enough to take a lot of pain. I wrote the book to let him know how much he had hurt me; it was the best way for me to do this.

The next sentence he wrote was, 'If you die in London I will be the first person to come and get your body and bring you back to your family.'

I was already depressed and now he was mentioning death. Dear Lord, please help me, why have you given me such a hard time? And why have you given me all these people? I do not deserve it, so please, give me a rest and some peace. All of sudden I got too emotional and tears spurted from my eyes, streamed down my cheeks and blended with the fluids dripping from my noise. They ran down the sides of my mouth and dripped from my chin. I tried to calm myself down but I couldn't fight it. I wished he could see my face and see how miserable and sad I looked, but I hoped it would be over soon.

Next he wrote, 'Let me know if you get married.'

I wished I was married. Of course he would be the first person I would tell. I wished that I was happy and that I could tell him all about it. But I wished nothing but the best for him, and I would always remember the song 'Because I Love You' by Shakin Stevens, which he always used to play to me when we were falling in love and life was so beautiful.

Then he said, 'I divorced my wife yesterday so I am free from her now darling.'

That news didn't surprise me at all because he had had trouble with his marriage for a very long time. I was sorry for him but at the same time I was hurt when he said, 'I am free from her'. So, what did he want me to do? He thought that I had been waiting for him all this time. He thought I was desperate to be married; even though I am, I would rather be single than married to him. My love for him was dead and had been buried many years before. The reason he didn't know was because I hadn't cared enough to tell him.

Finally, he wrote, 'Sorry for everything. I will love you always, your truly, DKK.'

I used to love him more than anything in this world, and he once held the keys to my heart, but not anymore. I still loved him but as nothing more than my best friend, in that way he will always be in a corner of my heart.

I replied to his email with a short message that didn't mention his divorce:

'The way you think about me is wrong; I have never changed, I am still the same Gina that I was the first moment you met me. You should know me better than that and you should know how hurt I am because of what you have done to my life. I love you too but only as a friend. You will be forever in my heart.'

CHAPTER 40

Feeling Sorry

It was around 8.30am on 19th March 2011and it was a beautiful morning. I sat in my living room enjoying grilled wild Alaskan salmon for my breakfast while watching *Day Break,* which is one my favourite programmes but not as good as *GMTV*. Suddenly my phone rang; it was a Malaysian number. I didn't recognise the number so I just ignored it but it just kept ringing non-stop. I almost sent a text saying, Who the hell are you? But then my phone beeped with a text message, which I quickly read. I was really surprised to see that the message was from Kazmin's girlfriend. It read, 'Hi, Gina! Dyana here, still remember me? Please call me; I need to talk with you about Kazmin Kuzi."

What the hell is going on now? I thought. How did she get my phone number? It was very exciting, I couldn't wait to find out what was happening, so I rang her and she explained: "Kazminhas cheated on me, like he did to you and Rosnah." (Kazmin's ex-wife.) "I have already told him that he belongs to you and I asked him to get back with you but he told me that he wanted to marry me. He talks badly about you, I don't believe it but he convinces me. I don't want to marry him, please, I need your help!"

Then I said, "I am quite busy at the moment but will call you in two hours."

The truth is, I wanted to finish my breakfast and also had no time to hear about stupid Kazmin's life again. But at the same time I felt sorry for that poor young girl. I had been through a hell of a lot with Kazmin, so I did understand her feelings. It was because of that that I promised to give her a call later.

Then she sent me a message that said, 'I really hope you call me, I don't know what to do and I don't have anyone to talk. I'm scared to make a decision

Life Behind the Silence 285

on my own. I have sacrificed my younger years for him. And recently I was sick and he said somebody perfomed witchcraft on me but my family have doubts and went to look for him.'

Exactly the same things had happened to me. In fact, I had been even younger then her. I replied, "Don't worry, and I will call you soon."

The whole hour before I spoke to her I was thinking, this is another episode in Kazmin's drama. Before his wife had given me lot of hard times and now his girlfriend needed help, and all just because of one crazy man. He was getting older and uglier, he had no money and no future and he was the biggest liar and cheater so why were they so crazy about him? Get a life, Kazmin!

Anyway, I had known Dyana two years; we had been introduced by Kazmin over the phone. We had only spoken a few times and since then we hadn't spoken again until I received her text. The reason Kazmin introduced me to her was because he wanted to marry me and at the same time marry her. He wanted to sleep with both of us in the same bed, and for us all to do things together. I had to listen to his entire plan and agree with a few words but really I was just pretending I wanted to know to see how far he would go with his mental plan. I gave him good suggestions, which made him very happy to stick with his plan.

As soon as I hung up the phone, I thought, thank God I am not in love with him anymore, thank God I did not marry him and thank you, God for taking my life away from him. He is just an evil man with a nasty heart. Since that day, every time he called me he talked about his disgusting plan and I felt really sick when I heard about it. A week later, I made the decision to open my heart to him and to let him know my feelings towards him, which I had never done before. It was really hard for me because he knew me as the Gina who always understood, who always accepted him and who would do anything for him, but that wasn't who I was anymore. He loved me but he didn't know who I was. I always hid things in silence, I had a lot of patience and did a lot of pretending.

Soon the phone was ringing and I knew it was him. For some reason my energy gave me the confidence to go through everything that I had kept hidden all this time.

"How are you?" was my first question to him and after a few minutes I told him directly, "I don't think I can marry you."

In a shocked voice, he asked me, "Why? Why are you doing this to me?"

"Sorry! I can't marry someone who wants me to share a bed with another woman. I am a woman and I have a heart and feelings. You should respect me as the first woman that you spent your life with, but you do not at all."

"Well! I was joking!" he answered.

"Something like this is not a joke. Who you think I am?" Tears of sadness started running down my cheeks, but I tried to make him understand.

"So you don't want to marry me?" he asked.

"No! You can marry your girlfriend, she is much younger than me, which is what you always wanted. You always say nice things about her. Who do you think I am?" I replied, still trying not to get too upset.

"You have really broken my heart, how could you do this?" He was still insisting that he was right.

As soon as he said that, I got really mad and said, "You are the one who has broken my heart, you have no idea how hurt I am because of what you have done. I have been suffering because of you for long time. I am sure you remember, when we started our life together I was so in love with you. I did everything you asked just to be with you. As you know, I worked hard for low wages, every day for weeks and months, always living in fear because you would get upset if I couldn't give you money when you needed it. I put my life in danger looking for and borrowing money for you, because I was scared of losing you. You never appreciated any single thing that I did for you. You wanted me to bleach my skin to become fair; you don't like my nose, you don't like my eyes, in fact you wanted to change my whole body."

He didn't say a single word so I continued to express my feelings, sobbing loudly at the same time. I said, "There is nothing that you like about me and I have never heard you say nice things about me so leave me alone. I will search for a new life, find happiness and build my future. Whatever you do, whoever you are with, I wish you all the best."

This was the first ever time that I had said all these things and expressed the feelings that I had kept quiet for almost my entire life. Now he knew that I was no longer the Gina that he used to know. I had been very stupid waiting and wasting my life for him. I was still waiting for him to say something, but he just kept silent; he was clearly lost for words. As I was too upset to continue talking, I said, "Fine, if you don't want to talk, take care." I hung up the phone straight away.

He only left me alone for a few months and then he started sending me texts and emails again. I ignored everything until one day I received an email that said, 'Can you please go and see my niece in hospital? She had a major operation and she needs some help."

He had three nieces living in London and I had known all of them for a very long time. Their parents lived in Malaysia so I was left with no choice but to visit his niece in hospital. From then on, communication between me and Kazmin started again but I tried not to be as close as we were before. He kept sending me emails but I only replied if it was something important.

Anyway, it was almost time to call Kazmin's girlfriend. I wasn't really looking forward to talking to her as I had already had experience of this with his wife. But I also wanted to find out what he had done with the money that he had asked for a week before his girlfriend called me. And I needed to find out what game he was playing now. So I dialled her number and she answered straight away.

"Hi, Dyana, it's me, Gina!" I said.

In her soft voice she said, "Hi, Gina! How are you?"

" I am fine thanks, darling! So what is happening?" I asked her without wasting any time.

"I just want to know about you and Kazmin. Does he still keep in touch with you? And are you both still in love?" I could tell that she desperately wanted to know the answer.

"Well, darling, here is the story if you want to know. The second time I decided to come to London, that was the end of our relationship, and I left him for good. I am no longer in love with him, I haven't been for a very long time but of course at first he didn't know that because I just didn't want to hurt him. Then when he introduced me to you two years ago, and told me all his plans, that made me tell him the truth, that I am no longer in love with him and I can't marry him. Because I have been hurt a lot by him. Since that happened we haven't contacted each other for quite some time." I explained this to her very clearly to make her understand.

"He promised me that he would not contact you anymore and he said that you were the one who always tried to call him. But I checked his mobile phone yesterday and I found your address, and I also checked his bag and found your book. When I asked him about your address, he said that you needed his help. I also asked about your book and he told me that you had never told him that the book was already published, he had found out by himself by searching on the website. Is what he said true?" she asked, hoping for good news. I thought, great, how fantastic, Kazmin is playing his usual games, he does the same to all women.

"OK, I am going to be very honest with you. He is the one who keeps pestering me with his emails and text messages, with all his sweet words; you also know that he is very good at that. But I ignored him for quite some time until one month ago when he needed my help with his niece in London. And for that reason I got in touch with him again. Recently he asked me for help, he needed some cash for something important that he had to do. So I sent him the amount that he needed and of course with it I sent my address. About the book, I was the one who told him it was published. That's all I can tell you, and it's the entire truth." Again, I explained very clearly so she was not worried about what was between me and Kazmin.

"But why does he lie to me about everything to do with you? How can I marry him if he doesn't change? Please tell me, what should I do?" She begged me for help.

"Darling, his life has been full of lies since the day I met him but I was such a stupid girl at that time, exactly like you. I sacrificed my young life for him but at the end of the day he left me and married someone else. Believe me, he won't ever change. You are such a young girl so please don't let him use you like he used me. Marriage is for life, and I don't think you want to marry someone who always cheats on you. Because if someone is a cheater they will always be a cheater, remember that. I am not the kind of person who likes to destroy people's relationships, I am telling you all this from experience. But if you think you can change him, that would be delightful and I would be more than happy to see him married. I an only advise you, the decision is in your hands and you are mature enough to know what is best for your life. What I have told you is the truth, from the bottom of my heart."

"Thank you so much for your time. You are the only one I can talk to and I will think about everything you have said." She ended the conversation sounding very frustated.

"Don't worry and don't think too much about all this. Take good care of yourself and if you need any help or you need someone to talk to, just give me a call."

27th March 2011; summertime had started and the clocks had gone forward one hour. It is only called summertime at that time, summer doesn't really start until June. Spring had arrived though, the clouds were blue and the birds were

Life Behind the Silence 289

singing and enjoying life. Spring is my favourite season of the year as it is full of joy. This is the time of the year to think about everything in life. Most of the trees wake up after being asleep for a few months, then soon they start to brings out young green leaves, some with flowers full of colour and divine smells; it feels like new life is beginning. Anyway, I had turned my clock forward the night before, which meant that I had lost one hour'd sleep. I felt my body roll sideways and my eyelids grow heavy. I dug my nails into my hands, trying to stop my eyes from closing again, and dragged my ass onto the chair to check my emails.

I decided to send an email to Kazmin. It said: 'Hi you! Just an email to let you know that even though we are not together as lovers, you will always be part of my life as a person who I can trust and talk to about everything in life, but from now on everything is over. So from now on I am not going to reply to your emails or return your calls because you are such a loser. You are so desperate for money, and I always help you without question. How dare you still lie to me? I never expected that you could do that. This is how you pay back my generosity? Shame on you! You know what, Kazmin, I am fine but you are never going to have a good life, and one day you will end up on your own. In the time I have known you, you have never stopped lying and cheating. Come on, get a life, MR Kazmin! You have no idea how much you broke my heart and I hope one day someone does the same to you. I had enough with your wife disturbing my life before so I don't want anymore hassle. Everyone since you has damaged my life, so please leave me alone. Do whatever you think is best for you and good luck for your future. Kind Regards, Gina.'

As soon as I sent it to him, I immediately closed my mind to it so I wouldn't think about how he felt. He did not deserve me feeling sorry for him. I hoped he would think about my feelings and I really hoped he would take my decision seriously. After spending fifteen years of my life with him, I have never had a single regret about my decision to leave him. I can't even imagine what it would have been like if I had married him, what would have happened to my life? Holy shit! I don't want to think about it. I made the right decision for my own future. I hope one day someone will hold the key to my heart and look after it for the rest their life.

CHAPTER 41

Trip to Australia

It was a beautiful Sunday morning, a fresh start to my day, but I still lay lazily in bed thinking, what should I do today? Go running in the park? NO! Sunday is my rest day. Should I go out for lunch with my friends? Um… No, I don't really feel like seeing anyone today. I thought, how about shopping? Yes! I love shopping and within a second I knew what I was going to buy.

As soon as I jumped out of bed though, the phone rang. Who the hell is calling me at this hour? I thought.

I was so surprised, it was my brother Nazeri calling me from Australia. I thought, it must be something important that he wants to tell me otherwise he wouldn't call. I couldn't wait to hear what it was but as always our conversation started with us laughing for no reason, especially as we hadn't talked for a few weeks. And as always he never stopped teasing, me which is very sweet of him.

Then he said, "Sis, I wanted to ask if you wanted to come over here to Perth."

As soon as I heard his invitation I was over the moon and really shocked, I just couldn't believe it. I wanted to visit him the day I found him but when I mentioned my plan, he didn't seem very happy about me visiting him. Well! I can understand that at that time it was maybe too early and maybe he was still in shock. But then after a few months I again mentioned that I could go over there to visit him but he was still not ready. I wondered why he was giving me so many reasons why I couldn't go. One day I spoke with his partner and she invited me to Perth to visit my brother. I wished she knew that he was not ready to welcome me yet. So I decided to be honest with her and said, "Shayan! Of course I would have loved to visit my brother the first time I found him, and I would love to see the place where he lives and works, but he won't allow me to

Life Behind the Silence 291

yet. And I don't want to come without his invitation, I don't want to upset him or arrive in Perth only for him to ignore me as that would really upset me."

As soon she heard my explanation she said, "Come on! Don't worry, I am here, I am sure he doesn't mean it. You should come here to see how he works, he really works hard and he is a good cook."

I told her, "Of course I would like to so could you do me a favour? Could you talk to him? But please don't say anything about what I told you."

Without question she agreed. So now I knew for sure that his partner had told him to invite me. Whatever the reason, I was very happy and of course I wanted to go but not at the last minute because I would have to fly back to London after two days.

So I told him, "Of course I would love to come and thank you for inviting me, that is very sweet of you, but not at this time, because I have a few things to do. It will be in the next few months though, I promise."

He agreed with my decision then after a few minutes we both said goodbye. After I hung up the phone, I lay on my bed and was so excited and so looking forward to my visit, especially as I had never been to Australia before. There was a big smile on my face as I thought, at last I can visit him. I was very thankful to Shayan!

A few months later, on 14th May 2011, Giovanni and I flew from London to Perth, via Malaysia. The flight from Malaysia to Perth took five hours. It was a good flight and it was night-time when we landed in Perth. I just couldn't wait to get out out of the airport and call my brother. My brother didn't know that I was coming, it was a surprise. But first we had to go through customs of course, like any other airport. They were checking people's passports like they had never seen one before. I have seen Australian customs officers on TV but I didn't expect them to be so strict. One of the customs officers was questioning an Asian lady. He asked her, "What is this charger for?"

The lady said, "It's a mobile phone charger."

The customs officer said, "Where's the phone?"

The lady said, "I haven't got it."

Then he replied, "We have to confiscate it!"

The poor lady, I felt so sorry for her. The customs officers were scaring her, they were really taking advantage of their position. I thought, Man! Are they stupid or what?

We still had to wait for them to check our luggage, and it was long fucking wait – excuse my language. They checked each person's luggage for more than an hour; they opened the luggage and checked every single detail and asked some stupid questions. We waited almost two hours. I got really pissed off, and I told Giovanni, "I would never ever come to Australia again, unless I had something to do,"

It was three in the morning and we were still standing waiting for our turn to be called. My legs were getting tired, so I sat on my luggage and at the same time my eyes kept looking at the customs officers, just hoping they realised that I had been waiting there long enough to be called.

I could see the two customs officers talking to each other and they both looked at me. I made myself look even more tired so they would hopefully feel sorry for me. Yes! One of them walked towards us. Thank God! Finally!

He said, "Are you two together?" I thought, are you blind? As he could see that we had stayed very close to each other.

I replied, "Yes, we are."

He answered, "Follow me." I quickly got up and followed him before he changed his mind.

He requested that we put our luggage on the table and open both of our suitcases so he could search them. When my suitcase was opened you could seee dozens of my panties lying on top of my clothes. I warned him. "I hope you don't sneeze, because I didn't wash them."

The truth is, I didn't want him to see my other belongings. Too bad, he didn't care about my warning and continued to search. If I had known they were going to be this strict, I would have put plenty of condoms inside my luggage, even though I never use them myself, then they could have asked questions about that, which would have be fun.

Then the customs officer asked us, "Why have you come to Perth?"

Giovanni answered, "On holiday."

The officer asked, "Why?"

Giovanni responded, "To see a different place and we thought it would be nice to come to Perth as it is only a five-hour flight from Malaysia."

Then they asked, "How did you pay for the ticket?"

Giovanni answered, "With money, of course."

They weren't too happy with Giovanni answering them back as it made them look stupid! I thought, when are these questions going to end? Then they asked, "Why have you only come for two days?"

Giovanni said, "Is that a problem? Don't people travel for two days?"

Then he asked Giovanni, "What do you do?"

Giovanni just looked at him and said, "Excuse me!"

He repeated the question to Giovanni, and Giovanni said, "I work for myself."

Then he asked me the same question and I told him I was an author and showed him my book, which he took away to check. Then he asked us, "Do you have money?"

Giovanni said, "Yes!" Then he asked how much.

Giovanni said, "You want me to count the money in front of you, to see how much I have? Here are my credit cards if you want to see them too."

Then the customs officer said, "Don't worry, that's fine."

I thought, they can see that we flew business class to Perth and are flying back to KL and London business class. Then he took our ticket and disappeared somewhere, then came back to question us, then left us again, and then when he came back for the third time, we were free to go. Jesus! It was about forty-five minutes before they would let us go. Before we left I asked him, "Why are you so strict? I will think twice about cominge back here again."

He smiled and replied, "Have a good holiday."

I look at him and said, "It better be after all this."

We took a taxi to the hotel where we going to stay, which took about twenty minutes. When we arrived at the hotel, no one helped us with our luggage. I went inside the hotel lobby and saw a man who worked for the hotel, but he just stood and smiled as he watched me carrying my heavy luggage in without offering me any help. What an idiot!

Suddenly a girl from reception asked me, "Do you need a trolley?"

I thought, are you stupid or what? Couldn't she see how big my suitcase was? Of course I needed one.

I gave her an angry look and said, "Yes please!"

The hotel was quite expensive but the treatment that we received was shit. By the time we entered the room, it was almost four in the morning. We were very knackered and went straight to bed, all because of the bloody customs officers.

In the morning I tried to call my brother but he didn't answer the phone. I thought he must still be sleeping because he had been working until morning. Too bad he didn't know I was already in Perth. My idea had been to surprise him but since our experience with the customs officers, I was really pissed off, especially as we were in the middle of nowhere.

The city is very big and very flat, and there was no shade but luckily it wasn't summertime, so the weather was perfect for me. There was nothing much to see, I found the city of Perth very boring. The people in Perth are very laidback. Everything is expensive; flight ticket, taxi, hotel, food – everything is an unbelievable price. I thought London was the most expensive city in the world. I wondered how my brother could live over there. Well! I guess he is probably used to it. Anyway, we decided to go into the city and have some lunch, but none of the food was exciting, so we ended up eating at McDonald's. I hate McDonald's and I couldn't remember the last time I had eaten there, but now I was in Perth having a McDonald's. Well! It wasn't as bad as I thought. While I was enjoying my French fries, I saw a few Aborigines walk in and sit beside us. I looked at them like they were life forms from a different planet. I hoped they didn't notice the way I looked at them. Now I was happy that I had at least seen something that I wanted to in Perth.

It was already five in the evening and my brother still wasn't answering the phone. I was starting to get a bit worried, then Giovanni suggested that I give him one last call; if he still didn't answer, he would take me to his restaurant later that night. I agreed then straight away dialled his number for the last time. He answered the phone at last, I was so relieved. We had a normal conversation, then he asked me, "Sis, where are you?"

I said, "In Perth."

He was shocked and replied, "NO! You must be joking. I thought you hadn't arrived yet. Why you didn't tell me? "

I laughed and said, "Well it was supposed to be a surprise, but you have only just answered my call."

We both laughed, and he said he would come and pick me up from the hotel and take me to his house.

We went back to the hotel to get ready for him. After an hour the hotel phone rang and Giovanni answered; it was my brother on the way up to my room. I stood in front of the door waiting for him, I was so excited! Then he walked out of lift and walk towards me with a big of smile on his face. He had lost a lot of weight, and he had cut his hair short. WOW! He looked very good, I was impressed. We hugged and kissed each other, I was so happy to see him.

He took us to his house and introduced me to his partner, Shayan, and Axel, his stepson, who is a sweet boy. His partner had a little bit of a hangover, but she was lovely and very friendly and she offered me a seat. I handed a gift that I brought from London to each of them. It looked like she was happy with my gift, I hope so!

A few minutes later my brother and his partner decided to take us for a drive and then to his restaurant, which was not very far from his house. It was a very nice night-time drive even though we couldn't really see much. On the way he showed me a few places which I do not remember at all; there is only one place that I still remember today and that is Swan River, which is very big and very nice. We arrived at his restaurant, which was very nicely decorated. He showed me the kitchen, where he is stuck all night cooking and at the weekend he only stops cooking at eight in the morning; my poor brother. But me and Giovanni were not very lucky this time, he had closed the restaurant for two nights because he had a pain in his elbow. As he had promised to cook for me, he took some food from the restaurant to cook at his house, so soon we were all heading home.

He cooked me my favourite dish, fish of course. WOW! It was so delicious. This is the first time I had eaten my brother's cooking, and it really impressed me. My brother, as usual, was very calm and didn't talk much. I can't even remember what he cooked for Giovanni. We had a blast with his partner, she was a fantastic host and very funny. The wine made her talk non-stop, which made all of us laugh, and we stayed up until five in the morning. We were having a lovely time on our first meeting. My brother showed me round his house and showed me his painting. WOW! The painting was magnificent. I never expected the quiet boy that I knew to have so much talent, but he had created such beautiful art. It was very impressive. He kept surprising me and I didn't know what to expect next.

We went back to the hotel and, after only a few hours' sleep, the hotel manager asked us to move to another hotel, because the rooms were fully booked. How stupid is Perth? So I had to wake up early to pack my luggage. As we were leaving the next day, I tried to make the most of my time with my brother. I wished I could stay a few days more but because of the ticket situation we managed to stay for only two days in Perth. Two days is a very short amount of time, and it was very rushed for us too, but it didn't bother me, I was just happy to see my little brother. Anyway, we settled into another hotel, and then we decided to go into town to look around while waiting for my brother to come and pick us around six in the evening. The city was very small and there was nothing much to see, but I kept looking around in case there were kangaroos crossing the road or koalas climbing the trees, but unluckily I didn't see any.

My brother came to the hotel at exactly six o'clock to take us to his house. He had promised to cook me steak, yum yum, but as soon as I entered the house I could see there was something different between my brother and his partner. She didn't look happy like the first time I had met her. I was sure something had happened between them. I wondered what the cause was. My brother's stepdaughter, Samantha, was in the house. We had spoken on the phone before but this was the first time I had met her in the flesh. She was very friendly, like her mother. We had a chat and got to know each other a little bit, it was very nice of her to come all the way from her house just to meet me.

We all gathered together at the dining table waiting for dinner to be served. My brother had become a chef at home and was busy in the kitchen cooking for us. I don't really eat meat, but because he always talks about how his steaks are the best, and how he makes the sauce with his secret ingredient, I was willing to try it. But I told him, I want my steak to be cooked very rare. I was watching my brother cooking and waiting impatiently, like a little girl, for the food to be served. Soon my brother put a huge steak in front of me. I was drooling, I just couldn't wait to put it in my mouth. Mama mia! I was lost for words, the steak was divine, and he had cooked the meat exactly the way I wanted it. The sauce was super too, and I ate a lot more than I had ever eaten before. He was so concerned, he kept asking me and Giovanni about his food. He was so happy when we told him that his steak was delicious, and then I said, "Adik, I salute you. Can you give me the recipe for your secret sauce?"

He gave me a big smile then said, "Sorry, sis, that's just for me."

I looked at him said, "You are bloody selfish."

He laughed then he said, "I will think about it."

Dinner went very well then some of them had to say goodbye, so that left six people including me. Again, we talked all night long, but I felt very knackered as the night before I had had just a few hours' sleep. But Shayan's face was fresh even though it was already four in the morning. She was still drinking her wine and saying lots of funny things, it was fun. I laughed so much but soon I had to excuse myself. I told them that I was very tired because I hadn't had enough sleep, which was true. My brother drove us back to the hotel. We would see him the next day, on my last day in Perth. The time was four thirty in the morning; as soon as I entered the room I passed out.

The phone rang at eight in the morning; it was my brother, but my flight was not until five in the evening, why had he come so early? It must be something important otherwise he wouldn't have got there so early. I jumped in the shower and left Giovanni to chat to him. As soon as I was ready, I found him on the sofa looking very sad.

I immediately asked him, "What's wrong?"

He said, "I argued with my partner."

I was not happy at all when I heard about that, and was really worried about my brother. I hoped their argument was not because of me.

Then I said, "Well! I knew it, because last night I could see your partner was not very happy, but why?"

He said, "She had been drinking too much and said some silly things to me, which made me very upset."

I sat and asked him to tell me everything that had happened. I had tears in my eyes but there was nothing much that I could do except give him loads of advice. I felt so sorry for him. If he wanted, I would take him with me. But he couldn't simply walk out because he had things to settle in his life, which I totally understood.

He took us to the airport. With his situation the way it was, it was hard for me to leave him. He had no idea how worried I was, it really put me under a lot of pressure. I knew he was big enough to take care of himself, but after only a few hours together I could already see the things that were happening to him. To know that he was having a tough life with his finances and an unhappy relationship made me so frustrated and it hurt me deeply. Whatever the problem was though, he had been with his partner for a very long time relationship so he could deal with it.

Before I left him I said, "I will help you however I can but sort out your problems first then come to me, I will wait for you in London."

He said, "Don't worry, sis! I will be fine and I promise I will come to London to see you."

I walked to the door and turned around to look at him, thinking, the last time he went to the airport was twenty years ago, when I left him to go to London for the first time. I was very sad when I left him behind alone, but I needed to chase my dream. And now for the second time he was at the airport and I was again leaving him to go to London, but it was a different situation this time. For some reason I was sad to leave him behind again because I couldn't do anything to help him. But I advised him to talk behind closed doors about his personal problems. I didn't want to get involved in their relationship. Then I walked away and never turned back, although my heart was full of sadness, but I was sure he was going to be fine.

CHAPTER 42

Hope

It is now time to free myself from the torture and anguish that has controlled my entire life. One of the best ways to rid myself of all the wretched feelings that I have carried inside me is to tell my life story through this book. I know when I read a personal story that touches my heart, I often wonder how the writer feels, knowing that the whole world now knows her story. Does she feel embarrassed or relieved?

Now I know; I have a feeling of great satisfaction and an overwhelming sense of relief.

I hope this book will help other young women who may find themselves in similar circumstances. I want them to know that they are not alone and that relief is possible. In Malaysia, my story is not an unfamiliar one. Those people will understand. For those who have never experienced such a life, they should count their blessings and appreciate the ones who love them. Things could have been worse.

For a long time I put on a brave face and pretended to myself and others that I was happy. With this book I wanted to bring out into the open the pain that I had kept inside me for nearly four decades. I needed to cast it off as it overwhelmed me. I believe that everyone's life carries important meaning. In this book I have poured out all my feelings in order to share them. I hope that writing this book and sharing my story will have some meaning. I can now move beyond the lies that I felt I had to live before. Now I can say, I am who I am.

I believe that one's dream can come true. Once when I was young, I found a magazine with the now-famous picture of the Beatles walking across the street outside the famous studio, and I told a friend that someday I would live in London, but they just laughed at me. Many years later, here I am. I found myself living just across the street from the Beatles' studio, almost at the spot where that photo was taken. I sent a picture of myself standing on that very spot to my friends in Malaysia, and they could not believe I was there. It was a dream come true.

I keep myself busy with my work, and I workout five times a week. But I need someone to bring a husband into my life. This is my mother's biggest desire. She wants me to be married and have a proper wedding in her home town. None of my siblings were married in a proper wedding. A formal wedding is a status symbol in Malaysia. My mother is constantly pushing me to get married as soon as possible. Every conversation we have, she starts out with the question, "When are you going to get married?"

When I was thirty-eight years old, I told her, soon. At forty, I gave her the same answer. I gave her the same answer at forty-five and I am still telling her the same thing but my mother puts a lot of pressure on me. I do understand that she is worried about my age. She has no idea that I have been worried for a long time, because I want to have children. But now I have given up and I am too tired to think about marriage. I have made my own decision about what I should do. No one can tell me what to do, not even my own mother. Sometimes I wonder if life is too short for quarrelling. I should make the most of it but the more I try, the more pressure I get. I am just hoping for a better life in the future.

CHAPTER 43

Decision

It was Thursday 22nd September 2011. The weather was changing and the mornings were cold now. I still lay in bed thinking about the next day as it was going to be a very special day. I didn't expect anything from anyone at forty-six years of age, because I was not looking forward to it myself. But I was sure Giovanni would surprise me with something to make me happy, especially as I was going through hard time at that moment.

When he arrived home that evening I thought, um…! Surely he will take me out for dinner or arrive with a present in his hand, but I got nothing that I was expecting. I found that a bit strange because he always celebrated my birthday at midnight on 23rd September. Anyway, I left him alone and checked my facebook to see how many people had wished me Happy Birthday. It put a smile on my face to know all my friends still remembered me and that made me happy throughout the night. But the person who I was expecting to wish me Happy Birthday, the person who was closest to me at that moment in my life, sadly he was soundly asleep and snoring loudly. I thought, how wonderful that I have this for my birthday. My lonely heart whispered, Happy Birthday, Gina! And I wished myself all the happiness in the world and that all my wishes would come true. All night I couldn't sleep thinking about my life at the age of forty-six, but sadly I was left on my own with no one to share my thoughts with, until I fell asleep.

I am an early bird so my eyes automatically opened at exactly the time that I usually wake up. I jumped out of bed, opened the curtains and pulled up the window to take a breath of fresh air. My hair was lifted by the wind and I could see swallows gathering in the blue skies. It was 23rd September, the beginning of autumn, and I felt so fresh, but also so sad inside. I was stirred by the black birds singing loudly and flying happily; such a happy morning they were having. I wished I felt the same as them, but sadly I was still hoping for a surprise.

I felt that there was something wrong but I tried to convince myself that he would never let me down on my birthday. I had turned down all of my friends' invitations just for him. All day I was expecting a phone call or a text message to wish me Happy Birthday but I received nothing, and I was waiting for him all day. Every hour that passed, my heart beat faster with anger, and every breath I took, I hated him more for what he had done. At last he turned up when the day was gone. Usually, as soon as I open the door on my birthday, I can see that he has something in his hand and I know it is my present, but not this time. I was completely fine with not getting a present, but at least he could have wished me Happy Birthday or have bought me a card because my birthday is very important to me. We had a very simple dinner at home and ended up sitting on the sofa without talking much to each other. I held myself together, trying not to let go of my temper, but it was really hurting me. I thought, this is like he has just blown out the candle on my cake and left me in the dark. I left him on his own and headed to bed. Lying down in the dark, I was lost for words. I did love him but from now I knew I had to love and care about myself more.

I couldn't sleep that night, my heart was waiting for him but my soul had decided what to do for my future. How could someone have the heart to do this to me? Why has no one never felt sorry for me in my life? How could someone be so selfish? Why? Why? I was so tired of asking myself that question. WHY? So I decided that from now on I had to start thinking more about my life than other people's. My life had been missing it's brightness for a few years, but I would gather back all my energy. My soul had the power to grow stronger so I would stand on my own two feet and get back to my own world. My heart had been screaming but my brain had been sleeping for a long time so I needed to wake up. It was now time for me make my own decisions about my own life. But which way should I go? And what did I want?

The next morning I woke up with a smile of relief because I had come to the stage that made me say, that's it! I am giving up. I am too tired to think about marriage, I have made my own decision about what I should do in my life. I decided to transfer my embryo into my womb and to get pregnant; that's what I wanted to do.

As far as I could see, Giovanni hadn't made any strong move to start a life with me so I knew where I stood. Whatever happened, whether I was married to him or not, I was going to get pregnant. The question was, should I think about my own life or my future baby's life? It was a very hard decision but things had to be done. I knew my life would be fantastic if I married him but I would never be happy, and that is the one thing that I didn't want to happen if I got married. For me, marriage is for a lifetime. Because it would be his baby, I had to discuss decision with him and tell him how I felt about our relationship. I did feel sorry for him, I am not a nasty person but I would rather be honest with him than hurt him. Because of his kindness and his caring nature I had tried everything to make our relationship work but it looked like it was only me who was really desperate to have a family, he didn't seem to care less. That's why he agreed with my decision. I knew my life would never be the same with him, unless he pulled back the relationship and repaired the damage that he had done. Why did he want it this way? I tried to search for the answer. He wanted to be with me but not have baby in the normal way, but what's the difference? What was in his head? I have had a few relationships but this was the first time someone had made such a weird decision and for the rest of my life I will never understand why, it has left me with a question mark in my head. It is very sad not to be married to him and be a family but he can always be part of my baby's life. He is such a lovely man and without doubt I know he would be a wonderful father to my baby.

The next day he called the hospital to make an appointment to have my embryo transferred but the hospital suggested that we see my doctor. I was so happy at that point, I just couldn't wait to be pregnant because I had been ready for long time to be a mother. The next evening I went to see my doctor in Harley Street, which is a very famous road for cosmetic surgery. We were there on time and after fifteen minutes of waiting I saw a young nurse with blond hair walk in the waiting room and call my name, so I said, "Yes! I'm over here."

I thought, you better be ready because fifteen minutes is long enough for me to be waiting for someone. As soon as I stepped in the room I saw my doctor. He was very cheerful and welcomed us with a big smile. He was so happy to see me and so happy to know that I was ready to get pregnant. After a discussion, he said, "He loves you."

When he mentioned that Giovanni loved me, it made me sad. I replied, "If he loved me, he wouldn't do it in this way but, but because I want the baby, these things have to be done. "

The doctor tried to comfort me so I wouldn't get emotional. He said, "Sometimes it is meant to be happen like this."

I wanted to answer back but I thought, I better shut my mouth before I get too emotional and burst into tears. After fiftenn minutes of listening to his explanation I was a bit disappointed. I thought that the hospital would transfer my embryo and I would get pregnant. I didn't know that I would have to follow a few procedures and have a scan before my embryo was transferred. I hate tablets but the good thing is I didn't need to have an injection; I hate needles. The doctor told me it wouldn't take too long to see how I was responding, it could be one week, two weeks or three weeks. I thought, that's not too bad, I can deal with that, so before we left the clinic I made an appointment for the week after to have the scan. I hate scans, in fact I hated everything about it but because I really wanted a baby, I had no choice. I tried to hold my temper and my emotions as much as I could, but the truth is I wasn't myself at all, especially as I didn't have anyone to share my problems with. I was heart broken and very frustrated about what he had done to my life. A thousand times I had told him what I wanted from him but he didn't do anything, and a million times I talked about our future and our life together but he didn't give a damn, in fact he just continued with his life and left me to deal with so much pressure. I knew his name but I didn't know much about his life and his family because he kept his life very private even though I was his girlfriend, or whatever he wanted to call me; I would never know.

A week later, we returned to the clinic for my scan. I just hoped everything was going to be fine. As soon as my foot stepped in the clinic my mood changed. I become angry but I tried to control my temper as much as I could until the scan was over. Then the dcotor explained that I had to continue my medication for another week because I was not ready for them to transfer my embryo. I was very disappointed but I completely understood. As soon as we left the clinic my temper blew up straight away in Giovanni's face. I asked him, "Why have you done this to me? Why couldn't you give me a normal life, and a baby in the natural way?" I was full of questions. WHY? I was so upset and burst into tears like a baby. But still I didn't get an answer. He just looked at me like nothing had happened and that made me wish I had never met him.

I had to continue taking my medication for another week, which I hated. I hate waiting; another week felt like another year. Every day my brain counted the hours until my scan so I could get pregnant and get on with my life without worrying. Exactly a week later I returned the to clinic for another scan,. Again, I just hoped for the best result. As usual we waited in the waiting room for the nurse come and collect us. After ten minutes I saw the same nurse as before. She came to get us and took us into a room, where she left me to get ready for the scan. But as soon as I saw the bed waiting for me to lie on for the scan, I started to get emotional.

I was lying on the bed, waiting for the doctor, and Giovanni was sitting at the side of the room. I turned around to look at him and I thought, don't you feel sorry for me? Suddenly he said, "Are you OK?"

That really made me mad and I replied, "Did you do to your wife what you have done to me?"

He just played dumb and I thought, you have such an evil heart. I turned my face away from him so I didn't have to look at him and tried to hold myself together. I was trying not to cry but it was so difficult at that stage.

Suddenly someone knocked the door. I quickly wiped my eyes and pretended that nothing was happening. When the door was pushed open I could that it was my doctor. He had a big smile on his face and said, "Hello, Madam, how are you? And hello, Sir, how are you?"

He made me smile and he shook Giovanni's hand. Then he asked me, "Are you ready?"

With a smile I said, "A big yes!"

He replied, "So am I. I'll keeps my fingers crossed."

He showed me the scan and at the same time he tried to explain to me the level that he wanted to achieve to ensure my embryo would survive, but unfortunately it hadn't reached that level at all. As soon as I heard his explanation, my heart dropped, my energy sank and tears ran fast down my face, like a river. When the doctor saw that I was crying, he tried to calm me down and told me that this problem was very common and could happen sometimes. I understood everything he said but I couldn't say a word because I was trying to stop crying. I was crying like a baby at forty-six years of age, I felt so stupid and ashamed of myself but I just couldn't help it. Suddenly the doctor came up with a solution to stop me crying. He said, "I am going to call the hospital to discuss if there is maybe something we can do."

Then he left of us both in the room while I got ready. I could hear him running around and making the call to the hospital. The nurses kept asking me, "Are you OK? Don't worry, everything is going to be fine."

I looked at them and said, "I am fine, thank you."

Life Behind the Silence

But I thought, stop asking me so many times, it just made me unable to stop crying. After fifteen minutes the doctor called us to his room. We sat in front of him and I tried to hold in my tears. He started to explain to me about my situation. He he had discussed things with the hospital and they had agreed to give me Viagra, which would help thing to move things along quicker. As soon as I hear d the word Viagra, I straight away said, "I want to stop, I have had nough."

He stopped talking and looked at me with a shocked face, then he asked, "Why?"

I started to cry again. I want to cry loudly, I wanted to scream and I wanted to express myself and share what I had been through in life but I could hardly speak and tears kept flooding my eyes. To stop myself crying I covered my face with both hands for a few seconds. Everyone was silent. I thought, I better behave myself, so I slowly slid my hands down. Bless my doctor, he was still sitting in front of me waiting for me to stop crying. Then he asked me, "Can I get you a glass of water?"

I said, "Yes, please!"

When I said yes, he didn't ask the nurse to get it, instead he quickly got up and brought a glass of water for me himself. He calmed me down and said a few words in his gentle voice that made me decide to continue my treatment. I asked, "If I continue for another week, is everything going to be fine?"

With confidence he said, "Yes, because the Viagra is going to make the line of the womb stronger and more durable." He explained about Viagra then he asked me, "Have you heard about Viagra? "

I just smiled. What could I ay? But he was so happy. He said, "Look at her, she's smiling now. Thank you for continuing the treatment, I am so happy. I don't want you upset when you walk out of the clinic, that will make me very worried."

I could see on my doctor's faces that he was so relieved and, before we left, the nurse made an appointment for us to return the clinic one week from that day.

CHAPTER 44

Happy Moment

I always look forward to November because throughout winter I run in the park at six in the morning. I do the same every year. But sometimes I get there too early and I have to stand outside the gates waiting for them to be opened. I do feel scared then because nobody else is in the park but then after fifteen minutes I start to see some other people running and I feel a bit more confident, but even then I keep looking behind my back every single second. There is not one moment when I feel tired with exercise, in fact I feel more tired if I don't train. Even when I am injured, I still run on my injured legs until they give up on me and then I get better without seeing a physiotherapist. There is no point me seeing a physiotherapist because I know what I have been doing. I support my body by training in that way.

The treatment was going very well except I could not be myself most of the time, that's why I didn't see any of my friends. I kept myself to myself; only my family and a few friends knew whatwas going on in my life. But my family lived on the other side of the world so I was all alone. I was angry with Giovanni, and cried night and day. To comfort myself I would walk alone in the park. I would lift up my eyes, lift up my heart and talk to my soul.

One day I had to go to the Malaysian Embassy to renew my passport. I had to send it off to the home office as my visa was going to expire in two months. I had been living in the United Kingdom since 1993 but I still paid for my visa. Well! You have to follow the rules. Soon after I heard that to stay permanently in the United Kingdom I would have to take the Life in the UK Test. I had been in this country for many years and this was the first time I had heard about this. Before my visa expired, and without wasting anymore time, I booked to take the test. It was to be a week from the day I called. From then on, what I had to do was get a book and study. When I looked at the book, it reminded me of when I was twelve years old and taking my exams. Well! I was glad because it so easy. When I read the questions it put a smile on my face, I wondered if it was real. I just couldn't wait to see what kind of people were taking the exam.

The moment came; I was taking the Life in the UK Test. My exam started at one in the afternoon but of course we had to be there thirty minutes before. As always, I was on time. As soon as I entered, I could see a number of people sitting down. I guessed that all these people were waiting to take the exam but all of them looked like refugees. I am sorry but it is true, and I felt like I was one of them. Anyway, I joined them and waited for the exam to start. While I was waiting, more people arrived. I guess they must have been waiting for everyone to arrive. When I looked at the time, I could see that the exam should have started ten minutes ago. I was really surprised, I was not expecting it to be like this at all, especially in the city of London. A couple of issues made me wonder if London is in a mess. I expected to walk into this place and see English people running the department. But instead it was Indian people with Indian accents and the exam was held at the Indian community centre; in fact, they also held them at an Iranian community centre. Anybody can register to take the exam to be a permanent resident in this country without an interview or anything. None of the people taking the exam with me were smartly dressed. I'm not saying that I am smart, what I mean is, I have struggled to stay in this country for many years and paid since I've been here and I have never claimed benefits. What do the government do? I don't underrstand. And I have heard a lot about English people who don't have jobs but there are jobs around and this is one of their jobs.

Anyway, a middle-aged Indian woman came out and called out everyone's name one by one and when she did everyone disappeared inside another room, including me. In the room we had one computer each and of course the person who was in charge explained the rules to us and told us what to do before the exam began. They were very helpful so I could tolerate the fact that we started twenty minutes late. We began as soon as she said, "You can start now."

I read each question and ticked the answer, jumping to the next question in under a second. Oh my Lord! I felt like I was ten years old taking the exam, it was easy-peasy. I'm not saying that I am a clever person but anyone could have done this, it was unbelievable. We had one hour to finish the exam but after five minutes I could hear people's footsteps starting to walk out of the room, one by one. I had finished the entire exam too but I took a bit of time double checking everything. As soon as I was ready to leave, I turned around. My God! Nearly every single person had gone. That just shows how easy the exam was. We all had to wait in the waiting room to be called for our result. I sat with the others but I didn't speak to anyone. I behaved like I was new to the country and couldn't speak proper English. I just listened to people around me talking. One middle-age guy sitting in front of me looked at me and I just looked down like I was stupid. Suddenly a woman sat beside him and they both smiled at each other then he said, "It was very easy."

She replied, "Yes!"

Then another women came over, she was a very happy bunny, and he talked to her too. He asked, "Where are you from?"

She replied, "'I'm from Japan."

Then a women's voice started calling our names one by one to receive our result. From the waiting room, I could see people jumping happily with their result and they had big smiles that reached their ears as they left the building. It didn't make me worried at all because I was sure I had passed; I really hoped I had anyway otherwise it would be so frustrating and embarrassing for me. Suddenly a voice called, "Miss Abdul Wahab."

Funnily enough I wasn't nervous, I walked in with so much confidence but I was still hoping that I had passed. As soon as I reached the table she asked me to sign the paper, which I did, then she handed me a copy and said, "Congratulations! You passed."

I looked at her and said, "Thank you very much, this is the best present that I have ever had."

She gave me a huge smile and I shook her hand before I left the room. What a lovely women. I was so happy but I still couldn't believe that I had done it and that I was now a permanent British resident. WOW! After so many years of struggling to stay in this country and paying for the visa, at last I was a permanent resident, and I deserved to be one. Outside Giovanni was waiting for me. I could see he was so excited to hear the result. As soon as I stepped out of the building he asked me, "Did you pass?"

I didn't say a word, in fact I made a frustrated face and handed him the paper and walked away because he was in the middle of talking to someone. While I was waiting for Giovanni, a boy walked past me with his result in his hand so I asked, "Did you pass?"

He turn around and said, "Yes, and you?"

I said, "Yes!"

We congratulated each other and he left with a happy smile. Gods bless him. I stood for a few minutes on my own and I felt a few drops of warm tears of happiness running down my cheeks. Goodbye visa, I thought, I am so proud to be British.

Giovanni ran towards me looking so happy, he just couldn't stop telling me how clever I was. Well! I didn't think so, I didn't even believe that I had done it. In five days' time I was going to have another scan and I hoped I would continue to receive happy news. I kept my brain busy by enjoying my moment with two of my dear brothers, because the day I took the exam I told them about it. Both of them wished me the very best luck and that made me so strong inside. I didn't do it just for me but also for Giovanni and my two brothers. Because they were waiting for my result and they believed in me, I was worried to death. Anyway, they both kept sending me text messages asking me for news. The first massage that came through was from my brother Zambri. It said, 'Sis! What happened with your exam? Did you pass?'

I replied, 'Zzzzooommm...! Ya bi da bi du! I passed. Zzzooommm...! Beep, beep, I am British.'

He replied, 'You're behaving like a child but congratulations, sis, I am very proud of you.'

That put a smile on my face. Then another message came through, this time from my brother Nazeri. It, 'Sis give me good news.'

I replied, 'Let me open my letter, Zzzooommm... I passed. Beep, beep, I am British!'

He replied, 'Ole, ole, ole, Congratulations sis, I knew you could do it so I'm going to have a shot of vodka.'

They are fantastic brothers. I might have been a bit silly but I just wanted to have fun with my brothers, it reminded me of when we were kids and I used to look after them and tease them, especially Nazeri. Behaving like this with them just made my day so much happier and kept my brain busy so I didn't think about the scan that was coming up.

Four days passed; my scan was the next morning. The night before I couldn't eat and I couldn't sleep much either. I was hoping that he would know exactly what to do but my hoping was hopeless. I went to bed feeling sad and lonely, just praying that tomorrow would go well; that was all I could do.

We were at the clinic on time and waited in the waiting room. Ten minutes later a young nurse came to tell us that a doctor would be arriving shortly. With an arrogant face I asked her how long 'shortly' was because I had been sitting there for fifteen minutes already. She looked nervous when I told her off and quietly ran off to find out from the doctor and let me know. That poor young nurse. I was a bad, bad girl. The night before I had promised myself that I would hold my temper around Giovanni as much as I could. He was talking a lot, I think he was trying not to make me angry at that stage. Only God knows how much anger I was holding inside me, it was burning like a fire and jumping high like a rocket, and my brain couldn't stop whispering, Come on, Doctor, where are you? Please give me good news today.

Giovanni excused himself to go to the loo and left me all alone in the waiting room, which I was very pleased about because I could then keep myself calm. Within a minute I could hear a big croaky man's voice from the corridor. I hoped it was my doctor but I knew it could be anybody. A second later two men walked into the waiting room and my heart stopped beating when I saw one of them. I looked at him and he looked at me; it was only me in the waiting room at that time. My eyes were blurry, I couldn't believe who I was seeing. He sat at the other side of the room and his friend left him, maybe to go to the loo. I put my head down and pretended to read a magazine but my heart was screaming, oh my God, I can't believe I've seen Rod Stewart! I really admire him and love all his songs, especially 'I Don't Want to Talk About It'. I wanted to look at him but I was too shy, but luckily Giovanni came back so I could talk to him and have a sneaky look at Rod Stewart's face. I wished he would look at us so I could give him a smile but he looked down at the floor. But then someone called him and he walked past us without turning around. WOW! He looked very good for his age. I wondered what he was doing in this clinic on Harley Street. Well! It was none of my business anyway, I was just so lucky to see him that day and I'm sure he brought me good luck.

The nurse called me to go up to the room because the doctor would be there any minute. I went into the room and got ready for the scan and today my heart felt so happy for some reason and I felt so confident. The doctor walked in and started the scan and within a second he looked at me with a big smile on his face and said, "Yes! That is exactly what we want. Now we are ready to transfer your embryo. I am very happy with the result, I am going to call the hospital to arrange your appointment."

He left us to celebrate the news but it didn't make the mood any different between me and Giovanni. I was just so happy that I was going to get pregnant soon but I didn't know about Giovanni because he didn't seem excited at all. Well! I expected that kind of reaction anyway because it was not a new experience for him.

Before we left the clinic, the doctor told us that he would call the hospital and in one week's time I would have my embryo transferred. For the first time, I left the clinic with peace of mind because I knew I would get what I wished for. I would have loved to share my happiness with Giovanni but I could see that he looked very normal, not at all excited, which was really sad because I would have loved to share the experience of my first pregnancy with him. I know a lot of men who are in love and lots of men who are married, and lots of men who are both, but I have never met anyone who is in a situation like me and I don't think I deserved to be treated like that. But on the other side I was confused because he is such a lovely person, so I was just waiting for him to tell me, "Move on with your life, Gina." Love sometimes brings life sweetness but it also brings pain; remember, love is always linked with pain. The next day it would be exactly one week that I had been waiting for my embryo transfer. I couldn't sleep all night long, and I cried tears of joy.

The day arrived when my embryo would be transferred; as a women I was mature enough to make my own decisions about my life. I had prepared myself to be a single mother. There are certain values and vows that I hold sacred, and it was this spirit that I had chosen to move forward with my life. I will forever cherish the time that I am going to spend with my little one. Marriage is one of the most beautiful things in the world but unfortunately it had never happened for me. It could still happen one day, I will always hope so. But my pregnancy will make my world and change my whole life.

I waited patiently for Giovanni to come and pick me up and take me to the hospital and I tried to hold my anger towards him as much as I could. The weather was very cold but I was looking forward to the winter. Giovanni phoned me to tell that he had arrived and was waiting in the car outside my flat. As soon as I stepped out of the house and walked towards Giovanni, I thought, come on, Gina, hold yourself together on this important day and don't let anything upset you. Well! I really tried hard but, ding dong, my temper exploded as soon as I sat in the car. I screamed hysterically and I cried like a baby, asking him why he had done this to me. But all this made my soul, my mind, my heart and my whole body weak because I would never get the answer, it just gave me so much pain and frustration. I knew that but I just couldn't help myself when I thought about what he had done.

We have arrived at the hospital and walked to the reception. Everything was fine and the receptionist asked us to sit in the waiting room until someone came to get us. I felt so tired, physically and mentally, but I just went with the flow. In the waiting room I saw a loving couple; why I can't be like them? I wondered. Then, ten minutes later, another couple walked in and sat beside me. They had big smiles on theirs faces and the woman held a picture and kept showing it to her partner. They were both so cheerful and happy; why couldn't I have what they had? Suddenly a pretty Indian women with a sweet smile (I guessed she was Indian by the way she looked) came and asked the woman, "How is everything?"

She replied, "Everything's fine."

The Indian doctor said, "I am so happy for you."

Then the doctor left them in peace and my soul whispered, whatever news she just received, I am very happy for her too and wish her good luck for her future. Giovanni and I were sitting side by side and facing each other but we were miserable. Every time he tried to talk, it just made me blow up. Suddenly I could hear a woman's voice call my name but my mind was miles away until she called my name a third time, then I said, "Here I am."

I rushed out of reception. A nurse in blue uniform stood waiting for me and she said, "OK, follow me."

We both followed her and she took us into the room where my embryo would be transferred. As soon as I walked into that room, I saw a bed with stirrups to put your legs up, and again I broke down in silence; it hurt me badly. I wanted a baby, that's why I was doing this, but what was hurting me was that I didn't understand why he was doing this to me. For security reasons the nurse asked me a few personal questions and then she explained everything. I heard someone push the door, then I saw the Indian doctor who I had seen earlier in the waiting room. She said hello to me and gave me a huge, beautiful smile, then she went to get everything ready for me. The nurse handed me a big piece of paper and asked me to go into the bathroom and remove my bottoms and wrap the paper around me. As soon as I came out of the bathroom the nurse asked me to lie on the bed with both of my legs resting in the stirrups. Tears kept flooding my eyes without stopping, without anyone noticing. Then the Indian doctor explained a few things to me in her sweet voice and someone from the laboratory brought out my embryo. The Indian

Life Behind the Silence

doctor said, "You can see your embryo on the big screen in front of you."

She pointed her finger at the screen; the light clicked on and then I could see my embryo. I felt like I was on a different planet and what I saw was like a little baby curling up nicely. My whole body shivered, I felt cold and as though my body was flying through the air to heaven. Warm tears of happiness ran down my cheeks because I knew someone new would be entering my life. The screen was switched off and then the nurse said, "Now you can see your embryo being transferred to your womb on the scream near you."

The Indian doctor was about to start transferring my embryo. She spoke very gently but my brain and my eyes were completely focused on the screen because I didn't want to miss a single bit of it. It was magnificent to watch, the most precious thing that I had seen in my entire life. After ten minutes it was done but they had to check to make sure it had been done properly. I started to get nervous when the doctor told me that they would have to do it again because my embryo hadn't gone in properly but she said that could happen sometimes. When I watched my embryo being transferred I promised myself that as soon as my embryo was safely inside my womb, whatever was upsetting me I would keep it to myself as much as I could. I knew it was going to be very hard but that I would make it. At last everything went perfectly and everyone was very happy; no words can describe my happiness. It was 6th December 2011, a Tuesday afternoon. Before we left the doctor told me to take a pregnancy test twelve days from the day my embryo was transferred. The Indian doctor wished me good luck and we left the hospital with peace of mind.

I thank you, God, for this most amazing day.

The journey through the treatment was such a difficult time and very emotional. And while I have been writing this part of the chapter, I have been getting really emotional but I just wanted to express myself as no one knows what I have been through in life. I have been talking to myself while writing this chapter, and every single word has come from my heart and from the beginning to the end I have been in tears without even noticing, that is how hurt I am. One day this book will be very important for my little one, it will explain everything and I am sure he or she will understand why I have decided to have them in this way and they will appreciate it more than anything in this world. He or she will give me the happy life that I have never had before. From now on I will try to makes myself happy as much as I can until I meet the little one.

I am now so happy to be a pregnant woman. Every morning and night I look at my tummy in the mirror getting slightly bigger. I rub my belly and say to myself, "Yes, I am pregnant. It is really happening." I just can't believe it. But I have no husband to touch my belly and to share my happy moments with. I would love to share this experience with a husband. Sadly my life has never been perfect but at least I have got what I wished for and that is the most important thing to me. This pregnancy has made me stronger every day and every day I count down the hours, the weeks and the months until my little one is born and I will be called a mummy and my life will be complete.

Then, once again my world became dark. My body dropped to the ground and I had no energy left, I cried without tears, completely drained. No words could describe how devastated I was, I had lost my pregnancy. This was the most precious thing that I ever had in my entire life and now it was gone and there was nothing I could do about it. It was so hard for me to accept the pregnancy had gone. But I tried to continue my life as normally as possible and it took me a few months to get over it.

I kept thinking over and over about what I should do next. And I almost gave up, losing hope, my heart broken, but my energy came back again and it pushed me to get stronger, to be a winner. I always said to myself, in life you have to be patient and never give up then you will achieve what you want. So I made my decision to use my last frozen egg soon and hope that this pregnancy would succeed, that was all I wanted at this moment. I am was very worried but I believed in myself, I believed in my soul and I knew that I had to think positive.

CHAPTER 45

My Father Leaves Me Forever

The last time I spoke to my father was September 2011; I never spoke to him again after that. He had had problems with his health and at one stage he ended up in hospital but everything was fine. I had worried a lot about his illness because he was paralysed in one hand and unable to move it so he was unable to work to support his family. It broke my heart to see him suffering with only one hand working so I gave him some money for his treatment; I just hoped he would use the money for that. I know he never cared about me, I know he used to abuse me and I know he never thought that I was his daughter but at the back of my mind, I always thought about him. He had a very difficult life financially and that made me worried as I didn't know how he was going to support his family. I never say no when people ask for help, especially my family. One day, my half-sister called me and asked me to send some money for my father, which I did. I know I shouldn't have helped him after what he had done to me but that is me, I can't help myself. I feel sorry for people when I see them having a hard time, and I felt sorry for my father. Anyway, my father was very grateful and he told me that the money that I gave him really helped him pay for his younger son's school. And I thought, you, Abdul Wahab, should be ashamed to ask the daughter that you used to call a bastard for help. I just did it as I thought it was my responsibility and that I might be in his situation one day, whose knows what will happen in the future.

In December 2011 my cousin Kamal phoned me and told me that my father had been to his house twice and asked him to ask me to call him; he told Kamal that I hadn't called him for quite some time. On his third visit, Kamal told me that my father wore a shirt that I had bought for him a long time ago and Kamal said he looked very smart. He wanted Kamal to take him to my mother's house but sadly at that time Kamal's car had broken down. Kamal said that his car would be repaired by my father's next visit and he promised to take him then. He returned home with an empty heart. But what Kamal didn't know was that was the last time he would see him; he would never return to Kamal's house again. I wanted to call him but because he didn't have a mobile I had to call his daughter's phone. I hate calling his daughters, they are very arrogant. If I didn't call them, they wouldn't even bother to find out about me. I wondered why he had asked Kamal to speak to me. Why hadn't he asked his daughter to call me if he wanted to speak to me? Then I thought, I will wait until he asks his daughter to call me. But for some reason I did think about him a lot.

On Sunday 29th January 2011, I received a text message from my brother Zambri to say that my father had gone into a clinic to have his arm checked and Zambri asked him to come to his shop when he was finished, which he did. Then all of sudden he wasn't feeling well and his arm was swollen and painful. Well, he had had a problem with his arm for more than a year so I didn't think it would be serious. But the next day I got another text message from Zambri, saying that my father had been admitted to hospital and was in the ICU. As soon as I heard that word I got so worried. I picked up the phone and dialled Zambri's number.

"Hi, sis!" he answered.

I asked Zambri, "Where are you?"

He said, "At the hospital visiting Dad."

Out of blue, and for no reason, I became hysterical and started screaming at Zambri, "You listen here, Zambri, I am going to tell you something that I have never told anyone in the family before. No one knows what our father did to our mother except me. I have kept it hidden in my heart for a long time and it has hurt me badly, and now for first the time ever I am going to tell you. It doesn't matter who's old and who's young, I might be gone before him as I am already forty-six years old. I am going to tell you now that from the day I was born he never wanted me as his daughter, he put chillies in my vagina, he cut my hair, he burnt my skin with a cigarette, he burnt my eyes with fire and he also tried to rape me. He says that I am not his daughter, so who I am?"

Zambri was silent as he listened to me then he said, "I am sorry but I will tell him."

Then I continued, "I have helped him a lot but he asked me not to tell anyone, especially mum, and I didn't but what upset me was that he didn't do anything for us when we were kids. The day I gave him the money, I sat with him inside the mosque. And that is the day that I wanted him to say sorry for what he had done, but I was really disappointed because he accepted the money so much easier than I thought he would. When I looked into his eyes it reminded me of the abuse that I had received from him. But I comforted myself and talked and joked with him and he laughed with so much happiness. But I wasn't happy. He thinks I have forgotten what he did. You know what, Zambri, every single time I look at him my heart hurts."

Zambri sounded so down when he said, "He should say sorry to us, especially to you."

I said," Yes, he should, and tell him what I have toldyou."

As Zambri was already at the hospital I allowed him to visit my father. He would let me know about his condition after he had finished his visit. As soon as I finished my conversation with Zambri I made a call to my mother. I told her the same story I had told Zambri. My mother was so happy that I had told Zambri what my father had done to me, I just hoped Zambri would tell him he knew. I never ever intended to hurt him, especially as he had a critical illness. I am not a bad daughter, I really don't know what came over me to make me explode and bring up something that I had been keeping a secret for my entire life. Every time I took my mother to see him, she would always say to me that I was nice to my father and that I had forgotten what he had done. But my mother didn't know my character; I am the kind of person who keeps things inside and pretends things are fine when really I am in a lot of pain but when the time comes something will happen. And now the time had come and I am sorry it happened when he was critically ill in hospital but I felt so relieved because I thought he would finally know that I was hurting because of what he had done.

That evening my heart felt that something was not right. For some reason I wanted to go back to Malaysia, just for a few days, to be with my family. I knew something was going to happen but I didn't know what. Zambri had sent me a text message to let me know that my father was going to be fine but

I still didn't feel right. Before I went to bed, I switched my mobile on and off many times just to check if I had received any news about my father. I tried to convince myself that my father was going to be OK even though I think about him in a negative way. Then I switched off my mobile and tried to sleep.

Tuesday morning; as usual my eyes automatically opened at the time I always set my alarm: 5.45 in the morning. The weather was shivering cold. Well, it was the coldest month of the year so I should expect it by now. Straight away I jumped out of bed to get ready for my run in the park. I looked at my mobile and thought, should I turn it on now or when I finish my run? I was so scared sbout receiving bad news about my father because my soul kept whispering to me that he was gone. I decided to turn on my mobile and hope for the best. A ton of messages came in; I was so nervous. The first text message that I read was from Zambri and it said, 'Sis, I am sorry but Dad has died.' As soon as I heard that my heart seemed to stop beating and I burst into tears. I asked myself, how can this have happened all of sudden? I couldn't believe that he had gone and left us without a single word. I ran to the living room to call Zambri to make sure that he was really gone from this world forever; I needed to hear it from Zambri's mouth. I dialled Zambri's number and he answered within a second. "Hello."

I immediately asked, "Has Dad died?"

He answered with one short word: "Yes."

As soon as he said yes, my heartbeat dropped and I burst into tears. At first I was at a loss for words completely but then I asked him, "Where are you?"

Zambri said, "At Mum's house."

I said, "Can I speak to Mum?"

Without a word Zambri passed the phone to my mother and she said, "Hello!"

I could hardly get any words out and I just couldn't wait to get off the phone but I said, "Mum, please go and see Dad. Whatever has happened is in the past and whatever he did to you, that is between him and God, just forgive him because he has left us forever. He used to be your husband and he is our father."

Then my mother said, "I am not feeling well, I have a big headache."

I know the day my father was admitted to hospital my mother was sick with fever but I insisted, "Mum, can you please go and see him for the last time."

Life Behind the Silence 319

As I was sobbing she said, "OK, but you don't cry too much, especially as you are pregnant now."

As soon as my mother agreed I hung up the phone without saying goodbye. I sat on the sofa as tears ran down my cheeks without stopping. I asked myself, why did he leave us without a single word? Why did it happen so fast? I know everyone will go when the time comes, we all stay only temporarily in this world, but I couldn't accept the way my father had died. Why must this happen to me? I thought. I know he used to be evil to me but now that he had he gone I felt I had lost something in my life. I know I couldn't accept him in my life but at least he allowed me to call him DAD. But now he was gone and would never come back, and I would never speak to him again. Why had he given me such a short time to be loved? Why did he leave me without saying SORRY? Why did he leave me with so many questions? Now I will forgive him for what he did, even though he hurt me, but that is between him and God. Whatever he did to me, he was still my father and I miss his voiceand his laugh. I did love him.

I was all on my own, crying and thinking about what had happened in the past. I was drained from crying non-stop from six in the morning until four in the afternoon. I just couldn't talk to anyone at that stage but Nas kept sending me text messages because he was worried about me and he wanted to know how my dad had died. Then I started to call everyone to find out but first I called my mother. She sounded fine but I only had a short conversation with her because I would have ended up crying even more and I didn't want her to get upset. I called Zambri and he told me that three days before my dad died, he went to the clinic to get painkillers for his arm as it had been painful for a long time. Zambri suggested that after he had been to the clinic he should stop at Zambri's shop to have something to eat, which he did. But then he complained that he had a headache and felt he wanted to vomit. My father asked Zambri to pack up his food so he could eat at home but Zambri didn't know what happened when he got home. But the next day Zambri received a call from my ste sister saying that my father had been admitted to hospital. Zambri went to the hospital but he didn't see my father because only a few people were allowed to visit and instead he asked his wife to see my father, what an idiot. Well, Zambri thought my father was going to be fine so he could go and visit him the next day. But the next day Zambri received a call from my stepsister saying that my dad was gone. I still wanted the full story about how my dad had died so I called my stepmother. She was very calm and explained to me that that night he couldn't sleep at all and he could hardly breath, that's why they had taken him to hospital. As soon as he got to hospital they X-rayed his hand and found out that his shoulder bone wasn't connected properly, then they made a small hole in his throat to make him breath properly and at the same time they put him on oxygen. But it didn't save his life, he died the next day from an infection in his body. It was a sad moment when he died because only my stepsister was with him. My mother, my stepmother, my brothers and the rest of his children didn't have time to see him on the last day of his life.

My heart pounded hard when I heard that and my soul whispered, Dad, I gave you money and I told you to get proper treatment so why didn't you do it? Dad, why have you left me when I need you in my life? Dad, why didn't you wait for me? Dad, why didn't you hear my voice before you went? I know I am your daughter and I forgive you, Dad, and I will always love you. I'll pray for you and that you go to heaven. I know everything that is alive in this world will die one day. I know everyone in this world is on borrowed time and when the time comes, God will take us and we have to give back that which belongs to him. I took a deep breath to try and hold myself up. I know he is in good hands and that he will rest in peace. But I am still in shock and it will take a long time to accept that he is no longer with us.

Thank God I at least did something good for him when he was still alive. My mother and my father didn't talk for many years after their divorce. In 2006 I decided to bring both of them together, which I did successfully and I am so proud of myself for doing that. My dad always told me that he missed my brother Nas terribly and I could see tears in his eyes when he said this so I promised him that I would bring my brother back as soon as I found him, which I also did and again I am so proud that I could do that for him. I hope that he is looking down on me from up there and saying, "She is my daughter, I am so proud of her and I am sorry for what I have done."

Before my father died, he had changed and become a good man. He had been a priest in his area for quite some time. He was well-known person and everyone loved him but he left everyone at the age of sixty-four and is now gone forever. As soon as they found out that he had died, everyone was in shock. Many people came to his house to pay their respects to his body before his final journey. I wished Nas and I could be there but it happened too fast so and unfortunately neither of us could be there to see his face for the last time. From a thousand miles away I said, "Goodbye, Dad."

CHAPTER 46

The Truth

For a long time I lived in silence, appearing to be what I wasn't, hiding who I really was, lying, being deceitful and never telling the whole truth. But there was always an important motive behind this deception. Sometimes it was because of my family fleeing from extreme poverty, sometimes because of personal embarrassment or because of a need to protect the ones I love. I felt trapped, locked in a cage of falsehood with no way out.

If I wanted to analyse the meaning of my life, I would not know where to start. I'm well aware that a lot of strange things went on around me, and I allowed them to continue because I felt I had no choice but to accept them. I also had no idea how to escape. When you are trapped in such difficult circumstances, you live in a dark and bewildered state, feeling small and powerless. I was overwhelmed. There were so many problems, so much turmoil throughout my family life, and so may emotions that I was left numb, desperate, depressed and anxious. Prayer was my only solace.

I did not have the courage to tell very many people my story through the years, even when I wanted them to know. I thought it would be a good idea to tell my story to the friends close to me in this book, because telling each person face to face would have been a heavy task. That is why this book seemed my best solution. I have been happy and content with my decision to do this project. To my friends: please accept this as my way of telling the truth to you. At least now you can understand the terrible circumstances that I had to live with that perhaps obliged me to act in an insincere manner. Here, now, you have the truth.

I want to thank my mother and my family for standing with me in my decision to tell the truth about our family. They are all brave, and we are all survivors. When I found my brother Nazeri I was still writing the book; as soon as I told him, he was so happy and proud of me. He gave me so much support and encouragement, and that's what I needed. My sister, Nurul, was so excited for me when I informed her that I had finished the book. She has always been excited for me and my dream. I consider myself very fortunate.

My story has turned out well, and many of my family issues have been resolved now. I will be able to write a happy ending to my life story.

Acknowledgments

I would like to take the opportunity to thank all those people who have collaborated in the writing of this book. I am deeply grateful to my dear mother for her support. I thank my sister, who helped a lot with directions while driving and who gave me many hours of comfort during my sad times. To my little brother, Nazeri, there was nothing more that I wanted in this world than to have you back in my life and to bring you back to our mother and to the rest of our family. And now, no words can describe how happy I am to have found you. I want to let you know that you are always in my heart and I love you more than you can imagine, and the same goes for the rest of the family. To my dear American friend, Paul Roberts, you are a wonderful and kind person. You have been so good to me, and I can never thank you enough for all your encouragement and your efforts helping me realise my dream of writing this book. You have always done what you said you would do. To my lovely Giovanni, a million thank yous for helping with and correcting my English in this book. You have done so much to help me on this book and you have been so patient; I can't even describe how thankful I am to you. You have the kindest heart that I have ever known. Finally, I owe my deepest apologies to Kazmin and my father, Abdul Wahab. If any words in *Life behind the Silence* hurt either of you, I am sorry but every word is the truth. Kazmin, I hope you can now truly understand how much you hurt me. My father, Abdul Wahab, you will always be my father; if you are watching from up there, I am sorry for writing all about what you did to me. I didn't plan to do this project yesterday, or last year, but thirty-five years ago. I forgive you and accept that you are part of my life. The damage that you have done has left a big scar on my heart and on my body, and I cannot ever recover. I hope in heaven you look down at me and say the word SORRY; that's all I need from you. I am happy that he had the daughters that he always wanted and I am sure that he loved them more than me. To all his children I say sorry from the bottom of my heart about what I have written about our dad but this is between me and him. None of you have ever been in my situation so you will never know what I have been through. I don't mean to hurt any of you and I don't mean to damage our father's status, I am just doing what I have promised myself I would for almost my entire life. The time has come for me to close the dark book of my life and let him rest in peace. When I return to Malaysia, I will visit his grave even though he did tell me at one stage that when he dies, I am not allowed to visit to his grave. I forgive him as a daughter and also respect him as a father who has gone forever, but I will go without his permission. He is the only father that I have and the happy times that we had togehther, even though it was only short, will stay with me for the rest of my life. Rest in peace, Dad; now you belong to heaven. I will love you always.